ECONOMICS OF THE
PHARMACEUTICAL INDUSTRY

Praeger Studies in
Select Basic Industries

ECONOMICS OF THE PHARMACEUTICAL INDUSTRY

John W. Egan,
Harlow N. Higinbotham,
and J. Fred Weston

PRAEGER

PRAEGER SPECIAL STUDIES • PRAEGER SCIENTIFIC

Library of Congress Cataloging in Publication Data

Egan, John W.
    Economics of the pharmaceutical industry.

    (Praeger studies in select basic industries)
    Bibliography: p.
    Includes indexes.
    1. Drug trade—United States. I. Higinbotham, Harlow N. II. Weston, J. Fred
(John Fred), 1916-   . III. Title. IV. Series.
HD9666.5.E34   338.4'76151'0973   82-572
ISBN 0-03-061803-7   AACR2

Published in 1982 by Praeger Publishers
CBS Educational and Professional Publishing
a Division of CBS Inc.
521 Fifth Avenue, New York, New York 10175 U.S.A.

© 1982 by Praeger Publishers

23456789   145   987654321

Printed in the United States of America

PREFACE

The ethical pharmaceutical industry has been the subject of intense scrutiny in recent years. The industry's direct relationship to national health and to the health care sector gives it unusual prominence as a public policy concern. Certain unique characteristics of this industry, such as its rapid rate of technological development, its reliance on patent protection, and its problems in a growing regulatory environment, have made it a popular arena for testing new concepts in the fields of industrial economics and policy analysis.

The growing literature has been more than academic in terms of impact. Starting with the Kefauver hearings in the late 1950s, the authors of various works in this field have testified and influenced legislative actions concerning the industry. With the enactment of the 1962 amendments to the Food, Drug, and Cosmetic Act, the role of the government in health care has had increased impacts on drug innovation and manufacturing. These impacts, in turn, are again a topic that has caused heated debates.

This study seeks to contribute to the ongoing debate by undertaking a review of the professional economics literature. It seeks to clarify past and present findings by analytic summaries of relevant published material. The study seeks to evaluate the issues based on a review of the literature, directed both to this industry and more generally to the study of industrial organization economics.

Our hope in publishing this work is to share with members of the academic, business, and technical communities our perspective on the evolution of ideas and concepts in this important area. We have endeavored to provide a framework for evaluating specific contributions and for identifying gaps. This framework may be of use in isolating public policy concerns and in formulating future research topics.

The research presented in this book is developed from a project initiated in 1978 by A. T. Kearney, Inc. Management Consultants, under the direction of John Egan and Harlow Higinbotham. Extensive contributions were made by two associates, Peter Kahn and Edward Yang, who researched much of the material and drafted a preliminary review. The research was updated and completed by J. Fred Weston in 1980-81. The authors would like to express their appreciation to the Pharmaceutical Manufacturers Association for its support on this project. The work benefited from the comments and suggestions of Samuel Mitchell, Ronnie Davis, Armistead Lee, and Thi Dao, members of the research staff of the Pharmaceutical Manufacturers Association. The contents and judgments expressed in the study represent the authors' sole responsibility.

CONTENTS

ECONOMICS OF THE PHARMACEUTICAL INDUSTRY

1

INTRODUCTION AND BACKGROUND

The pharmaceutical manufacturing industry has achieved great advances as demonstrated by a high rate of introduction of new drugs, downward price trends, extended human longevity, and substantial reductions in the costs of maintaining good health. Yet the industry is frequently criticized for its methods of marketing, high prices and excessive profitability (Schifrin, 1967, p. 894). The present study seeks to place these issues in their proper economic and financial framework.

THE ECONOMIC AND SOCIAL ENVIRONMENT

The Health Care Financing Administration (HCFA) estimates that health services and supplies expenditures in 1980 were over $247 billion. This represents 9.4 percent of the $2.6 billion gross national product (GNP) for 1980. While GNP grew at a 12 percent rate during the previous decade, national health expenditures during the same period increased at a 14.5 percent annual rate.

Of the expenditures on health services and supplies in 1980, about $100 billion was spent on hospital care, with a growth rate during the decade of 15 percent per annum. Expenditures on physicians' services in 1980 were about one-half the outlays on hospital care, with a growth rate of about 13 percent. Expenditures on nursing home care grew at an 18 percent rate, reaching $21.6 billion by 1980.

Outlays on drugs and medical sundries reached $19.2 billion in 1980, representing 7.8 percent of total health services and supplies, down from 11.8 percent in 1970. The growth rate in the outlays on drugs was at a 9.5 percent rate, reflecting high productivity and price increases below the rate of increase in the consumer price index as a whole. In addition, an important contribution of advances in drugs has been to reduce the costs of hospitals and physicians' services.

Escalating medical expenditures have given rise to concerns and proposals to control costs. In part the rising costs have been a result of the substantial role of third party payments, which have stimulated consumer demand for health care services. Cost–based reimbursement systems have limited incentives to provide medical care by the least expensive methods. Instead they stimulate the use of innovative, technologically advanced methods that raise costs.

Another factor contributing to the rapid rise in the costs of medical services has been the role of government in financing health care expenditures. Financing by all government is now over 40 percent with the federal government paying for 70 percent of such financing.

In efforts to control costs, hospitals have sought tight control over inventories. Purchasing groups of hospitals have been formed to seek quantity discounts. Laws allowing or compelling pharmacists to fill prescriptions with generically equivalent drugs have been passed in 48 states. At the federal level, efforts have been made to increase the number of drugs covered by maximum allowable cost (MAC) limits at which the reimbursements for Medicaid prescriptions are made. The government has also taken on an increased regulatory role.

BRIEF HISTORICAL BACKGROUND

The research-based pharmaceutical industry as we know it today is relatively young. Its life begins in the mid-1930s with the development of sulfanilamide. This led to further research in molecular modification, which resulted in the development of as many as 5,000 sulfonamides (Wardell, 1979a, p. 7).

The isolation of penicillin was begun in 1938, leading to its first human use in 1941. Mass production was achieved by 1943. Several thousand penicillin-type compounds with different applications have been developed. Within a decade following 1943 a number of important advances had been made in antibiotic therapy. In 1961 ampicillin, the first gram-negative acting penicillin was developed. Research on drugs has spread into many other therapy areas. The pace of technological innovation has increased at a rapid pace.

Other important changes took place in drug production. Before the 1940s, pharmacists used essentially a handicraft method for preparing drugs as required for each prescription. This handicraft method became increasingly expensive as wages increased. At the same time, the retail pharmacists could not compound the new antibiotics or antihistamines. The pharmaceutical manufacturers began the production of virtually all drugs, leaving the retail pharmacist with the function mainly of packaging and labeling the prescription. The mass production of drugs by manufacturers has substantially reduced costs.

SOME PERFORMANCE ASPECTS OF THE DRUG INDUSTRY

Because of the mass production of drugs and productivity improvements, drug prices on average have either fallen or not risen as fast as the consumer price index. The increased effectiveness of drugs has also reduced the costs of other health care services. The costs of doctor care, hospital care, and the duration of therapy all are substantially lower than they otherwise would have been without the progress in drugs and their favorable price trends.

New effective pharmaceuticals have virtually wiped out death rates from diseases such as poliomyelitis, whooping cough, and tuberculosis. The use of tranquilizers has substantially reduced the number of mental patients in hospitals. As one author (Schwartzman, 1975a, p. 6) has noted, "New tranquilizers and anti-depressants helped reduce the number of patients in mental hospitals from 558 thousand in 1955 to 339 thousand in 1970. During those years the average hospital stay dropped from 8 years to 1.4 years."

Even critics acknowledge the tremendous achievements of the drug industry in terms of the benefits accomplished.

It is difficult for many modern workers to realize that most of these accomplishments have been recorded during only the past forty years, a period in which more practical advances were made in medicine than during the preceding forty centuries. Largely as a result of such therapy, along with the widespread use of vaccines to provide immunity against such infections as diphtheria, whooping cough, tetanus, and smallpox, the average life expectancy at birth in the United States has risen from fifty-four years for a child born in 1920, and sixty for one born in 1930, to seventy for a child born in 1970. The change can be shown similarly by maternal mortality rates, one of the most widely used health indicators. In 1930 there were about 680 maternal deaths per hundred thousand live births in the United States; in 1940 there were 376; in 1950 there were 83; in 1960 there were 37; and in 1969 there were 25 (Silverman and Lee, 1974, p. 14).

Not only have death rates been greatly reduced but also the reductions in the costs of illness have been very great. Estimates of the dollar magnitudes of the benefits have been made. For example, it has been estimated that

> the use of these and similar drugs has had an impact on the economic costs of illness that amounts to savings of many billions of dollars a year. Thus, one cost analysis showed, the reduction in hospitalization made possible by new antituberculosis drugs yielded gross savings of roughly $4 billion during the period 1954–1969. Estimated savings resulting from the use of polio vaccine are now of the order of $2 billion per year. The new measles vaccine has given annual savings of about $180 million, in addition to averting millions of cases of acute measles and thousands of cases of mental retardation each year (Silverman and Lee, 1974, p. 14).

These general estimates of savings in illness from improved drugs of many billions of dollars per year are corroborated by careful individual studies. For example, it has been estimated that over a ten-year period the savings from tranquilizers have amounted to a present value of over $12 billion. The basis for this estimate is set forth in Table 1.1.

Thus the benefits of the performance of the pharmaceutical industry are widely agreed to amount to "many billions" of dollars per year. Its accomplishments have led to the development of pharmaceutical manufacturing as a major industry whose salient characteristics are profiled in the next section.

A PROFILE OF THE U.S. PHARMACEUTICAL INDUSTRY

The global sales of the pharmaceutical industry in 1980 are estimated at some $22 billion. Global research and development (R & D) outlays were just under $2 billion, representing about 9 percent of global sales. About 1.5 billion prescriptions per year are filled. There are more than 100,000 health care establishments, including hospitals and nursing homes. Distribution is greatly influenced by the professional buyers for drug purchasers—more than 200,000 physicians and veterinarians. Of the total of manufacturers' direct dosage form sales, about 53 percent are made to wholesalers, 23 percent directly to retailers, and about 20 percent to hospitals of various types.

The nature of the functions performed in pharmaceutical manufacturing is indicated by financial patterns based on data for succesful firms. Production expenses are almost one-half of the total costs of a drug manufacturing operation. The nominal costs of materials may represent less than 10 percent of the selling price of drug products. The value of a drug product, however, is not determined by the weight of the materials it

TABLE 1.1. Estimated Savings from Tranquilizers (values as of 1970)

Years after Introduction	Patient-Days Saved (millions) (1)	Present Value of Savings ($ millions) (2)
1	1.02	$ 25.3
2	13.44	303.3
3	42.17	865.4
4	49.70	927.6
5	40.13	680.0
6	32.39	499.3
7	44.61	625.4
8	51.13	651.2
9	52.35	606.5
10th and subsequent years	66.00 per year	6,944.2
Total		$12,128.2

Notes: Column (1) is calculated as (1.650 patient-days in mental hospitals per capita in years 1955–64) × 1970 population.

Column (2) is calculated as $27.33 × column (1) discounted to the present at 10 percent. $27.33 = 1970 daily personal income per capita ($10.70) + 1970 daily per patient expenditure at mental hospitals ($16.63).

Source: Sam Peltzman, *Regulation of Pharmaceutical Innovation: The 1962 Amendments* (Washington, D.C.: American Enterprise Institute for Public Policy Research, 1974), p. 65.

contains. The value of a drug product reflects the R & D capabilities brought to bear in creating the product, the skills and quality control exercised in its production, and the information on product characteristics communicated to the medical profession on its utilization.

Some writers state that the batch processes in the production of pharmaceuticals do not lend themselves to economies of scale. While this may be true for physical manufacturing operations alone, a successful drug firm must develop an effective organization of R & D, production, quality control, and marketing activities. For a drug manufacturing firm, fixed costs may represent as much as 50 percent of total costs. Hence unit costs are likely to be quite sensitive to volume changes.

Recent evidence shows economies of firm size in R & D activities in the drug industry. Also capabilities in the basic sciences underlying pharmaceutical research efforts are applicable in diverse therapeutic drug classes whose groupings are artificial from the standpoint of research, production, and marketing organizations. Diversifying across a number of research areas is a necessary business imperative of adjusting to the inherent risks of the pharmaceutical industry.

Promotion and marketing activities of drug manufacturing firms constitute about 25 percent of each sales dollar. The marketing of prescription drugs has characteristics different from the marketing of other consumer goods generally, including the marketing of over-the-counter (OTC) drugs. Where the purchasing decision is made by the ultimate consumer, advertising and promotion methods can be directed at the ultimate consumer on a mass basis in an attempt to "pull the goods through" the retail establishments by consumer requests. For prescription drugs, however, the purchasing decision is made by the professional doctor rather than by the ultimate consumer. Hence, the largest percentage of marketing outlays is used in the activities of the field representatives who call upon physicians, pharmacists, and hospital purchasing agents. Field representatives number some 25,000 involving outlays of more than $600 million a year. This represents a cost of about $2,000 per practicing physician per year, if the costs of field representatives are assigned to physicians alone.

SOME ISSUES THAT HAVE BEEN RAISED

The increased costs of medical care generally have led to questions about whether the costs of drugs are as low as they could be. Some have argued that both drug prices and the profitability of pharmaceutical companies reflect some monopoly elements.

Some critics have argued that promotion and marketing costs of drug companies are too high. They have argued that relatively less should be spent on promotion and more on research and development. They argue that while the record is good it could be even better with a shift from promotion to greater innovation.

Many issues have arisen with regard to the use of the patent system and the creation of private brands. With an emphasis on cost control, some have urged that greater possibilities of substituting generic drugs for private brands be implemented. Some have argued that the patent period is too long. Others argue that it is too short. Some propose compulsory licensing of successful drugs

New drug developments have slowed down during the last decade. Some argue that this is due to the 1962 drug legislation. Others argue that it is due to a depletion of research opportunities. Still others feel that the increased role of government regulation and its implementation have been the prime cause of the slowdown in the development of new drugs. Others are concerned that the innovation rate in the United States has declined relative to the rest of the world. Before the new drug law of 1962, the rate of new chemical introductions in the United States was about one-half the worldwide rate. Subsequently, the U.S. rate dropped to about one-fifth of the worldwide rate. Thus the U.S. decline represents a smaller proportion of a decreased innovation rate.

Prior to 1962 virtually no studies of the pharmaceutical industry appeared in economic journals. Interest in the industry was stimulated by the hearings on the drug industry held by the Subcommittee on Antitrust and Monopoly of the Senate Committee on the Judiciary between 1959 and 1962. Between 1959 and 1967, ten other congressional investigations and hearings on the pharmaceutical industry were held. The early articles on the industry drew on these hearings. The early studies presented negative evaluations of the behavior and performance of the drug industry.

Even by the early 1970s, information about the drug industry was outdated. It continued to be based on the congressional hearings of the 1960s. During the 1970s much new data and a broad new literature on the drug industry were developed. This new literature on the pharmaceutical industry has given rise to the present study.

OBJECTIVES OF THE PRESENT STUDY

The central purpose of this study is to present a critique of the new economic literature regarding the ethical pharmaceutical industry. This includes an examination of the relevant research and an evaluation of the public policy issues that have been raised. The basis for this review is a bibliography of over 300 books, articles, and other references concerning drug industry economics.

There are a number of reasons why the pharmaceutical industry represents a research area of general interest. It represents a technologically dynamic industry of the type that is of prime importance for the future health of the U.S. economy. In addition, of course, the importance of its products to people's health places it in a prime position for public policy concerns. As a representative of dynamic industries, the pharmaceutical industry has characteristics that require innovative theories of economics and industrial organization to understand and explain the developments in the industry.

The newer studies of the industry reflected the important distinctive characteristics of the pharmaceutical industry. The industry is characterized by a high growth rate based on technological breakthroughs. There is a long development period for new products. A high proportion of investment is in intangible assets such as research and development and in expenditures on promotion. There are high risks associated with intense competition to discover innovative drugs and to obtain protective patents. Favorable price trends and outstanding performance by some criteria were considered against the possibilities that price and other elements of performance could potentially have been even better. Issues have been raised with regard to concentration and possible monopoly elements in some sectors of the industry.

Since the structure-conduct-performance (SCP) paradigm is the dominant approach to industrial organization, the basic pattern of the chapters follows that framework. Accordingly, the pattern followed in the present survey of the evolution of the economic literature on the pharmaceutical industry considers in sequence its structure, its conduct, and finally its performance. These topics are treated in the following order: Chapter 4 covers structure; Chapters 5 and 6 cover conduct, and Chapters 7 and 8 cover performance.

Within chapters we have divided the material into major and minor subject areas. Generally each chapter or major subject area discussion begins with a statement of a central concept or problem falling within the SCP paradigm. Early contributors (1962–68) are discussed and then contrasted with the work of subsequent writers.

To help clarify the evaluation of concepts and results, we introduce simple path charts at various points in the text. These charts identify the historical flow and development of hypotheses (designated by single arrows) as well as the presence of conflicts (designated by double arrows) between writers with opposing views. Our objective in creating these path charts is to provide a one–page summary of major subject areas as well as an aid for identifying points of conflict, disagreement, or gaps in the literature.

The SCP framework is essentially static in its orientation. Hence the function of Chapter 2 is to consider alternative models that will help deal with the more dynamic aspects of the pharmaceutical industry. A central feature of the literature on the pharmaceutical industry is the changing context within which issues are developed and analyzed. Generally, the history of pharmaceutical economics has been one of gradual broadening in the perspective assumed by the analyst. Static concepts of market structure are expanded to include the pattern of entry and exit over time; pricing policies are evaluated in the dynamic context of continuing innovation and discovery; and the pharmaceutical industry itself is viewed in the larger perspective of the overall health care problem. Chapter 2 introduces these concepts in terms of the traditional literature of industrial organization economics. It also describes an emerging view of dynamic industrial competitive behavior that stands in contrast to its more static predecessor. Thus the pharmaceutical industry provides a useful subject area for testing innovative theories of industrial organization.

2

ALTERNATIVE ECONOMIC MODELS OF
THE PHARMACEUTICAL INDUSTRY

The traditional view in industrial organization economics has been that structure determined the conduct and performance of an industry. The key premise was that high concentration in conjunction with barriers to entry facilitated joint action and resulted in tacit if not explicit collusion.

A more recent alternative view is that its structure is the result of competitive processes in an industry. This view holds that the relative market position of a firm reflects the degree of success it has achieved in identifying the market's multidimensional needs and meeting them.

The policy implications that flow from each of the competing models of the drug industry differ radically. Good public policy depends critically on which of these models—the standard microeconomic model of atomistic competition or the dynamic model—best explains how the pharmaceutical industry works and best predicts what kinds of economic behavior leads to desired outcomes.

STATIC COMPETITION

Decisions in the traditional economic literature for the model of atomistic competition are simple and straightforward. The demand curve for an industry is the sum of the demands of all individuals involved. The supply curve is the sum of the marginal cost functions of individual firms. Thus given an industry demand curve and an industry supply curve a market clearing price is determined by the intersection of these two curves. This is the price then taken by the individual firm whose decisions are limited to selecting the output to equate marginal cost to price. It is assumed that the individual firm can readily match the best cost functions achievable in the industry and its decision process is essentially an output adjustment decision process.

Under the monopoly case derived under the atomistic competition theory, the industry demand function is given in a similar fashion, but one seller equates marginal revenue and marginal cost and the industry price and output are thereby obtained. The traditional model is silent on how a monopoly comes to pass, nor does it inquire as to the conditions under which the monopoly position may be subject to erosion.

When we move from the simple atomistic competition and monopoly models to the more sophisticated progeny—monopolistic competition and oligopoly theory—the models are somewhat more complex but the standard models are still highly simplified relative to the complexities of the actual world. Under the monopolistic competition model temporary profits or rents are achieved by creating favorable situations with downward sloping demand curves facing individual firms. At full equilibrium, however, there are no excess profits, even though there is excess capacity in the sense that the tangency conditions take place to the left of the low point of the long-run average cost curve.

Under oligopoly, of course, we have a cluster of models ranging from the relative simplicity of the Cournot-type model to highly complex formulations expressed in game theory exercises. The latter, which yield somewhat indeterminant results for public policy purposes, assume that awareness of interdependence results in either tacit or overt collusion; but these models are developed under assumptions that all decision variables except price and output are held constant. When additional variables such as product quality, product innovation, sales organizations, and selling strategies, are taken into account, the number of variables and their numerous gradations make it difficult, if not impossible, to predict rivals' actions and reactions. Hence tacit collusion becomes much less likely and even overt collusion is difficult to formulate and to monitor.

On the other hand, while no tacit collusion is assumed under price leadership models, the price, output, and profit results shift from competitive norms and approach in varying degrees under varying assumptions toward the monopoly result. The situation is similar for the limit entry models, which postulate that there are some dominant firms already in an industry who set prices somewhat below the cost levels entrants would experience for output levels available to them after pre-emption by the existing firms. Most forms of limit entry models yield final equilibrium results equivalent to those under monopolistic competition or under one or another oligopoly model. The congruence depends upon the nature of the assumptions built into the structure of the more math-ematically sophisticated limit entry models, which nonetheless are oversimplified from the standpoint of the complexity of the real world.

DYNAMIC COMPETITION

The theory of atomistic competition outlined above may be contrasted with the assumptions and economic processes under the alternative model of dynamic competition. These are shown in parallel columns in Table 2.1.

Simply put, the atomistic competition model assumes a world of certainty, stability, and simplicity. The world of the dynamic model is more like the world most of us live in—uncertain, changing, and complex.

Broad environmental influences, combined with the constraints presented by existing products and firms in the market, lead the firm to develop adaptive policies with respect to product, quality, prices, sales methods, promotion efforts, service organization, and financial facilities. These decisions, in turn, have an influence on the quality and type of fixed investments and on the level and behavior of other costs. Even on patented new products, constraints are set by the market, since new products substitute in some degree for older products.

Strategies are formulated to offer either breadth or specialization in a range of combinations of product characteristics. Iterated reviews of product quality characteristics, materials characteristics, production methods, and marketing methods seek the optimal product quality, cost levels, and marketing attractiveness. Since administrative discretion is exercised in selecting among alternative combinations of choices under uncertainty involving pricing decisions in relation to the other variables, atomistic firms as well as firms in concentrated industries may be said to have price policies.

DECISION PROCESSES UNDER DYNAMIC COMPETITION

Thus decision making in the real world of uncertainty is greatly different from the processes described by the static equilibrium models of atomistic competition. The familiar partial equilibrium diagrams in textbook presentations of output decisions greatly oversimplify and distort the decision process in both small and large firms. It is artificial, for example, to separate pricing from the broader framework of investment-product-market strategies.

Figure 2.1 sets forth a matrix of factors influencing investments and product market decisions. It begins with a set of constraints presented by existing products and firms in the market. The first constraint is basic product characteristic vectors. A second is price vectors in relation to product characteristics. The price vectors should be considered as relative prices as well as absolute prices. The third constraint is the nature of the

TABLE 2.1.   A Comparison between Two Alternative
Economic Models

Assumptions and Economic Processes under the Model of Static, Atomistic Competition	*Assumptions and Economic Processes under the Model of Dynamic Competition*
1. Large numbers of sellers and buyers.	1. Small numbers of sellers and sometimes small numbers of buyers.
2. U-shaped average cost curve, economies of scale exhausted at relatively small size.	2. Relatively sharp decline of costs until some point of minimum efficient size (MES), then slowly declining costs.
3. Decisions limited to adjusting output to market-determined price.	3. Dimensions of decision making are numerous and of many gradations. Decisions on technological leadership, product quality, promotion including selling organizations, advertising, and price discounting, relative cost efficiency, and so on.
4. Supply of entrepreneurs is readily available: The best production technology and product quality are instantaneously matched.	4. Time, organizational experience, and organizational learning are involved in the development of an effective economic team so that advantages and disadvantages between firms are not quickly equalized.
5. Cost conditions are the same and firms are of similar size.	5. Cost functions are of different shapes, and firms are of different sizes.
6. Entry into an industry and exit from it are virtually instantaneous.	6. Entry and exit are not easy or speedy because of relatively large MES and the time, costs, and uncertainty of matching the efficiency of existing firms.
7. Collusion is precluded by the large numbers of sellers.	7. Collusion is made difficult by the numerous decision processes in a dynamic environment.
8. Efficiency is stimulated by the need to keep costs below the industry price.	8. Efficiency is stimulated because large advantages or disadvantages are not readily matched.

Source: Compiled by the authors.

sales or dealer organization vectors involved in selling the product. Finally, there are the advertising and promotional effort vectors. These are the familiar four Ps of marketing: product, price, place (or channels of distribution), and promotion (including advertising).

Other factors could be important depending on the nature of the product. For durable goods, both the existence of a service organization to provide for continuous effective performance of the product and credit availability, since a large unit investment is required, represent additional important sets of vectors. The firm must also formulate strategies and tactics in connection with its own product quality variations, sales or dealer organization, advertising and promotion effort, service organization, and financing facilities.

As Figure 2.1 suggests, environmental forces also exert influences. These include a set of social vectors such as population growth rates, its composition and location. There are also political vectors representing various types of government policies with regard to taxes, monetary policy, and import and export stimuli or restraints. Important technological factors represent the rate of new product and process development in the industry. A large number of economic environmental influences also must be taken into account. These include the international economic outlook, the national economic outlook, and the fundamental determinants of industry volume arising from the nature of the products produced.

To limit the costs of compiling and processing information, goals and tasks are "factored," and operational targets are employed at several levels of the firm. Business executives typically emphasize four types of financial targets: return on investment, growth in sales or earnings per share, checkpoints with regard to liquidity and solvency as measured by cash flows or leverage analysis, and a favorable valuation relationship between the earnings of the company and the market price of its stock.

After the planning and budgeting decisions are made, managerial attention becomes focused on critical variables influencing the results of operations, such as market share. It does not, however, follow that managements substitute market share for profit maximization. Market share is not a goal but a managerial check-point in the following adaptive process: An important factor in corporate resource allocation decisions is the potential sales volume for a product line. To provide a basis for capacity decisions, management must estimate its expected sales volume, which in turn depends on estimated market share. The size of the divergence of actual from expected returns will be a function of the divergence between the targeted and realized market share or total dollar value of sales. Thus, market share is likely to be regarded as an end in itself. Targets or rules thus need to be distinguished from organization goals; targets are used to coordinate operating divisions in the achievement of corporate objectives.

FIGURE 2.1. Matrix of Factors Influencing Investment and Product-Market Decisions

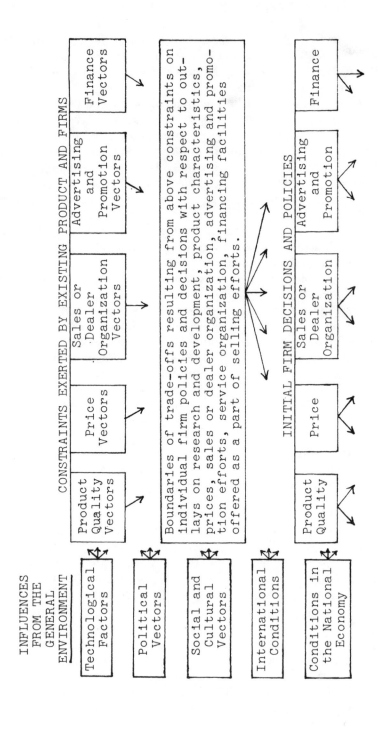

14

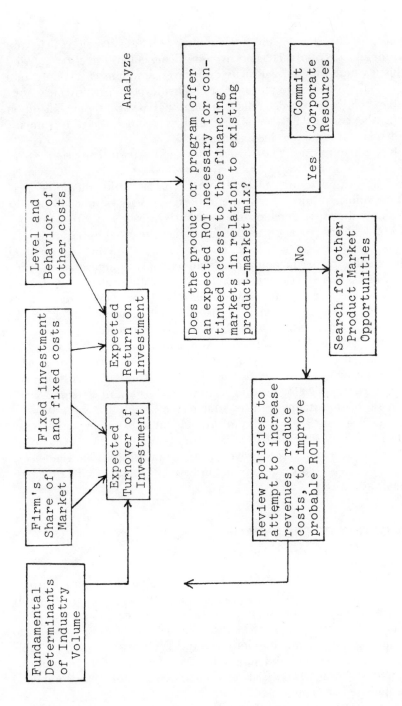

Analyze

Level and Behavior of other costs

Fixed investment and fixed costs

Firm's Share of Market

Fundamental Determinants of Industry Volume

Expected Return on Investment

Expected Turnover of Investment

Does the product or program offer an expected ROI necessary for continued access to the financing markets in relation to existing product-market mix?

Yes

Commit Corporate Resources

No

Search for other Product Market Opportunities

Review policies to attempt to increase revenues, reduce costs, to improve probable ROI

Source: Compiled by the authors.

15

Because of change and uncertainty, emphasis is on review and adjustment of decisions. The nature of satisficing behavior is also suggested by this learning process. Satisficing objectives represent checkpoints in a firm's continuing effort to move toward higher levels of performance. Thus whether rules and targets reflect nonoptimal behavior depends upon whether they are used flexibly or whether they are employed as instruments in a dynamic information feedback process.

It is sometimes argued that an atomistic industry structure is necessary to direct decision making toward increased efficiency. Although this view is consistent with a deterministic model, in a dynamic world other forces may produce similar results. One is the importance placed on achieving cost reduction and cost leadership. In a dynamic environment with numerous forms of rivalrous behavior, and with long lags involved in responding to actions by rivals such as changes in product quality or product differentiation, cost reduction reduces vulnerability to unfavorable events. Cost leadership reduces vulnerability to a rival's strategies. A related emphasis is on price reductions over time. The rationalization provided was "enlarging the market," which is consistent with a static model; but secular price reduction also is a strategy for dealing with uncertainty. A massive type of risk faced by business firms is competition from new and substitute products. Since product substitution involves performance-price comparisons between existing and new products, continued efforts at price reduction is a strategy for insuring against this form of uncertainty.

In short, uncertainty induces strategies reflecting the same types of pressures for efficiency and performance improvement ascribed to atomistic industry structures in a deterministic model. Some evidence in support of this hypothesis is provided by analysis of price movements in concentrated versus less concentrated industries generally and particularly in the drug industry.

APPLICATION OF THE DYNAMIC VERSUS THE STATIC VIEW IN PRICING

The usual textbook treatment of decision making in the firm is overly simplistic. Particularly in the area of pricing the dimensions are simply pricing and output, with all other variables held constant. Within the dynamic framework, however, the formulation of policies with respect to price must take many variables into account. These are conveyed by Table 2.2. Numerous demand and supply factors influence price. In addition, economic, political, and social factors as well as other environmental constraints must be considered.

With such a large range of variables, no simple formula can be devised to formulate prices or price lines. Explanations of pricing policies and patterns are not readily communicated in simple criteria, yet critics of drug pricing have ascribed simple rules to pricing.

Value in use is only one among a large number of factors influencing prices and price changes. Certainly it is one of the demand influences, but it is a distortion of industry practice to characterize value in use as the sole or main determinant of price.

Nor would it be sound to have prices determined by costs. Without taking demand factors into account, some products would be priced so high in relation to user income that consumer health care needs would be met to a much less desirable degree than they are met today. Without placing pricing in the context of the economics of the industry and the total planning and resource allocation processes of firms, a distorted view of the pricing process will be produced.

It should be evident from the earlier discussion on the firm's decision–making process that standard microeconomic theory is guilty of unjustifiable overgeneralization of simplified price analysis. It is convenient in developing the theory of the firm in microeconomic theory to *assume* for analysis of some types of problems that all variables are at their optimum values and/or are assumed to be held constant, while permitting only price and output to vary. In this type of partial equilibrium analysis, a demand curve and average and marginal costs curves are "given." For an atomistic firm, marginal costs are equated to (average) price to determine the firm's "output" rate. Even for short-run analysis, this is a vast oversimplification in assuming that the demand and cost curves are known. Even for a given scale of plant, demand and cost factors are subject to uncertainty and change. In a long-run context, in which changes in scale of plant may take place, the assumption of known and certain demand and cost functions may provide useful exercises but are misleading as guides to industry policy. They fail to capture the strategies, policies, and processes by which firms seek to deal with change and uncertainty. Nevertheless, the formal partial equilibrium analysis of standard microeconomic theory will be set forth as a point of departure.

The static partial equilibrium model is based on a number of assumptions: absence of economies of scale, a large number of sellers, a large number of buyers, perfect knowledge of factor input prices and qualities by producers, perfect knowledge of product prices and qualities by buyers, perfectly homogeneous products, and instantaneous mobility of factors.

Under these assumptions, the demand function facing the individual atomistic firm is horizontal with infinite elasticity and marginal revenue equals average revenue equals price. If a firm faces a demand function that has a negative slope to some degree, marginal revenue will be less than

TABLE 2.2. Pricing Considerations in the Pharmaceutical Industry

Demand Factors	Supply Factors	Environmental Factors
1. Product characteristics defined by acceptability, efficacy, and absence of side effects.	1. Number and types of competing products.	1. Size of the economy.
2. The therapeutic qualities of a drug in relation to other products.	2. Number and types of competing companies.	2. Percentage of income spent on health care.
3. Classes of physicians who are the most likely prescribers.	3. Rate of future prospective development of competing products.	3. Nature of and expectations toward health care systems.
4. Price schedules for related products.	4. Research, production, and quality control requirements expressed in required investments and cost levels.	4. Consumption habits and patterns with respect to the use of pharmaceuticals.
5. Daily dosage quantity and expected duration of patient therapy.	5. Nature of distribution systems required for effective marketing.	5. Standard of living in the economy.
6. Dosage or treatment costs in a health care program.	6. Size, forms, and strengths of products to be marketed.	6. Size and distribution of gross national product.
7. Effects on related costs in a health care program.	7. Expected shelf life of products.	7. Characteristics of the political environment.
8. Extent and characteristics of probable users, considering age group, income levels, and so on.	8. Patent position of the firm in relation to other products and firms.	8. Role of government in payment for health care.
9. Elasticity of demand with respect to price.	9. Other products produced by the firm and their prospective prices, costs, volume, and returns.	9. Role of government as a regulator and inspector.

10. Cross elasticities of demand with respect to price and product qualities.
11. Elasticity of demand with respect to income.
12. Probability and timing of appearance of new competing products.
13. Projected volume at various prices.
14. Duration and pattern of probable product life cycle.
15. Extent of use of prepayment plans, insurance plans, and government programs in paying for health care and drugs.

10 Ease of limitation or improvements by others.
11. Location of production in relation to markets served; domestic versus exports.
12. Sources of raw materials.
13. Differences in required associated services to the medical profession.
14. Tax patterns.
15. Government regulations and procedures required for certifying drugs.
16. Sources and costs of capital.
17. Types of scientific and technical capabilities required.
18. Production and quality control supervision by regulatory agencies.

10. Rate of growth of government as regulator and inspector.
11. Economic instability or stability.
12. Patterns of price changes in the economy as a whole.
13. Import, export, and foreign exchange regulations.
14. Antidumping regulations.
15. Laws with respect to patents.
16. Laws and administrative policies with respect to compulsory licensing.
17. Licensing regulations.
18. Comparative licensing regulations among different countries.

Source: Compiled by the authors.

average revenue. The firm will equate marginal cost to marginal revenue and part of the difference between price or average revenue and marginal cost is a measure of "consumer welfare loss."

Under the atomistic competitive theory the mechanisms for eliminating above-normal profits are entry, the revaluation of fixed assets, and rebidding on other costs. Exit is the mechanism by which supply conditions are reduced to increase price and the revaluation of assets downward takes place through reorganization and bankruptcy to eliminate the losses of submarginal firms and to bring their profits up to normal levels.

THE PHARMACEUTICAL INDUSTRY
AS VIEWED IN A DYNAMIC MODEL

A number of dynamic characteristics have been observed in the pharmaceutical industry. A new patented product has an element of uniqueness. The entry of new products and firms is slowed only when the therapeutic performances of the existing products are high and superior. Historically, however, no leading product has maintained its market share position for more than a limited number of years. The general pattern is one of temporary preeminence but with relatively rapid displacement of leading products. This is strong, solid, overall empirical evidence of relatively high cross-elasticities of demand. This suggests that in a long-run context there are not likely to be wide departures between long-run marginal costs and price for most drug products. In addition, departures from technical optimal pricing tests must be related to advances in innovation, product improvement, and new products evaluated in relation to consumer welfare. Put another way, static welfare analysis and negatively sloped demand functions must be compared to consumer welfare gains from innovation, which may quickly exceed the hypothetical benefits of making demand functions less inelastic as prescribed by static welfare analysis.

Some empirical tests suggested by the dynamic model include the following. Price flexibility analysis should not be limited to list prices. Price lists represent initial offering prices from which various discounts and deals are frequently made. Different policies on services and returns have the effect of price changes. Price flexibility studies must analyze actual transactions prices and other indirect measures of variations in manufacturing prices.

In addition, drug prices need to be analyzed over time. The dynamic model directs analysis to: trends in an index of drug prices over time, movements in the prices of drugs that held a leading market position at the start of the time period for analysis, and the relationship between the prices of leading drugs and the appearance of substitute drugs.

In a static model, above-average profits are taken as an indication of poor performance. In a dynamic model it is inappropriate to view profits either standing alone or for a particular year. Profits have to be viewed over longer time periods to observe their role in dynamic resource allocation processes. Profits in an industry may be high for some segments of time as a result of temporary factors, such as a high rate of new successful product introductions. Or profits may become depressed because of a surge of the flow of resources to areas that have reported high profitability rates. While reported drug industry accounting returns exceeded the average for all manufacturing for earlier time periods, in recent years the difference between the drug industry and all manufacturing unadjusted rates of return have virtually disappeared.

Profitability rates have to be related to the rate of new product successes and failures for individual firms. Overall, profitability measures for individual firms or leading firms represent only part of the picture in a dynamic framework. Profitability measures for an industry must include not only the successful survivors but also those that attempted entry and failed, those firms that actually entered but subsequently failed, and those firms that reported negative profits on individual product entries into drugs even though the home industry of the firm may not have been the drug industry.

Accounting measures of profitability require some adjustments for meaningful comparisons or analysis. One adjustment is outlays that are likely to have capitalizing versus expensing effects for more than one accounting period. Thus R & D outlays and selling expenses are likely to have effects that persist at least to some degree in years after the outlays are made. Capitalizing such expense outlays will have an effect on cost and investment measurements. For a given year, the effect of capitalizing outlays that otherwise would be expenses depends on the extent to which costs are reduced by capitalizing an expense (net income is increased) as compared with the extent to which investment is increased by capitalization (which affects the rate of return).

A second adjustment may be required to take into account the effects of persistent high rates of inflation. These adjustments include effects of leads and lags on revenues and costs generally and tax effects related to inventory and depreciation accounting. Gains or losses from the firm's net position in monetary assets and liabilities or real assets and liabilities must also be considered.

Another characteristic of the cost characteristics of pharmaceutical company operations needs to be taken into account. A high proportion of the costs of a pharmaceutical manufacturer, compared to manufacturing generally, are not allocable to particular products. The reasons are that R & D outlays may be allocated to broad research areas that result in both failures and successes. Detail men and other selling efforts encompass a number of products. Over a period of years manufacturing facilities are shifted from one family of products to another. The earnings from a very few products must cover the losses on aborted R & D projects and must not only subsidize the service drugs but also partially subsidize the less successful drugs that are brought to the market. This complicates the pricing decisions including government policies to influence prices. It would not be appropriate cost accounting to attempt to assign costs and profits to individual products. The relevant "product" is a group of individual drugs.

In a dynamic framework the interactions between prices, profits, and innovation need to be taken into account. Lower prices may mean a lower rate of progress and innovation. Constrained prices and profits therefore may constrain competition and innovation in a longer time framework. The incentives of competitive striving for new products and the competition between products and innovational efforts can have impacts on cost controls, cost reductions, and subsequent reductions in prices over time. In a dynamic context what is most relevant to the consumer may be not the profits of the producers, but the economic efficiency and economic incentive effects of profits that produce improved products at lower costs and lower prices.

In a dynamic framework it is sometimes said that the price and quality performance of the U.S. drug industry has been a fortuitous result of the inherent technical dynamism of the industry; but the technological fertility of the drug industry may itself be an effect produced by the quality of entrepreneurship and management that has been stimulated by appropriate incentives.

Other dimensions for evaluating innovation in the drug industry may be utilized. One is the international dimension. One test is the export surplus or deficit generated by the U.S. drug industry. Another is the relative source of patents for drugs used in the United States and in other countries.

Finally, government regulation itself needs to be viewed in a dynamic framework. Regulatory processes that seek to protect users from ineffective or harmful drugs can in a longer-run framework have the opposite net effect. Undue delay of effective drugs has the same effects as inadequate control of ineffective and harmful drugs: increased costs of illness and unnecessary deaths. Unduly restrictive regulatory drug approval processes can be as harmful or more harmful than unduly lax review processes. Thus tradeoffs are involved and appear to call for the exercise of independent professional judgment.

Similarly, government rules on drug pricing may achieve reductions in the short run but result in higher drug prices per unit of quality in the long run. The initial impact of price controls on successful products may be lower prices; but the decreased prices will result in lower returns from successful products. Both the incentives and the ability to conduct research for innovative drugs are thereby reduced. By lopping off the top of returns from successful products, overall returns are decreased, but if no provision is made for offsetting the losses from unsuccessful R & D efforts, incentives to undertake high-risk projects will be reduced. If account is taken of unsuccessful research efforts and unsuccessful drug products, this is equivalent to taking the overall profitability position of the firm into account. If this occurs, perverse incentive effects will begin to take place.

Thus the static view of industry analysis directs attention to prices, profits, and new products at some point in time. A dynamic approach views these patterns in a longer-run framework. In addition, it takes into account interaction effects that are likely to be produced over a longer-run period. These longer-run effects are amenable to prediction using the standard microeconomic principles derived from static theory but placed in an analytical, dynamic framework.

In view of the central role of product competition and innovation in the pharmaceutical industry, the description and evaluation of performance of the industry must employ a dynamic framework. The use of standard, static, structural models is an inappropriate analytic framework for viewing the process and behavior of the pharmaceutical industry. The dynamic approach is both more realistic and more sound from an analytic stand-point. Theory and practice come together in that the appropriate dynamic tests for an industry are similar to those faced by the managements of individual firms. The central questions relate to what are the strategic and fundamental policy decisions that must be made by the firm in order to enhance its long-run position in the industry. In a dynamic framework this question poses the central test for survival and progress of an individual firm as well as for effective performance by the industry as a whole.

PHARMACEUTICALS AND THE HEALTH CARE INDUSTRY

Many of the above topics have been examined in the economics literature devoted to the pharmaceutical industry. A relatively new area of analysis, and one we feel deserves greater attention in the theoretical and empirical work, concerns the relationship between the ethical pharmaceutical industry and the nation's overall approach to health care problems.

The dynamic paradigm outlined above already suggests an approach. The dynamic model directs analysis to effective price decreases through reductions in the costs of illness. In addition, the impact of the increased effectiveness of drugs in reducing the costs of other health care services needs to be taken into account. In this framework, analysis needs to be made over time of the costs of doctor care, hospital care, and the duration of therapy. Illustrative is an estimate that the reduction in hospitalization made possible by new antituberculosis drugs yielded gross savings of some $4 billion during the period 1954-69. Similarly, Peltzman (1974) estimated the savings from tranquilizers (in 1970 prices) as over $12 billion. These are the kinds of comparisons that are implicit in an analysis of any industry in a dynamic rather than static or structural framework.

In the broader perspective of the nation's total health care delivery system, considerably more work remains to be done. The pharmaceutical industry represents only a small, if important, segment of this system. Major policy issues and economic needs in this domain include such concerns as the role of preventive medicine, the design of medical insurance programs, health care needs of the Third World, the structure of the medical profession and the intensive care industry, and the developing crises in chronic disease and care for the aged. The contributions of drug technology of these problem areas has been enormous and will no doubt continue in the future. Just as the economic literature to date has succeeded in providing a dynamic context to the economic policy questions facing this industry during the 1960s and 1970s, so we would hope for a more broadened market perspective in which to view this industry's contribution in the 1980s.

3

MARKET DEFINITION AND INDUSTRY STRUCTURE

INTRODUCTION AND HISTORICAL BACKGROUND

The study of seller concentration has been an important aspect of industrial organization economics. The characterization of industries as competitive, oligopolistic, or monopolistic has been in large part determined by the number of sellers in the market. The theory underlying this approach is that the "fewness" of sellers produces market power.

The U.S. pharmaceutical industry has not escaped this type of scrutiny from economists and politicians. Following the Kefauver hearings from 1959 to 1962, the industry has been charged with possessing monopolistic market power in the form of high rates of return, excessive prices, patent abuse, product differentiation, and wasteful promotional activities (for example, see Steele, 1962; Costello, 1968; and Schifrin, 1967). Demsetz (1973, p. 1) in a review of empirical studies testing the market concentration doctrine, described it thusly:

> . . . the doctrine holds that the structure of a market gives a reliable index of monopoly power—more specifically, that monopoly power is associated with the degree to which the output of an industry is concentrated in a few firms. Market concentration has been linked through this doctrine to price inflexibility and inflation as well as to monopoly power.

If these allegations are to be substantiated, economic theory dictates that high seller concentration has to be a significant characteristic of the pharmaceutical industry. Unfortunately, the art of measuring seller concentration or market power directly is far from established among economists on either a theoretical or empirical level.

In reviewing the alleged cause-and-effect relationship between seller concentration and performance, Demsetz (1973, p. 1) finds that newer data contravene the conventional wisdom:

> A consistent pattern seems to emerge from the review of past studies and from new data presented in this study. Whereas older studies have found empirical support for the market concentration doctrine, newer studies have not. In the latter, correlations between market concentration and various measures of monopoly power turn out to be less persistent and considerably weaker or even nonexistent than in the earlier work. New data also indicate strongly that the productive efficiency of large firms relative to that of small firms is correlated with market concentration.

A similar evolution in thinking has occurred among economists who have focused on the pharmaceutical industry. Early critics pointed to high concentration, particularly in therapeutic submarkets, as prima facie evidence of excessive market power. Newer studies, however, based on analysis of pharmaceutical markets over time, do not support the conclusion that high concentration is consistent with sustained market power.

APPROACH OF THE CHAPTER

This chapter presents the various approaches that have been considered by economists, with special attention to the applications to the pharmaceutical industry. It should be noted that a large part of the chapter is devoted to the theory of concentration measures developed in the field of industrial organization. Part of this chapter deals with analysis not peculiar to the pharmaceutical industry, since the measures are meaningless unless they can be applied to all industries. We will proceed with the following topics: theoretical aspects of market definition, measurement of concentration ratios, alternative estimates of the number and size of therapeutic submarkets, and dynamic approaches to measuring concentration. The progression of topics through the chapter follows that of the related economic literature, from relatively narrow, static investigations of market concentration and structure to more refined, dynamic studies of market segmentation and stability.

THEORETICAL ASPECTS OF MARKET DEFINITION

A standard economic definition of a market is given in Stigler's *Business Concentration and Price Policy* (1955, p. 152):

An industry should embrace the maximum geographical area and the maximum variety of productive activities in which there is a strong long-run substitution. If buyers can shift on a large scale from product or area B to A, then the two should be combined. If producers can shift on a large scale from B to A, again they should be combined. Economists usually state this in an alternative form: All products or enterprises with large long-run cross-elasticities of either supply or demand should be combined into a single industry.

In brief, the key to defining a market is the degree of substitution. Demand substitution depends on the characteristics of the good and the preference pattern of the consumers. Supply substitution depends on production technology and input mobility. There are also other variables, such as institutional constraints, geographic barriers, and imperfect information that affect the measure of substitutability of a good.

Limitations of Cross-Elasticity Measures

Since the estimation of cross-elasticities requires very strict assumptions, many of these problems are disregarded for analytical purposes. Bishop (1952) criticizes the ceteris paribus assumptions of the elasticities measurements. The change in quantity of the *ith* commodity with respect to change in price of the *jth* commodity is defined with the condition that the price of the *ith* commodity does not change. Such a condition depends, however, on the degree of interdependence of firm decisions in the market. At this point, the question becomes tautological since the interdependence of firm decisions within an industry is exactly the issue underlying market structure studies.

Demand versus Supply Elasticity in the Drug Industry

The choice of economically relevant pharmaceutical markets is made very difficult by the wide difference between the substitutabilities of demand and supply. For example, Measday (1977, p. 262) considers the four-digit level concentration ratio to be too broad:

In short, concentration ratios for the pharmaceutical industry as a whole convey a somewhat misleading impression of the industry, although they are useful in the broad sense of supplying information on the number and approximate size distribution of drug firms. From a standpoint of the influence of industry structure on competitive behavior, however, it is necessary to go beyond the industry-wide ratios and examine concentration in therapeutically significant categories and in bulk drug production. On this basis it appears that high concentration in these separate categories, rather than the moderate concentration of the entire industry, is the dominant structural characteristic.

But then Measday continues: "Entry into the industry is not inherently difficult. The technical expertise and ability to maintain the high quality necessary for drug manufacturing are well within the reach of small enterprises. Nor are capital requirements for production any barrier."

This contradiction shows that there is a high cross-elasticity of supply between two therapeutic markets, while the demand cross-elasticities between two drug markets may be quite small. Unfortunately, there is no established method of incorporating such differences, although we know theoretically that both demand and supply substitutabilities are important.

MEASUREMENT OF CONCENTRATION RATIOS

Even the simple measurement of concentration of an industry has long been a controversial area for economists. Between the severe limitations of data and the imperfection of the various methods, agreement on a measure of seller concentration for industries has been rare (the pharmaceutical industry is again no exception to this situation).

The simplest and most accessible measure is the market concentration ratio computed by the U.S. Bureau of the Census. It is the percentage of total industry sales contributed by the largest firms (commonly four or eight), ranked in order of market shares. The Census defines four-digit as industry class, five-digit as product class, and seven-digit as product or commodity level. The concentration ratios in 1972 for several representative industries, including the pharmaceutical preparations industry (SIC 2834), are shown in Table 3.1.

There are more sophisticated formulas that take account of the number of firms and their size distribution, such as the Gini coefficient, entropy, and the Herfindahl index, but each of these methods still has weaknesses even if the data were available.

Studying Table 3.1, one might conclude that the pharmaceutical industry is by no means concentrated. The industry serves as a good example of how the problem of market definition hampers any form of concentration measure. On the four- or five-digit level, many industries are defined either too broadly or too narrowly, resulting in downward or upward bias in the concentration ratio. The central problem is the difficulty in defining an economically meaningful market that reflects the degree of substitutability on both demand and production sides.

TABLE 3.1. 1972 Concentration Ratios for Representative Industries

S.I.C. Code	Industry Description	4-Firm Ratio	8-Firm Ratio	Number of Firms
37111	Passenger cars (five-digit)	99	100	n.a.
3211	Flat glass	92	n.a.	11
2043	Cereal breakfast foods	90	98	34
3511	Turbines and turbine generators	90	96	59
3641	Electric lamps	90	94	103
3632	Household refrigerators and freezers	85	98	30
2111	Cigarettes	84	n.a.	13
3672	Cathode ray television picture tubes	83	97	69
3334	Primary aluminum	79	92	12
3011	Tires and inner tubes	73	90	136
3331	Primary copper	72	n.a.	11
36512	Household television receivers (five-digit)	66	93	n.a.
3721	Aircraft	66	86	141
3411	Metal cans	66	79	134
2822	Synthetic rubber	62	81	50
2284	Thread mills	62	77	61
2841	Soap and detergents	62	74	577
3691	Storage batteries	57	85	138
3221	Glass containers	55	76	27
3873	Watches, clocks, and watch cases	55	67	183
2082	Beer and malt beverages	52	70	108
3562	Ball and roller bearings	53	73	99
3523	Farm machinery and equipment	47	61	1,465
3621	Motors and generators	47	59	325
3312	Blast furnaces and steel mills	45	65	241
2873	Nitrogenous fertilizers	35	53	47
3143	Men's footwear, except athletic	34	51	118
2041	Flour and other grain mill products	33	53	340
2911	Petroleum refining	31	56	152
2211	Cotton-weaving mills	31	48	190
3552	Textile machinery	31	46	535
2051	Bread, cake, and related products	29	39	2,800
3241	Cement	26	46	75
2834	Pharmaceutical preparations	26	44	680
2651	Folding paperboard boxes	23	35	443
2851	Paints and allied products	22	34	1,318
3541	Metal-cutting machine tools	22	33	857

TABLE 3.1 *(continued)*

S.I.C. Code	Industry Description	4-Firm Ratio	8-Firm Ratio	Number of Firms
2026	Fluid milk	18	26	2,026
2421	Sawmills and planing mills	18	23	7,664
2711	Newspapers	17	28	7,461
2512	Upholstered household furniture	14	23	1,201
2086	Bottled and canned soft drinks	14	21	2,271
3494	Valves and pipe fittings	11	21	643
2335	Women's and misses dresses	9	13	5,294
3273	Ready-mixed concrete	6	10	3,978
3451	Screw machine products	6	9	1,780

Source: F. Scherer, *Industrial Market Structure and Economic Performance* (Chicago: Rand McNally, 1980), p. 62 from U.S. Bureau of the Census, *1972 Census of Manufactures*, "Concentration Ratios in Manufacturing," MC72(SR)-2 (Washington, D.C.: U.S. Government Printing Office, 1975).

Considering the case of the pharmaceutical preparations industry (SIC 2834), Scherer (1970, p. 54) observes:

> The worst offender is pharmaceutical preparations, which lumps together dozens of drugs for which there are no adequate substitutes (except perhaps greatly extended medical care). Economically meaningful market definitions must generally be found in this case at the seven-digit level of detail, given that substitution in production is often blocked by patent barriers.

It is clear that the seller concentration of the pharmaceutical industry would have to be measured in smaller submarkets; but the question of "how small" remains. Numerous investigations before and after Scherer have attempted to produce alternative measures in terms of pharmaceutical submarkets. The difficulties of defining therapeutic markets is well illustrated by the wide dispersion in results.

ALTERNATIVE ESTIMATES OF THE NUMBER AND SIZE OF THERAPEUTIC SUBMARKETS

Vernon (1971), for one, begins by examining the relationship between substitution elasticities and market definition. The difficulties involved in choosing the submarkets can be readily seen from the beginning of his article (p. 247):

On the demand side, the answer is reasonably clear that the categories are meaningful as markets. Of course, all of the drugs are ethical (prescribed by doctors), and it is generally accepted that the choice of drugs by doctors is relatively insensitive to price. ... On the supply side, the justification for the meaningfulness of the therapeutic markets is weaker. That is, to what extent would a price increase in sex hormones induce entry into that market by a supplier of other drugs.

Vernon finally divides the industry into 18 therapeutic markets (see Table 3.2) and proceeds with his concentration formula.

Cocks and Virts (1974) also use the therapeutic-class concept to prepare their data base in a study on the pricing behavior of the ethical pharmaceutical industry. The theoretical background of their approach is clearly presented (p. 350):

The grouping is based on the concept that sets of products of one therapeutic class that intersect with sets of products of another class can be combined to form an overall set of products. Intersection is based on the way physicians actually use various drugs, and it is the intersection of these sets in use that is used to establish the boundaries of a total set. Judgment is involved in the grouping of these products, and they may or may not represent relevant economic markets. Further research is necessary to determine the way drug markets can be delineated.

The National Disease and Therapeutic Index (NDTI), which is compiled by the market-research firm IMS America, Ltd., was used to establish the intersections of various therapeutic classes. The data reflect the prescription decisions made by the physicians in each submarket. The result is the ten product markets shown as follows (Cocks and Virts, 1974):

Antiinfective market
Analgesic and antiinflammatory market
Psychopharmaceutical market
Cough and cold market
Antihypertensive and diuretic market
Vitamin and hematinic market
Oral contraceptive market
Anticholinergic and antispasmodic market
Antiobesity market
Diabetic therapy market

In another study, the management consulting firm A. T. Kearney, Inc. (1974) examined entry and exit in the pharmaceutical industry. As mentioned earlier, this is an alternative measure of market power; high rate of entry means that existing firms lack the ability to develop high entry barriers. Entry is defined as the percent of a therapeutic market share held by firms that were not active in the market at a previous specified date;

TABLE 3.2. Concentration of Sales in the U.S. Ethical Drug Industry, by Therapeutic Markets, 1968

Therapeutic Market	Four-Firm Ratio
Anesthetics	69
Antiarthritics	95
Antibiotics-penicillin	55
Antispasmodics	59
Ataractics	79
Bronchial dilators	61
Cardiovascular hypotensives	79
Coronary-peripheral vasodilators	70
Diabetic therapy	93
Diuretics	64
Enzymes-digestants	46
Hematinic preparations	52
Sex hormones	67
Corticoids	55
Muscle relaxants	59
Psychostimulants	78
Sulfonamides	79
Thyroid therapy	69
Unweighted average	68

Source: John M. Vernon, "Concentration, Promotion, and Market Share Stability in the Pharmaceutical Industry," *Journal of Industrial Economics* 9 (July 1971).

specifically, it is the share of firms in 1972 that were not in the market in 1963. The study was particularly interested in the variables determining the entry and exit rate.

The industry is subdivided into 17 therapeutic drug submarkets (A. T. Kearney, Inc., 1974):

Anorexics	Oral contraceptives
Anthemintics	Osytocics
Antibiotics (B&M)	Penicillins
Anticonvulsants	Psychostimulants
Antihypertensives	Sedatives and hypnotics
Ataractics	Sulfonamides
Bronchial dilators	Thyroid preparations
Coronary vasodilators	Trichomonacides
Diuretics	

The 17 submarkets vary in size, growth rate, number of participants, degree of maturity, and product efficacy. One of the findings showed that markets with high growth rates induce more entry. This supports the hypothesis that market demand growth causes market share instability.

Telser et al. (1975) have continued the research to study the supply response of the pharmaceutical industry. The data base of the two studies are the same 17 therapeutic markets. Telser et al. comment (p. 457):

> The rationale for a category is hard to describe since it depends on both supply and demand conditions. Categories based solely on demand conditions would include all drugs designed to treat a single illness. Were supply conditions the sole criterion, then the category would include all those drugs with a high cross elasticity of supply regardless of the final uses of the drugs.... It is probably more accurate to say that demand conditions are more important than supply conditions in defining the therapeutic categories.

Telser et al. thus have stressed the cross-elasticities on the demand side in classification of drug submarkets.

The number of therapeutic submarkets increased drastically to 69 in Hornbrook's study on market domination and promotional intensity in the pharmaceutical industry (Hornbrook, 1976). Before reaching the empirical section of the study, Hornbrook discusses at length the problem of market definition and the use of cross-elasticities.

He brings out an important but neglected point: The assumptions of competition by price are not necessarily entirely realistic in oligopolistic markets. By definition, cross-elasticity depends on changes in quantity induced by changes in prices. This becomes questionable in an industry like the drug industry, because the firms compete by innovation and promotional activities as well as by price.

This means that other aspects of competition somehow have to be incorporated into the process of market definition. Hornbrook also questions the ceteris paribus condition of cross-elasticity estimation. The discussion is similar to the one presented by Bishop (Hornbrook, 1976; Bishop, 1952).

Hornbrook also makes a novel attempt at resolving the problems of market delimitation by exploring the Lancaster (1966) characteristics approach. The Lancaster approach considers that consumption activities are not directed to goods and services per se, but rather to the characteristics they possess. For example, any food is composed of different degrees of different characteristics such as nutritional content, taste, odor, and palatability.

Drugs can be simply one component of good "health." Hornbrook (1976, p. 18) elaborates:

> Health is both a consumption and an investment good. "Health" can be viewed as a bundle of characteristics—"well-being," "vitality," "physical

fitness," etc.— that are enjoyed directly and that enable the individual to engage in consumption activities that produce other satisfaction-producing characteristics. Households produce health for their members by combining their own time and skills as well as market goods and services to produce nutrition, rest, medical care, and other inputs required for health. Prescription drugs constitute one set of market goods that households use in the production of health, or to be more accurate, a reduction in the state of ill-health.

The characteristic of a drug that the consumer demands is really its "therapeutic effect." The substitutability of these characteristics should dictate the classification of drug markets. In breaking the industry into so many submarkets, Hornbrook is assuming that when physicians make prescribing decisions, they do not consider the degree of therapeutic overlap among drugs to be high.

DYNAMIC APPROACHES TO MEASURING CONCENTRATION

Even when accurately constructed, static measures such as four-firm concentration ratios may be totally incorrect in the long-run. Scherer puts it succinctly (1970, p. 125): "Another quite different view of the processes by which market structures emerge has been postulated by some economists. Let us begin by stating the hypothesis in its boldest, most radical form: the market structures observed at any moment in time are the result of pure historical chance." The problem is of course inherent in any comparative static economic analysis that assumes the observed phenomenon is one of equilibrium. What is needed is a measure that can reflect the changes in the firm's market position through time.

Turnover Measures

Joskow (1960) pursued the concept of firm turnover rate by correlating the rank changes of the firms through time. Hymer and Pashigian (1962) considered such a measure "not very useful" and proposed the concept of change in market shares. The new measure creates a market instability index, I, defined as:

$$I = \left[\sum_{i=1}^{n} \frac{a_{t,\,i}}{A_t} - \frac{a_{t-1,\,i}}{A_{t-1}} \right]$$

where
n = the number of firms in the industry
a = the assets of the *ith* firm at time t
A = the total industry assets at time t
The number of firms and degree of turnover among small firms have little effect on the index because the index sums up the differences between the ratio of firm to industry assets.

About the same time, Gort (1963, p. 51) also was dissatisfied with the Census concentration ratio: "In judging the intensity of competition in an industry, the ability of leading firms to maintain their relative position in a market is probably more significant than the extent of concentration at a single point in time." Gort proceeds to construct another market instability measure that depends on the correlation coefficient for market shares of leading firms in two periods. He also points out the absence of a relation between his stability measures and changes in the common concentration ratio.

Hymer and Pashigian (1962, p. 86) also reached a similar result: "A priori, one might expect to find greater market share stability in the more concentrated industries, but the contrary appears true."

It is obvious that the new measure cannot be used indiscriminantly in testing market power. As a matter of fact, it is the growth in demand that often causes the market to appear unstable and prevents us from drawing any conclusion about the degree of intrinsic market power. This growth effect is described by Gort (1963, p. 55):

Rapid growth generates instability in two ways. First, given imperfect foresight, some firms adjust their scale of production to anticipated growth faster than others and this leads to shifts in market share. Second, assuming there are recurrent lags in the adjustment of supply to rapid changes in demand, earnings will recurrently rise above a "normal" (opportunity-cost) rate of return. This should lead to entry of firms in the industry—hence to changes in market shares.

Along this line, Weiss (1963, p. 70) proposed an opposing view on the use of the instability measures. He argued that present high instability often means future high concentration. "When industries with very unstable market shares in (small-scale) classes finally settle down, most small firms have either disappeared or become big firms. Most of the remaining firms are in the large scale ranges where market shares are stable."

In discussing stochastic determinants of market structure, Scherer (1970, p. 129) observed: "One final point implicit in the discussion thus far should be made explicit. The more variable firm growth rates are, the more rapidly concentrated industry structures will emerge, other things being equal."

It seems that by moving the concentration measure to a dynamic level we have opened up new problem areas about the structural evolution of an industry. When a dynamic approach to market concentration is used, the definition of market tends to become larger. This happens because all elasticity measures increase as the time horizon expands. Gort and Hymer and Pashigian noted that there are mainly two components influencing changes in market shares. One is the movement of variables that are exogenous to the market structure, such as growth in demand and change in technology. The second is the effect of actual seller concentration, which all previous methods tried to identify.

Even this simple distinction—while clearcut—may be misleading. For example, changes in demand may not be exogenous but instead dependent upon changes in technology *within* the industry. Put another way, changes in market share and the structure and scope of market concentration may not be explanatory variables but symptoms of a dynamic process whereby innovation breeds competitive uncertainty, which in turn competitors try to reduce through further innovation and so on. It seems clear that a theory is needed that illuminates the interactive effects of the many variables influencing concentration.

Entry and Exit Measures

Another measure of market power, consistent with the "dynamic approach," is the entry rate of an industry. Telser (1975) has considered entry from the viewpoint of the optimal supply response to a given demand condition. In this analysis the supply curve shifts in response to growth in demand, that is, there is an inflow of new firms. Telser, in his empirical study of entry into the pharmaceutical industry, measured entry by using the proportion of sales in 1972 in the therapeutic category by companies that were absent from the category in 1963 or some other previous date.

One of the main findings in Telser's study is that high concentration ratios coexist with high entry rates. The implication is that there is no effective entry barrier protecting the market power of the present firms. The result supports the previous studies, where instability measures were used. Telser's finding is crucial because it is based on a theory of optimal firm behavior; growth in demand is now being built into the market analysis. Again, it is difficult to perceive the existence or absence of market power due to the strong influence of growth in demand.

SUMMARY AND AREAS FOR FUTURE RESEARCH

The Trend toward a Dynamic Approach

The static Census concentration ratio has been proven to be quite uninformative for the pharmaceutical industry. Meanwhile, trying to relate seller concentration to monopolistic market power has also been vigorously criticized. See Figure 3.1 for an evolution of views. The conflicting results from the static and alternative measures of drug industry competitiveness render the former method archaic and impotent. Market instability and entry rates have given the issue a dynamic dimension that the field of market structure badly needs. Great strides are also being made in testing the relation between these new measures and the familiar market variables, such as promotional intensity, pricing behavior, and R & D innovation. However, there is still plenty of ground left uncovered in this direction.

The key finding from analysis based on a dynamic perspective is that market concentration at any given point in time is not necessarily associated with anemic or nonexistent competition. Thus, the finding of concentration loses its force as a justification for concluding lack of competitiveness. High concentration over time is another matter whose implications do not appear to have been fully explored; but this question has not been one of compelling interest for economists analyzing the drug industry, since over time changes in market share have been volatile.

Lack of market share stability does not mean that drug companies do not gain market power—at least temporarily. Put another way, the shift from a static to a dynamic perspective does not mean that the issue of market power—the ability to command prices in excess of marginal costs—disappears. A finding of market power, however, is not tantamount to a criticism that the industry's performance is inconsistent with the public interest. Before an evaluation can be made one way or another, more fundamental questions must be addressed, specifically:

- What does market power really mean?
- Since fast growth generally increases entry rates into an industry, does fast growth imply competitiveness?
- Is there any evidence that companies in the pharmaceutical industry actually achieve market power in a dynamic context?
- Does the competition between newer products and older products even before patent expiration reduce the significance of patents in making possible a divergence between marginal cost and price?

FIGURE 3.1. Path Chart of Drug Market Definition

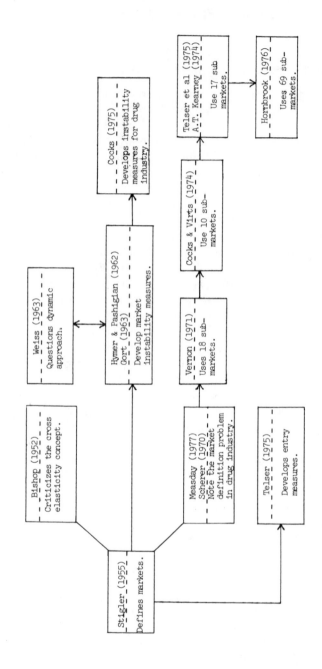

Source: Compiled by the authors.

On the Market Definition Problem

For the most part, the wide range in the different number of sub-markets used in empirical studies on the pharmaceutical industry (from 10 to 69) can be accounted for by the following factors:

- Lack of consensus among economists on an applied definition of a market in all economic fields.
- The particularly wide difference between demand and supply cross-elasticities in pharmaceutical products.
- Whether the analysis was based on a point in time or a period of time. Cross-elasticities of supply will be higher if the analytical perspective is dynamic, that is, takes into account the passage of time.

Although sometimes seriously criticized, the cross-elasticity concept still dominates the theory of market definition. The concept is attractive because it is built upon a body of well-established microeconomic theory. Through cross-elasticity, the idea of economic substitution in both demand and supply is clearly expressed; but the underlying assumptions are too strong to be applied to the field of imperfect competition, where many of them become unrealistic. There is also the question of "how large or small" the cross-elasticities should be in identifying the markets. Through further research, these problems may be solved by innovative adaptation of the microeconomic theory and solid understanding of the industry on a case-by-case basis.

We suggest the following:

An empirical study of the demand and supply cross-elasticities of pharmaceutical products. Given the approach's limitation, the study can serve as the first step toward establishing some form of quantitative benchmark on the issue.

An empirical study on the evolution of market structure in the pharmaceutical industry. This helps to create a perspective on the dynamics of the industry.

A drug demand study, using the Lancaster approach. Hornbrook's idea that drugs are only components of a larger package, a "health service," suggests an alternative approach to measuring demand for drugs. The suggestion is particularly attractive, considering the progress that has been made in the uses of characteristic equations for automobiles, housing, clean air, and so on.

4

PRICING BEHAVIOR OF
THE DRUG INDUSTRY

INTRODUCTION AND HISTORICAL BACKGROUND

The behavior of output prices in the drug industry is a major facet of the nature of competition in drugs. It has been frequently contended that the drug industry is in an excellent position to exploit the consumer. This arises as a result of: low overall demand elasticity, a set of drug submarkets that seem to be well-established at least on the demand side (as discussed in Chapter 3), and perceived entry barriers on the supply side (discussed in Chapter 5). In this paradigm the drug firms are seen as oligopolists who use a variety of devices to maintain their market position (for example, quality competition as opposed to price competition, and insistence on the inferiority of generic drugs as compared to brand-name, major firm products). Pricing practices are cited as evidence of oligopolistic behavior: For example, price inflexibility is seen as evidence of a "kinked" or "kinky" demand curve, a construct believed to be typical of oligopolistic market structure.

We will deal with the literature pertaining to these issues in this chapter. A related series of issues is dealt with in Chapter 5, and in a sense the two chapters should be seen together as focusing on the claim that the industry's competitive performance is indicative of inadequate competition. In general, issues arising on the demand side of the market are dealt with in this chapter; the issues having more to do with the supply side of the market are treated extensively in Chapter 5.

This chapter and the next bear witness to a sharp distinction between static and dynamic analysis as it pertains to the drug industry. Charges against the industry are frequently phrased in terms of the traditional static view of market structure; the industry is most frequently, and most effectively, defended by emphasis on dynamic analysis and the life cycle of drugs. It is demonstrated how competition can occur in nonprice dimensions such as quality, therapeutic characteristics, and seller services. The industry's defenders emphasize the costs of research and development, and the necessary repayment to innovation. This latter point is a relatively new approach, and many theoretical and empirical questions remain to be answered before it can be said that a fully developed dynamic model "explains" drug industry behavior.

APPROACH OF THE CHAPTER

A useful way to proceed would be to look at the actual behavior of drug prices, as described in the literature, and then to proceed to an examination of the controversy over whether price is an effective instrument of competition, with a particular focus on price competition between brand-name products and generically labeled versions of multisource drugs. Hence, the discussion of prices will be ordered as follows: price trends in drugs, the price flexibility issue, price competitiveness, and competition between generic and brand-name products.

PRICE TRENDS IN DRUGS

In both the Consumer Price Index (CPI) and the Producer Price Index (PPI, formerly wholesale price index, WPI), the components for prescription drugs have either declined or risen by less than prices generally. Since this evidence is contrary to the notion that the industry enjoys exceptional monopoly power, it has led to some criticism of the price indexes, either on the grounds of having inadequate samples or because newer and more expensive products are "linked in" at a neutral level that (allegedly) exerts a downward bias on the index.

The Thesis of Increasing Drug Prices

An example of the line of argument challenging the reliability of the Bureau of Labor Statistics (BLS) price indexes of prescriptions (in the CPI) and of ethical pharmaceutical products in the PPI was provided by Seymour Harris (1964, p. 75):

The point has been made time and again that the increase in the price of drugs since prewar has been modest indeed. The BLS Consumer Index has not been entirely satisfactory in this area. In view of the dramatic changes in chemotherapy, the relative stability of items used in the index and the slow changes in weights of the BLS index, the BLS index is subject to criticism.

Charging that the sample coverage and weighting of the prescription drug components have not been adequately updated to reflect changes in consumption patterns, Harris concluded that a more accurate indicator of actual price trends at retail would be provided by the average prescription charge, which was rising during the 1960s, at the same time the CPI for prescriptions was falling.

The decline in the CPI, according to Harris, was attributable to the fact that new drug products were introduced at a high price and could move only in a downward direction. Given their relatively large weightings, this characteristic of the "wonder drugs" gave the index, he charged, a continuous downward bias. He went so far as to allege (p. 76) that "it is clear that the price of *prescription* drugs has increased much more than the general price level and than total medical care."

A similar skepticism about the CPI is voiced by the U.S. Department of Health, Education and Welfare (HEW) report, *The Drug Users* as part of the Task Force on Prescription Drugs (1968e). The focus of their critique is that the basket of goods included in the index does not accurately reflect the consumption importance of the included goods and excludes many drug products believed to have risen in price. They again cite evidence that the average prescription price has risen steadily, and they suggest that it is a more reliable guide to "actual drug costs."

Hence the major evidence cited for an increasing trend in prices is rising average prescription prices, sluggishness of changes in the BLS product weights, and relatively high prices for new products. An additional cause for skepticism about the BLS index is the strong prior belief that the drug industry is monopolistic in nature.

Evidence Supporting the Price Indexes

The criticisms of the price index of prescription drugs, by Harris and (in a milder form) the HEW Task Force (1968a-f), were not so much an attack on this particular index, or on the pharmaceutical industry, as they were a criticism of price indexes in general for not being adequate measures of *expenditure*.

Having recognized this, in September 1969, the Pharmaceutical Manufacturers Association asked the commissioner of Labor Statistics to comment on that section of the Task Force report, and particularly on the suggestion that an index based on the average prescription charge would be a more appropriate measure of the price changes of prescription drugs. In his answer of October 23, 1969, the acting commissioner, Ben Burdetsky, commented in part:

> Such an index would measure changes in average prescription charges, or prescription expenditures. It would not measure price trends within the concepts of the CPI or WPI, since it is affected by factors other than price changes, such as changes in the quantity and type of prescription drugs sold at different periods. In calculating the CPI and the WPI, on the other hand, we attempt to hold all factors other than prices constant between two time periods.

The letter continued with the assertion that for the purposes of the CPI and the WPI, the size of the samples of prescribed drugs and the frequency of review of the sample weights seemed adequate to the Bureau, although they recognize that "there are other purposes for which a more precise measure might be needed, and a larger sample required."

On the central issue, however, the acting commissioner was firm:

> It is not a function of a price index to measure changes in expenditures, which are affected by such factors as changes in income, tastes, availability of products, and standards of living, as well as price changes. Therefore, when comparing trends measured by an index of expenditures and a price index, the essential difference between the two measures should be kept in clear perspective.

Empirical support for this position has been furnished by John Firestone, who, for almost 20 years, has been preparing price indexes based on much more comprehensive samples of prescription drugs, with annually revised weightings. Yet his results roughly parallel those of the BLS. He does, however, show pharmaceutical prices declining in the 1960s somewhat less, and rising in the 1970s somewhat more, than would be indicated by the BLS indexes, although the differences are relatively minor and not always in the same direction.

Firestone (1970, p. 17) ascribed the somewhat smaller decline of his index during the period 1961-70 to the fact that it is much more comprehensive: "It is well known that the broader the coverage of an index in terms of the number of items included, the more sluggish it tends to become." His comprehensive index showed a decline of 9.2 percent in manufacturers' prices for ethical pharmaceuticals during the ten years covered, compared to a decline of 10.7 percent in the corresponding BLS/WPI index.

During the 1960s, Firestone also maintained a separate price index for patented drugs and one for those not covered by patent. This study provided a refutation of the widely held assumption that price reductions occur only after a product emerges from patent. In fact, there was very little change in the index of nonpatented drugs. With 1949 as a base, it was 100.8 in 1960, 98.2 in 1962, and 101.1 in 1966. By comparison, the separate index of patented products was down to 92.4 in 1960, to 87.1 in 1962, and to 85.9 in 1966. It was clear that innovators had been lowering prices before the patents expired.

Perhaps the most important contribution of Firestone, however, was his measurement of changes in average prescription size. He showed that there had been an increase of 27.3 percent, between 1960 and 1969, in the size of the average prescription. This finding, also confirmed by subsequent statistics, illustrates the importance of the point made by the acting Commissioner of Labor Statistics on the need to keep a price index from being affected by extraneous expenditure factors, such as changes in taste or in the size of the unit being purchased. The importance of this size factor alone was illustrated by Firestone in providing data on changes in the average prescription price (or charge) when adjusted for changes in size. Before adjustment for size, the average prescription charge in 1978 ($6.44) was exactly 100 percent higher than that of 1960 ($3.22). After adjustment for the 66.3 percent increase in average prescription size, the change in unit price was shown to be an increase of only 20.2 percent, according to Firestone. Since this was not substantially greater than the change in the retail prescription price index (a rise of 15.1 percent according to BLS and of 14.8 percent according to Firestone's comprehensive index), it would follow that the other nonprice element in expenditure—the trading up to newer products at higher prices—could not have carried as much weight as implied by the criticisms of Harris.

While Firestone's work has been essentially statistical, helping to support the BLS position and methodology, other writers have applied this evidence to the question of whether the industry's market power is excessive. In an article defending existing patent protection against Schifrin's proposal of compulsory licensing, Forman (1969) pointed to declining drug prices during the 1960s as incompatible with the assumption of exceptional power over prices. Writing in defense of the industry's performance, two British economists, Reekie (1978) and Teeling–Smith (1975), have demonstrated that there is no inherent conflict between falling prices and monopoly (or rising prices and competition). While conceding that the trend in prices may not be conclusive by itself, the industry defenders continue to insist that if manufacturers had excessive market power, they would hardly have been expected to reduce prices in the 1960s and raise them so much less than other prices in the 1970s. If demand were indeed inelastic, as the critics claimed, an opposite pricing behavior might be expected from profit maximizers.

THE PRICE FLEXIBILITY ISSUE

Writing in 1935, Gardiner Means set forth the hypothesis that certain industries, whose prices showed relatively infrequent change, were exercising power to "administer" their prices. The hypothesis gained numerous adherents, and the term "administered prices" was selected as the title of the Kefauver hearings into the drug industry in the early 1960s.

To establish the thesis that price stickiness and oligopolistic market structure are causally linked, Sweezy (1939) offered another hypothesis: the kinky demand curve. He argued that firms in an oligopolistic industry recognize their mutual interdependence as to pricing and demand. They must then attempt to deduce the behavior of rivals in response to their own actions, since their rivals' behavior will affect the demand curve facing them. The kinky demand curve theory assumes that firms make the least favorable prognosis possible. They assume that if they raise their own price, their rivals will not follow suit; consumers will desert their product and go to their rival to purchase the commodity. On the other hand, if they lowered their price, other firms *will* follow their lead. Since all firms have the lowered price, the initial firm will attract fewer new customers than it would have if it were the only one to lower the price. Hence neither price increases nor decreases are profitable.

There are many problems with this theory, not the least of which is simply that there may be many plausible interpretations of infrequent price changes, and either oligopoly or competition is consistent with either frequent or infrequent price changes. Nevertheless, given the charge of administered prices against the drug industry, it was inevitable that some attempt would be made to count the number of changes occurring in drug prices. Two studies have been done: Cocks and Virts (1974) and Primeaux and Smith (1976).

Cocks and Virts group the industry into ten dominant markets. They then derive price indexes for each group, and for drugs overall. With these indexes, they examine price flexibility by counting the number of price changes. They use transactions prices instead of quoted prices, which Stigler and Kindahl (1970) showed to be both more accurate and more flexible. They also correct for prescription size. They conclude that prescription drug prices have not been rigid.

Primeaux and Smith (1976) obtained similar results. They test two implications of the kinked-demand hypothesis: first, that if the drug industry were oligopolistic, price changes would be rare; and second, price decreases would be followed by competitors, but price increases would not be. Individual drug products were classified as either monopolistic, duopolistic, or oligopolistic, depending on whether and how many competing drugs exist. The behavior of ologopolists was then examined relative to the two others. Their conclusion as to price flexibility was: "Price rigidity in the duopoly, oligopoly and total oligopoly market structure exceeded that in the monopoly market structure by only a minute degree" (pp. 191–92). For their second hypothesis, own price changes and rival's price changes were noted in nonmonopoly markets.

> It is clear . . . that pricing behavior of the combined set of all oligopoly products did not confirm the kinky demand curve theory . . . although there was nothing in the data to suggest that drug industry pricing behavior supported the kinked demand curve, the duopoly patterns were more nearly compatible with the theory than were the oligopoly patterns. The kinked demand curve was supported by 36% percent of the price changes in duopoly market structures but only by 24% of the changes in the oligopoly market structure . . . . Overall, the results of this study contradict the underpinnings of the kinky demand curve (pp. 195–96).

One problem with Primeaux and Smith's methodology is that it is very hard to distinguish in practice between oligopoly, duopoly, and monopoly; yet the study is based on comparisons between these rather arbitrary categories defined for their approach.

On the basis of the evidence cited, it seems that there is not much foundation for the conclusion that the drug industry behaves according to the kinky demand curve theory. However, this alone does not necessarily mean that the drug industry is competitive in structure. It might, instead, mean simply that the kinky demand curve is (as Stigler argued in 1947) a poor indicator of oligopoly structure.

PRICE COMPETITIVENESS

A further source of controversy about the drug industry has been the apparent willingness of drug companies to compete in ways other than price. Growing out of the perception of the major drug firms as oligopolists relying on administered prices, some writers pointed to the large amount of research and innovation (much of it deemed duplicative) as the inevitable result of an unwillingness to compete in terms of price. Starting from this hypothesis, writers like Henry Steele (1964, p. 200). argued that patents should be abolished, since they constitute "a most formidable barrier in restricting competition."

The response to this argument by other analysts includes two major points. They contend first that research and development constitutes a perfectly acceptable alternative form of competition; and second, that the industry has been willing to compete in price and has in fact done so.

Nonprice Behavior as Competition

Michael Cooper (1966, pp. 154–55) responds to Steele's position by saying, "The falseness of these arguments is the result of a refusal to depart from traditional price competition and to recognize the force of substitution as a form of competition in its own right." He points to the frequent changes in top–ranking firms in different therapeutic submarkets and argues that this is evidence of competition between competing products; firms introduce new products in submarkets to compete with current market leaders. He believes that "as long as there are not artificially contrived barriers to entry, this is as efficient a market structure as any" (p. 157).

This leaves open the question of whether new drugs are in fact innovative, or, as has been frequently contended, "mere molecular manipulations" as alleged by some witnesses before the Kefauver and Nelson committees. The popular use of this phrase, as though implying the waste of resources on the development of marginal drugs, prompted a number of books and articles by biochemists and pharmacologists pointing out that some of the most important pharmaceutical advances were discovered, often by chance, through the modification of existing molecules.

Other writers have pointed out that an improvement, even if it turns out to be marginal, may be meaningful to some subcategory of patients and is thus comparable to price competition. Michael Cooper (1966, p. 88), for instance, writes:

Whether a drug is a minor or major advance depends largely on one's viewpoint, at least initially whilst the product undergoes the test of time. To its inventor it is a genuine improvement for no company would risk time and money to launch a drug only to have it proved worthless twelve months later. The firm would lose in reputation, its most important intangible asset, and probably make a heavy financial loss in withdrawing the drug before it had covered its research overhead or the initial high promotional outlays.

Brozen (1975) develops a similar concept, which he labels "multidimensional competition." His analysis is developed within the framework of the classical theory of the firm. He asks how a firm decides how much of each input to buy, and he derives the standard answer: Each input should be used until it contributes no more to total cost than it contributes to the value of output. He then asks analogously how a firm decides upon the quality and other characteristics of its output; again, he argues that each characteristic should be added until its marginal benefit and marginal cost are equated. Similarly, the most profitable way to attract customers from rivals is not necessarily only to lower price; product improvement and innovation will also contribute to profitability, and at the margin, the ratio of the benefit added to profit by lower price to the benefit from further innovation should be equated to the ratio of their respective marginal costs. Furthermore, he argues, not to take other dimensions of competition besides price into account would be inefficient, just as using only one kind of input would be inefficient.

Price as a Means of Competition

The idea that a pattern of competitive behavior could be found in drug price movements was put forward recently by Teeling-Smith and Reekie. Teeling-Smith (1975) argues that drug introduction follows a "skimming price" behavior, which is essentially price discrimination over time. When a new and radical drug innovation is put forward and patented, Teeling-Smith states, the initial price is high; this maximizes profits since in the short run the demand for a highly useful and innovative product is likely to be inelastic. As time passes and substitute products are found by competitors, and as patent expiration approaches, price tends to fall toward its marginal variable cost. This form of price behavior is defended on the grounds that it is necessary for the survival of the industry. The marginal variable costs of producing a unit of virtually any drug product are minimal. In order to cover the initial fixed costs of the research necessary to develop the product, additional consumers' surplus must be captured by the firm in order that total revenue exceed total cost. This can be done only by price discriminating. On the other hand, for the noninnovative product, which may be an imitation of another firm's innovation, the price is likely to be low (called "penetration pricing" by Teeling-Smith) since the demand curve for that product is likely to be more elastic.

This model is tested for the British market by Reekie (1977); later he tests the model using U.S. data (1978). Reekie attempts to show in both of these studies that skimming behavior does occur for drugs with a high innovative content and that penetration pricing occurs for drugs with low innovative content. In both cases he finds his hypotheses confirmed. We will discuss here only the later study using U.S. data, since the two studies are essentially similar and derive similar results. Reekie puts forward three hypotheses. First, he divides new chemical entities (NCEs) in the period 1958-75 into three groups (those with important therapeutic gain, those with modest gain, and those with no gain) on the basis of a classification scheme used by the Food and Drug Administration (FDA). He finds that at the time of introduction the first group tends to be priced at a higher level (relative to therapeutic competitors) than are drugs in the second or third group. This he feels is consistent with the simple competitive model. Second, major breakthroughs, he finds, tend to be reduced in price over time as new competition becomes more and more likely. Third, he estimates a demand model that suggests that the demand elasticity for individual NCEs increases over time and that demand is less elastic for "important" drugs than for "modest" innovations (though, interestingly, his results also show that drugs with "no innovative content" are the least elastic of all).

This evidence is cited by Reekie as proving that drug prices follow a competitive model. However, it is clear that price discrimination between markets with different demand elasticities (whether by time or some other criterion) is frequently considered evidence of monopoly or some other noncompetitive market structure (see, for example, Stigler, *The Theory of Price* [1947], Chapter II). It does appear that drug firms are quite responsive to price and that changes in price are seen as profit-maximizing options, contrary to implications of the kinky demand curve theory.

In his Technical Appendix to Teeling-Smith's article (1977), Reekie comments:

> Price discrimination is *not* a pejorative term. It indicates merely that a product (or similar products) is (are) being sold at different (non-marginal cost related) prices. Skimming price . . . can be justified on welfare grounds in that it enables a firm to appropriate to itself consumer's surplus and so increase consumer's surplus and so increase producer's profits. This is economically desirable where marginal costs are very low (as pointed out to be so in pharmaceuticals) or are zero.

In short, price discrimination is justifiable because it allows goods to be produced that otherwise would not be, thereby generating "consumer's surplus": the division of the surplus between consumers and producers is of no interest in welfare terms.

These sentiments may be repugnant to some economic traditionalists who see any example of the discriminatory pricing as proof of monopoly power and who feel that the price of each product should be based on its marginal cost. A moment's reflection, however, will reveal many examples where this is impossible. The extreme case is that of the lighthouse, which can provide warnings of danger to an additional ship at a marginal cost of zero. Other examples abound: Most public utilities and carriers (rail, air, or bus lines), if their prices or fees were set at the level of marginal costs, would never be able to cover their average costs.

An analysis of these situations in terms of public welfare has been provided by William Baumol and David Bradford (1970). In essence, they observe that certain industries are characterized by heavy unallocable overhead costs. This means that variable costs, which can properly be allocated to each product or service, will represent a lower share of total costs than would be the case for industries as a whole. In such a situation, if the company sets its initial price at the marginal cost (based on allocable direct or variable costs), it will never cover its average costs. It is a prescription for bankruptcy.

In such industries, whether power companies, airlines, or research–based pharmaceutical manufacturers, average prices exceed marginal costs. The question then arises as to whether this excess, or differential, should be uniform for each product in the line and for each segmented market in which the company operates. The answer supplied by Baumol and Bradford is a clear "no." The differential should vary, and it should vary in terms of the elasticity of demand for each product and in each segmented market. Such a policy is dictated not simply by considerations of profit maximization. It is demonstrated by Baumol and Bradford as necessary to maximize consumer welfare as well.

It has been observed that direct production costs are a much smaller share of total costs for the full-service pharmaceutical manufacturer than for the typical firm in other industries. Company controllers make a valiant effort to identify the R & D costs associated with individual products, but they are the first to admit that these allocations are, for the most part, arbitrary. Any observer of the industry will confirm that it is typical for a company to be highly dependent on a very few extremely successful products to carry the major share of overhead and make the major contribution to earnings. These intrafirm transfers or subsidies are characteristic of public utilities as well. In the drug industry they are particularly pronounced. This characteristic is independent of the form of ownership. A state-owned pharmaceutical manufacturer would have to operate in the same fashion. Similarily, where markets are segmented, as they are internationally between sovereign countries, or as between hospitals and pharmacies domestically (because of the nonprofit exemption to the Robinson-Patman Act), it is typical (in the United States and abroad) to find lower prices for those products, and in those markets, where competition is more elastic to price.

Those who deplore this as immoral in the marketing of life-saving medicines, in "charging what the traffic will bear," are implicitly asserting that in this sector (unlike others) prices should be determined solely by the costs of supply, not by the interaction of supply and demand. They are also ignoring the Baumol-Bradford demonstration that this "price discrimination" actually maximizes social welfare.

In his study of pricing, Weston (1979, pp. 95, 96, 89, and 82) concluded as follows:

> The evidence on trends in market shares and in drug prices in the individual therapeutic classes supports a number of generalizations:

1. A leading patented product has an element of uniqueness. This must be so or the patent would not have been achieved in the first place.
2. No product is completely unique in a longer-run context. "Uniqueness" is a matter of degree and what appears to be absolutely unique in the short run is less unique or less competitively superior as time elapses.
3. Product imitations and product substitutions result in high cross elasticities of demand over broad groups of drugs and define a therapeutic product class.
4. Entry of new products and firms is slowed only when the therapeutic performance of the existing product is high in relation to its price.
5. Historically, no leading product has maintained its market share position for more than a limited number of years. Preeminence is temporary.
6. There is also competition in prices among a wide array of competing drugs. This competition has resulted in a downward trend in prices of new drugs in the years following their introduction. Thus drug prices compete over their life cycle with the prices of other drugs over their life cycles. In addition, the data demonstrate that the trends of drug prices, relative to other consumer products, have continuously trended downward.

Schwartzman (1976a, pp. 255–72) examines the history of prices in antibiotic markets as well as in other markets. Some of the leading manufacturers of antibiotics cut their prices substantially before the expiration of patents and prior to the actual entry of other firms. In some antibiotic markets the new entrants initiated the price cuts and the leading firm delayed their own price cuts. The firms with smaller market shares were aggressive price cutters seeking to increase market shares so that the firms with the larger market shares were eventually forced to cut their prices due to losses in market shares.

Schwartzman observes that the prices of some generic products manufactured by relatively small companies are lower than the prices of major companies' products. In such cases the price of antibiotic products would not have been reduced to marginal costs. Price differentials for generic products may result from uncertainty in comparing the quality of the products and the reputation of their producers.

Product Competition:
Barrier or Stimulus to Price Competition?

One of the most fundamental developments in the literature on pharmaceutical industry economics has been the change in economists' perception of the relation between price competition and product competition. Until the mid-1970s, the prevailing view was that promulgated by Steele in the early 1960s: Such devices as patents, product proliferation, and heavy advertising were anathema to price competition. Moreover, this perception by no means has completely died out. Comanor (1979, p. 66) succinctly summarized this line of thinking: " . . . rapid innovation may indeed be at the expense of substantial price competition. Whether this is the case is a major question regarding the role of competition in the pharmaceutical industry."

Challengers to the Steele tradition stand the classic view on its head. Far from being a barrier to price competition, product competition—when viewed over time—stimulates price competition. Weston (1979, p. 71), based on his analysis of pricing in the market for antiinfectives, summarizes his findings as follows:

> The traditional short-run partial equilibrium analysis of standard micro-economic theory represents an oversimplification of the pricing mechanism. The price of a drug product is its nominal price plus quality factors, and price competition takes place on many dimensions of quality. These dimensions include, for example, efficacy, safety, clinical evidence and experience, information communicated to physicians, and the reputation of the man-ufacturer. Product competition results in continuous price reductions on older products. Furthermore price competition takes place in the discounts and rebates to wholesalers and other distribution outlets. There are relatively high cross elasticities of demand between drugs in a product group, and there are not likely to be wide departures between long-run marginal cost and price for most drug products. Possible departures from technical pricing tests are more than offset by advances in innovation resulting in substantial benefits to consumers.

If the appropriate test of a theory is its conformance to the empirical evidence, the newer, dynamic view of the interaction of product and price competition would appear to deserve acceptance. The massive amounts of price data used by Weston, for example, simply were not available to earlier analysts, who therefore had to rely much more on traditional theory rather than facts.

It should not, however, be inferred that Comanor and Steele are entirely wrong. If at a given point in time the market for pharmaceuticals were made less responsive to product differences, prices on existing drugs would be some unknown extent probably fall. According to the dynamic view espoused by Weston, however, if the result was that it became economically unattractive to engage in a new drug development, prices for existing drugs would—over time—be higher than if product competition had remained robust. This happens because the introduction of new drugs causes the prices of old drugs to decline, and in response prices for new drugs are reduced from their introduction levels.

It should be remembered, however, that the dynamic view rests on an assumption whose validity is not something that economists are equipped to measure: The size of the mine of biochemical insights has not even begun to be fully explored much less exploited. Put another way, major therapeutic breakthroughs are waiting to be found.

COMPETITION BETWEEN GENERIC
AND BRAND-NAME PRODUCTS

If more heat than light seems to have been generated over this issue, part of the problem is semantic. The term "generic" should perhaps be used only in connection with a prescription: the physician is prescribing generically when he writes the generic name of the drug rather than a particular trademarked or brand name of an individual manufacturer. When prescribing generically, he has delegated the responsibility for source selection to the pharmacist.

Over the years, however, popular usage has applied the term "generic" to certain drug products. When this is done, confusion arises because of difference in interpretation. To some, a generic drug product is simply one that lacks a brand name and is marketed under the generic name (which *all* drug products have). By this criterion, the thyroid tablets of Armour Laboratories, and the nitroglycerin tablets of Lilly or Parke Davis, would be considered generic products. For other writers, a generic product is simply one that is marketed by a "generic company," that is, one that either manufactures, repackages, or merely distributes copier versions of multisource drugs but that lacks an R & D capacity and hence does not innovate new drugs. For those in this school, the above-cited thyroid and nitroglycerin tablets would not be considered "generic," whereas versions of the same drugs marketed by "generic houses" would be, even though they might carry brand names, as about a dozen versions of nitroglycerin from such companies do today.

The problem is further complicated by the spread of the so-called branded generics. Is SK-Tetracycline to be considered a brand (Smith-Kline) or a generic (tetracycline) drug product? If it is to be considered a brand-name product—since only one manufacturer is entitled to use this name—then how does one justify the general treatment of "Kesso-Tetra" as a generic product? The distinction here seems to be that Smith-Kline is a research-based manufacturer while McKesson Laboratories is a generic house.

A still different interpretation of the term has been offered by Halperin (1979). He has proposed that all versions of a multisource drug other than the innovator's should be considered as "generic," whether or not they carry brand names. The difficulty with this concept is illustrated in the case of ampicillin. If only one version is to be considered "brand name," should it be Polycillin, the brand of Bristol-Myers, which was first on the U.S. market and is still the most expensive, or Totacillin, the brand marketed by Beecham, the real innovator of ampicillin, which finally introduced its own brand (at much lower prices) on the U.S. market?

Articles in newspapers and popular magazines typically deal with the antisubstitution laws—which still exist in six of the 50 states—as though conveying to the trademark holder a government-protected property right. Since even in these six states the physician always has the opportunity to delegate source selection by writing generically, the "property right" is circumscribed. It is comparable to the legal requirement that when a customer asks for Coca-Cola he should not be served Pepsi Cola without his permission. The essential issue raised in this debate over the antisub-stitution laws is whether the physician should be deemed to have delegated authority over source selection to the pharmacist unless he takes some positive and overt step to prevent substitution. The Federal Trade Commission has proposed, in its "model" product selection law distributed to the states, that this overt action should be in the form of handwritten certification that the particular brand-name drug is "medically necessary" for this patient. Experience has shown that when the law is phrased in this fashion, physicians will generally not exercise their prerogative to withhold permission to substitute; possibly they lack evidence to declare a particular brand as absolutely essential, even though it is one they know and prefer.

The scholarly literature thus far has not addressed the issue of the economic impact on the funding of R & D by the research-based companies should the FTC and other agencies succeed in making "product selection" by pharmacists virtually universal. The issue is an important one, however, because government efforts that in effect mandate that price must be the all but exclusive criterion for selection among multisource drugs can significantly affect expected returns from R & D and therefore industry's willingness to engage in R & D. Although there is not much literature on the economic aspects of the competitive ground rules between research-intensive and nonresearch-intensive companies, much work has been done on the scientific aspects of the issue. Specifically, a substantial number of studies and articles have been done on the scientific question of equivalency (or nonequivalency) of different versions of the same drug. These were reviewed by Schwartzman (1976a, pp. 226-50) and are summarized as follows:

FDA Potency Study (1966): The FDA tested samples of drugs from 245 manufacturers and found 8.1 percent of the sample to be inadequately potent. The FDA inferred poor performance by the industry generally. The results were later questioned and to some extent defects in the study were acknowledged by FDA.

The Steers Study (1967): The National Center for Drug Analysis attempted to provide information about the quality of drugs on the market on an ongoing basis. Their initial survey found many manufacturing defects and wide variation in the level of potency. Schwartzman infers, from the presence of defects, that they are the fault of generic producers, and not of major brand names. Such an inference is without evidence.

The Pitts Report (1971): Dr. Roy Pitts of the University of Minnesota reported to the commissioner of the FDA that many marketed drugs were substandard (25 percent of his sample) and called for closer FDA monitoring of manufacturing processes.

McCaffree and Newman (1968) described the outpatient drug program of the Group Health Cooperative of Puget Sound and suggested reasons for its relative efficiency and success. The main characteristics of its drug program were adherence to a drug formulary, administrative control, and the economies inherent in generic bulk purchases. Controls within the organization ensured quality in the generic purchases.

Defense Personnel Support Center (1967): The DPSC conducted preaward surveys of 149 domestic drug producers; 48 were disqualified from awards on the basis of either low quality or poor "housekeeping." Senator Nelson has argued this technique overstates the risk from generics.

General Accounting Office (1973) stated that the FDA had inadequate resources to fulfill its plant inspection obligation. The GAO found that nearly 20 percent of plants had not been inspected in their sample.

Drug Bioequivalence Study, Office of Technology Assessment (1974): In consideration of HEW's proposal that maximum allowable cost be the basis for governmental drug purchases, the Congress asked if bioequivalency could be equated with generic equivalence. The OTA's report found that the standards on which generic equivalence are based are inadequate and hence even chemical equality between generically identical drugs may be questionable. Furthermore, the FDA's inspection program is inadequate.

Gumbhir (1971): Gumbhir surveyed pharmacists on their opinions as to the relative quality of generic and brand name drugs. The questions emphasized the physical appearance of the drugs. About three-fourths of the pharmacists surveyed believed brand-name drugs to be of higher quality than generics. However, the more critical dimensions of efficacy and safety were not discussed and conclusions about them should not be drawn.

Fitelson Laboratories Study: This study tested 20 samples from 20 manufacturers of three drug products as to identity, weight, and disintegration time. All drugs tested met USP (United States Pharmacopaeia) standards. The conclusion was that the risk of poor quality is negligible regardless of source.

Reserpine; Conjugated Estrogen: These studies were performed by private laboratories under contract to the major manufacturers of the respective products. Samples from many manufacturers were tested for conformity to USP standards. Both studies found that a substantial proportion of the copier versions failed to meet the compendial standards as represented by the standard products of the innovators, that is, Serpasil in the case of reserpine and Premarin in the case of conjugated estrogens.

SUMMARY AND AREAS FOR FUTURE RESEARCH

Drug pricing behavior has been used as an indication of the degree of competitiveness to be found in the pharmaceutical industry. The degree of price competition varies considerably by therapeutic class and by product. Where patient needs are highly specified and varied, where technical problems of uniformity, purity, and bioavailability lead to a higher risk of quality failure, competition between suppliers of multisource drugs is more likely to be on a nonprice basis. Similarly, as between sole-source drugs treating the same condition, the product offering unique therapeutic advantages will face a relatively inelastic demand curve and be able to command a price premium. Here again, competition is apt to be more on the basis of quality than price.

On the other hand, for the more mature multisource products—including many of the older antibiotics—where examples of nonequivalence have been relatively rare, price competition has been pronounced and has been demonstrated in the market research data either by an overall price decline (relative to other prices) and/or by a marked erosion of the market share of the innovator's product when priced at a substantial premium over the prices of other versions.

The model of Teeling-Smith, relating relative introductory prices to quality (that is, to the appraisal by expert pharmacologists of the degree of therapeutic uniqueness of the new product), has been tested and apparently validated by Reekie, using both British and U.S. data. This does *not*, however, mean that all price differences are to be fully explained and socially justified in terms of attributes of quality. In all commodity markets, surely, there is an element of the irrational, of brand loyalties not based on well-controlled studies. There is no reason to assume that prescription drugs should be different and exempt from all cases of irrational product differentiation.

If pharmaceutical manufacturing and marketing are to be studied in

FIGURE 4.1. Path Chart of Drug Pricing Policy

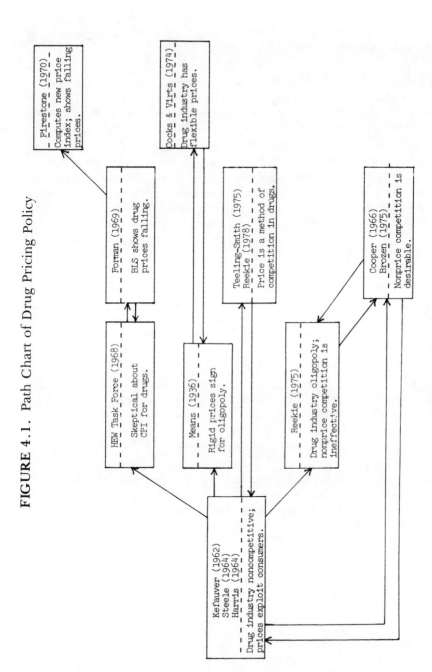

Source: Compiled by the authors.

57

context rather than in isolation from the rest of the economy, the relevant field for socioeconomic research is not whether the industry conforms to the classical model of perfect competition but whether it differs from that model in such a manner and degree—relative to other industries—as to justify some government intervention to protect the consumer. Even if it should be found that pharmaceuticals are characterized by some unique degree of oligopoly or market power on the part of the principal suppliers, it would still need to be determined whether government intervention would be able to correct the situation and provide the public a substantial *net* and longer–term saving. Would the saving exceed the direct administrative costs borne by physicians, pharmacists, and even consumers? What would be the impact, on the industry's ability to continue to innovate, from various possible interventions, such as the curtailment of patents or the adoption of price ceilings to eliminate all prestige premiums on multi-source drugs? The existing literature is filled with strongly differing views on these issues.

There appears to be a clear discontinuity in the literature vis-a-vis the issue of the relationship between product and price competition (see Figure 4.1). The newer, dynamic model of the drug industry says that *over time* periodic "market power" can induce price competition. The classic view, based on analysis of the industry at a given *point* in time, argues that product competition is at the expense of price competition.

Since, however, their respective time perspectives are different, the two views are not necessarily contradictory. The dynamic model acknowledges that product-based competition in the present may entail a pricing structure that is higher than it would be if competition were based on price alone. As will be discussed in detail in Chapter 6, the policy question that arises is whether greater price competition among today's drugs benefits the public more than a competitive process where price competition is a by-product of product competition. Put another way, is less innovation and more price competition more beneficial to the consumer than a hybrid competitive system based on an evolution of product characteristics as well as on price?

5

ENTRY AND STRATEGIES

The pharmaceutical industry was the main target of the Kefauver Committee's hearings of 1959 through 1962. During these hearings, much publicity was given to the allegation of various witnesses that manufacturers in this industry enjoyed an exceptional degree of monopoly power.

While these charges did not result in legislation requiring compulsory licensing of drug patents, or other punitive measures recommended by some witnesses, they did give rise to a lively academic interest in the economics of pharmaceutical marketing as a case of imperfect competition.

The basis of this discussion dates to the 1930s. Joan Robinson (1933) did much to legitimize the idea that large segments of a free-market economy may be routinely monopolistic. However, Edward Chamberlin's *Theory of Monopolistic Competition* (1936) represented the first attempt to provide a theoretical foundation for a view of the U.S. economy that captured noncompetitive elements and was also descriptively believable. Chamberlin emphasized the degree of product differentiation to be found among firms in a vaguely defined "group" or industry as the basis for monopolization. Chamberlin's concept of a link between product differentiation and monopoly gained currency over the next few decades. In 1956 Joe Bain's study, *Barriers to New Competition* (1956), set forth a series of entry barriers that included product differentiation and helped to define the concept more rigorously. He argued (p. 60) that

> product differentiation is propagated by differences in the design or physical quality of competing products, by efforts of sellers to distinguish their products through packaging, branding, and the offering of auxiliary services to buyers, and by advertising and sales-promotional efforts designed to win the allegiance and custom of the potential buyer . . . . He [the seller] can

> presumably raise his prices somewhat above those of his rivals while retaining
> some but not all of the customers who prefer his product . . . . In order to
> secure a market, the entrant may have to accept a lower price than established
> firms . . . [until] he establishes "buyer acceptance" for his product. Or he may
> have to incur appreciably higher selling costs per unit of sales volume.

As a result, product differentiation may inhibit free entry into an industry and thereby create monopolistic advantages for the established firms.

THE LONG SHADOW OF HENRY STEELE

The wide influence that Bain's ideas attained did much to lay a foundation for the charges that were soon made against the U.S. drug industry. In 1962 and 1964 Henry Steele published papers, based on the testimony in the Kefauver hearings, that remain the definitive attack on the drug industry. Steele's arguments may be separated into demand and supply categories. On the demand side, Steele (1964, p. 199) argued that, since doctors prescribe for patients but do not buy, price is not a factor in the purchase of drugs; indirect demand creates inelastic demand.

On the supply side, approximately constant returns to scale apply in production, he argues, so that large drug firms have no competitive advantage with small firms in production. Steele (1964, p. 162) also argues: "The only important economy of scale in most drug markets seems to be that of large-scale advertising and distribution." Monopolization occurs in drug submarkets through use of patents and brand names to create a false differentiation of product. Advertising leads doctors to use brand-name products; deliberately chosen obscure generic names forestall use of generic products. Patents favor large firms, since for a small firm, "a patent is merely an invitation to costly litigation, and the only advantage a small firm can take of a patent is to sell it to a rival" (Steele, 1962, p. 138). Furthermore, big firms "disparage" the products of small firms; advertising favors large firms. Furthermore, Steele (1964, p. 222) argues, drug industry research is not an important argument for maintaining patents, since most drug industry "research" amounts to no more than yet another way to differentiate products, this time by "molecular manipulation"; foreign countries without patent protection and nonindustry researchers are said to be more productive of fundamental innovations. Steele's major argument is against patents as the fundamental entry barrier: "In general, the presence or absence of price competition in drugs depends upon the presence or absence of patent protection" (Steele, 1964, p. 158). His policy proposals hence center on eliminating spurious product differentiation by eliminating legal protection for product or brand-name ownership.

A number of things can be said about Steele's arguments at this point.

In the first place, his argument on the behavior of suppliers is based o concept of *product* differentiation. Advertising, brand names, patents, a research are to him all ways to separate one product from another. Steel points out that no significant scale economies exist in drugs (outside of those pertaining to advertising); and no absolute cost advantages are said to accrue to established firms that are not available to new entrants. Steele depicts an industry in which entry into the overall market would not be too difficult but for the existence of distinct submarkets in which supply elasticity is reduced by the success of manufacturers in establishing the perception of product differences. This technique, as he sees it, further restricts and subdivides the effective or relevant market for each product, and thus, by raising the concentration rate, increases the degree of monopoly power. It will be apparent that the issue of product differentiation, emphasized by Steele, is closely linked to the question of concentration and market definition discussed in Chapter 3.

Second, the product-differentiation argument presents an essentially comparative-statics framework of analysis. The purpose is to explain how profit rates or prices may be, at a moment in time, greater than the level of profits or prices that would be expected if competition were textbook perfect and based exclusively on price. As a result, Steele's analysis is not well geared to take time-related phenomena into account. To some extent, the evolution of thought in response to the issues raised by Steele and others has been toward an explicit inclusion of dynamic elements into industry analysis.

Third, Steele has failed to place product differentiation in pharmaceuticals in a proper context. If, as observation suggests, it is equally characteristic of manufacturers in other commodity markets to seek to differentiate their products, the relevant questions would then appear to be whether this technique is more or less prevalent in pharmaceuticals compared to other industries and more or less subject to the constraint of having to support performance claims with scientific proof. The fact that each claim for a prescription drug product must be demonstrated, to the satisfaction of a highly critical regulatory agency, and with "substantial evidence" in the form of controlled clinical trials, would lead one to suspect that product differentiation in this industry is more likely to be authentic, and less easily contrived, than in industries not subject to the same vigorous standards of proving the accuracy of the information disseminated. Product differentiation is not, by definition, a uniform evil. It is an example of product differentiation that the modern antibiotic actually cures an infection while the Victorian elixirs did not. In brief, the drug industry might deserve the strictures of Henry Steele on this point if it were really evident that product differentiation is completely artificial and contrived. The evidence to date would not appear to support this conclusion, however.

Finally, Steele not only accepted the accounting rates of return as

for comparing the profitability of pharmaceuticals
ıt he attributed the striking differential shown by
return on investment to monopoly elements
ᴗrentiation. His basic articles, of 1962 and 1964,
ᴗppearance of the studies demonstrating that profits
ᴗompany annual reports are overstated because of the
treatment of R & D. Steele's work also was done before the
ᴗarance of empirical studies demonstrating that advertising and
promotion in pharmaceuticals have been used primarily to gain entry for
new products rather than to protect the market shares of existing products,
in short, as a means of encouraging, rather than inhibiting, competition.
(See discussion of Telser in Chapter 3).

APPROACH OF THE CHAPTER

A taxonomy of major considerations covering drug industry entry
barriers and conduct would be the following:

- Advertising as a barrier to entry: observed correlation between advertising and
  profitability, and alternative explanations; rational versus image-oriented
  consumer-search and Veblen effects; and economies of scale in advertising.
- Patents and research: optimal length of patent life; "artificial barriers to supply-
  side substitution" versus "necessary innovations", and "repetitive and trivial
  innovations" versus "fundamental breakthroughs."

ADVERTISING AS A BARRIER TO ENTRY

Relationship between Advertising and Profitability

In his 1956 *Barriers to New Competition*, Bain set forth the doctrine that
advertising creates barriers to entry through artificial product differentiation. Telser (1964) and Backman (1967), however, subsequently concluded
that this hypothesis did not conform to the empirical evidence. Telser
found that the correlation between the advertising/sales ratio and the level
of seller concentration is not statistically significant. In concluding that
advertising is relatively innocuous, Telser spoke from a long tradition in
economics that tended to see markets as competitive except in unusual
circumstances. In response to Telser's initial investigation, Comanor and
Wilson (1967) presented an extensive empirical analysis of the effect of
advertising on profitability. They argued (p. 424) that "concentration
ratio [used by Telser] measures only one dimension of market structure,
and is therefore an inadequate indicator of market power.... The weak

correlation between concentration and advertising simply indicates that these are independent rather than collinear variables."

Profit rates, they argued, represent a more reliable measure of market power than concentration ratios: Regressing the average profit rate for the period 1954–57 for 41 U.S. industries on a variety of market structural variables such as economies of scale, concentration, and capital requirements as well as advertising, they found that advertising was the only consistently significant explanatory variable, while concentration ratios were consistently insignificant. The implication Comanor and Wilson (p. 437) drew was that "investment in advertising is a highly profitable activity . . . . It is likely, moreover, that this . . . is accounted for by the entry barriers created by advertising and the resulting achievement of market power."

They justified their results with an appeal to Bain's theory of entry barriers. They argued that advertising by established firms creates brand loyalty; entrants must incur penetration costs to overcome this obstacle. These penetration costs are the entry barrier. Furthermore, these costs may be related to scale, creating an absolute scale barrier to entrants.

This statement of the effects of advertising remains the definitive statement of this position: Ayanian (1975a, pp. 479-80), writing eight years later, called Comanor and Wilson's argument "to my knowledge the only rigorous attempt to explain how advertising creates a barrier to entry." In addition, Comanor and Wilson's empirical work has remained the principal and most definitive statement of the general position.

An article published contemporaneously with Comanor and Wilson's by Mann, Henning, and Meehan (1967) presented an analysis very similar to that of Comanor and Wilson. They try to show, by Bain's theory of product differentiation, that differentiation as measured by advertising intensity per dollar of sales is associated with concentration. Hence their analysis is very close to Telser's, but they get exactly opposite results. Their results, like Comanor and Wilson's, point toward a positive link between concentration and advertising, though their statistical work is rather less sophisticated. They claim the differences with Telser's results are a result of their more careful measurement of variables. Combined with Comanor and Wilson's charges against Telser, the result was to provoke an empirical controversy over the advertising/profitability relationship.

In response to Comanor and Wilson's paper, Telser (1968) responded with what amounted to a new view of advertising: Far from creating an entry barrier, advertising was a means of entry, since firms used it to create consumer disloyalty, not loyalty. Relying on a view of consumers as rational, instead of motivated by image, Telser argued that experience with good products, not advertising, created loyalty; if a product failed to perform to anticipation, all the image in the world would not hold the consumer. Advertising functioned to inform consumers of alternatives to their current consumption behavior. He points out that if advertising could be relied upon to create entry barriers and high profits, all firms would invest more in advertising than they do. Finally, he made a point that became fundamental for the issue: that Comanor and Wilson's measures of profitability and assets failed to account for the asset nature of advertising, and hence they understate true firm assets and so overstate the profit rates.

Accounting versus Economic Profits

This latter point was extensively explored by Weiss (1969). Though the point is equally applicable to all forms of intangible capital, and in particular R & D investment, Weiss concentrates entirely on advertising capital. Advertising is expensed fully for tax and accounting purposes, but should not be, he concluded. Only true capital consumption should be charged. Observed profits are less than true profits by the amount of net investment in advertising capital. Likewise, equity should be increased by the undepreciated portion of past and current advertising expenditures.

What determines the relationship between true and observed rates of return? The true rate of return can exceed or fall short of the observed rate of return depending on whether profits or equity have a greater proportional adjustment. Moreover, the gap between true and accounting profits will be greater, the greater is the rate of growth of advertising and the lower the depreciation rate; the rate of return will be over- or understated depending on whether the accounting rate of return exceeds or is less than the rate of growth of advertising.

Using these concepts, Weiss reestimates Comanor and Wilson's advertising-profitability regressions and finds that the results hold up well when the true rate of return is substituted for the accounting rate; since none of the relationships changes significantly, he concludes that advertising is positively related to profitability. Furthermore, he argues, since taxes depend on the absolute level of profits, and not on rates of return, it is clear that true profits have been understated by expensing of advertising and hence there is a tax subsidy to firms with relatively long-lived advertising. He believes the subsidy favors brand-name advertising, which probably depreciates more slowly than other forms; futhermore, this subsidy, by his estimates, is unevenly distributed: 42 percent went to drug, soap, and soft drink industries. He proposes that the subsidy be eliminated by requiring that advertising be depreciated; the IRS should issue depreciation guidelines, as it does for other forms of capital. This, he feels, would reduce advertising and excessive emphasis on brand names.

There are a number of questions that arise from a review of Weiss' study: It is possible that advertising is depreciated over too short a life span, thereby understating true profits; and he does not include other forms of intangible capital in his estimates, again probably biasing his results toward an optimistic view of accounting rate accuracy. Later studies have attempted these adjustments.

Also it is very important to keep in mind that Weiss' calculations pertain to absolute profits, not profit *rates*. If a firm were to change the accounting treatment of R & D from expensing to capitalizing, the result would be to increase taxable profits. In the first year of the transition, there would also be an *increase* in the profit rate; but after full depreciation of successive years of R & D investment, the effect would, typically, be to *lower* the profit *rate*.

In short, it would not be appropriate to infer from Weiss' results that higher profits are the same as higher profit rates. The reality in fact is the reverse in those cases where advertising is expensed rather than capitalized, and the accounting rate of return exceeds the growth rate of advertising.

Finally, there is a more fundamental problem. Weiss' conclusion rests on the assumption established by Bain, which has been convincingly challenged in recent years, that advertising is essentially anticompetitive. If, as Telser and others have argued, the net effect of advertising is to strengthen competition, then advertisers may have a stronger case for retaining what is admittedly a tax incentive. Furthermore, it may be difficult to justify removing this incentive from advertising while retaining it for the other major form of intangible investment, R & D.

The Question of Causality

The question of causality, assumed in earlier papers to flow from advertising to profits, was raised in an important book by Richard Schmalensee (1972). He showed, in a model assuming profit-maximizing behavior by firms, that firms with high profit rates will have higher optimum advertising/sales ratios than firms with low profit rates. His empirical work tended to bear this out, though the direction of causality is never clear in his regressions; also, his results are confined to firms "in the same market situation," that is, firms that operate in markets where the effectiveness of advertising and the conjectured behavior of rivals are the same. Since a finding of a correlation (in regression analysis) does not necessarily imply a causal relation between two factors, the proof that a correlation exists between advertising and profitability—demonstrated by the work of Comanor and Wilson—still does not signify that advertising intensity is a cause, direct or indirect, of above-normal profitability. It could be that some third variable, such as innovation, was the more significant causal factor and that advertising was simply a concomitant of this factor.

Vernon (1971) attempted to answer the causality question by estimating a series of equations that attempted to explain concentration ratios and promotion/sales ratios separately, cross-sectionally across therapeutic markets in the drug industry. His results are inconclusive, not so much because no relationship exists, but because of the simultaneity bias and other statistical problems present in his methodology. In explaining concentration, his best equation—a simple linear regression of concentration ratios on promotion/sales ratios—drops from an R^2 of .34 to .09 when he moves from 1964 to 1968 data. Likewise, when explaining the promotion/sales ratio, the major explanatory variable is the concentration ratio, and that is only marginally significant at best. The upshot is that simultaneity and specification bias render invalid this attempt at defining causal direction; besides, the model is not capable, given its structure, of indicating whether concentration depends on promotion or vice-versa. The issue of causation is still unsettled.

Recent Studies

This assumes, however, that the *presence* of a relationship is agreed upon, something that a series of writers in the early 1970s have strenuously disputed. Harry Bloch (1974) charges that Weiss' study is hampered by aggregation bias as a result of using industry instead of firm data. Weiss used advertising expenditure figures for an industry by adding up from the firm data to derive an industry figure. Bloch argues (p. 273) "values of [advertising stock and flow] calculated in this manner tend to overstate an industry's advertising assets and net investment whenever firm advertising expenditures have long-lasting negative effects on the demand facing other firms, . . . evidence indicates . . . that these effects are substantial." Bloch reestimates the relationship using firm data and finds that the positive relationship between advertising and profitability vanishes. Bloch uses a uniform depreciation rate of 5 percent, and again the consequence of the intangible capital bias is that profit rates are pushed up and absolute profits down.

In a 1974 paper with Siegfried, Weiss corrects his 1969 paper for a variety of minor errors but does not concede the accuracy of Bloch's reestimate of his refinement of the Comanor-Wilson regression; he says that "the reestimates of the Comanor-Wilson regressions are not affected by Bloch's criticism."

Comanor and Wilson had implicitly assumed a depreciation rate for advertising equal to one. Weiss attempted to correct the bias resulting from this by assuming a depreciation rate of .33. Bloch rejects this figure for statistical reasons and chooses a 5 percent rate. The first attempt to estimate a depreciation rate for the drug industry came in a 1974 doctoral dissertation by Robert Ayanian. (This work was extended in two later papers [1975].) Ayanian (1975a, p. 483) first derives the conditions under which true and accounting rates differ; his findings, like those of Bloch and Weiss, are that

> the calculated rate of return diverges from the true rate of return as an assumed advertising retention rate (one minus the depreciation rate) diverges from the true advertising retention rate; as the advertising to equity ratio becomes larger, and as the accounting rate of return diverges from (the percentage advertising growth rate).

His retention rate estimates reveal that advertising depreciates relatively slowly in the drug industry (an average retention rate of .913, as compared to an unweighted mean of .849 in the industries he considers, which are all heavy advertisers); hence the bias is relatively large for drug firms. He then reestimates Comanor and Wilson's regressions; using identical data and functional forms, he finds that the t-statistic of advertising intensity on rate of return drops from 3.445 (highly significant) to 0.884 (insignificant) when he substitutes the corrected rate of return for the accounting rate. Ayanian (pp. 501–02) concludes, "The results of this paper are completely at odds with the 'barriers to entry' view of advertising. Over a wide range of advertising intensity and diverse products there appears to be no systematic relationship between advertising and profitability."

Ayanian also presents an argument that points to a fundamental flaw in the advertising-as-entry-barrier view of Comanor and Wilson. He argues (1975a, p. 480):

> They construct a model in which they claim that new firms have higher costs than established firms at every level of output. The reason for this is that in addition to production costs and advertising costs faced by established firms, new entrants also have "market penetration" advertising costs ... I interpret this as saying that market penetration expenditures are an investment with infinite life and zero depreciation rate. That is, the only cost of market penetration is foregone interest on penetration expenditures. Now since all firms in the market must at one time have entered the market, all firms in the market must have had penetration expenditures. But since in this model penetration capital does not depreciate, all established firms must have their penetration capital intact, and ceteris paribus, be incurring interest costs equal to those faced by the new entrant. Thus in Comanor and Wilson's model there is no cost differential between new and established firms and thus no barrier to entry by new firms.

This may be a problem with the way Comanor and Wilson present the model, but as for the existence of entry barriers, it only appears to raise the questions of how quickly entry capital depreciates and of whether initial entrants and later entrants bear different levels of entry cost. Perhaps the well-known fisheries problem applies: as each additional firm enters the market, the returns fall, or the costs of entry rise. Since this has not, apparently, been commented on in the literature, it seems to be an area for future research. Also, Hornbrook (1978) presents the argument that this understates the costs facing new entrants, since the costs borne by established firms are, by definition, the costs borne by those who penetrated the market successfully; the true range of costs facing new entrants includes the costs (possibly higher) borne by unsuccessful entrants.

Two recent studies have tried to incorporate research and development expenditures in intangible capital: Ayanian's essay in Helms (1975), and Clarkson (1977a). Despite the differences in methodology, the two reach identical conclusions: that drug firms' rates of return are less different from the economywide return to capital when all accounting adjustments are made. Ayanian estimates a decline in rate of return from 17.7 percent to either 14.06 percent or 13.69 percent, depending on depreciation assumptions, for 1973. Again for 1973, Clarkson reports a decline from 17.76 percent to 10.64 percent upon adjustment of data. The differences can be attributed to several alternatives: Clarkson uses much higher depreciation rates than Ayanian (33 percent as compared to 9 percent or 13 percent); Clarkson uses separate depreciation rates for advertising and R & D, while Ayanian uses a single rate; finally, there are minor conceptual differences in the accounting methodology used to correct the rates of return. By comparison with other industries, Clarkson presents identical calculations and corrections for 11 major industries. Pharmaceuticals have the highest rate of return among these industries, both corrected and uncorrected rates. When not corrected, pharmaceuticals are 7.09 percentage points, or 63.3 percent, above the average. When corrected for intangible capital, the difference falls to 3.29 percentage points, or 34.27 percent above average (Clarkson, 1977a, p. 64). Hence the corrections for intangible capital erase about half of the difference between pharmaceutical rates of return and average rates of return.

Stauffer (1975) also emphasizes the problems in estimating true profit rates when time-dependent costs and returns are present, such as R & D, and warns that the presence of these factors will consistently invalidate standard accounting procedures. The length of the time process and the ratio of working capital to fixed assets also affects the size of the bias. The paradoxical result is that an increase in the delay, or gestation time, on new product approvals can at the same time lower the firm's actual profits while increasing the nominal profit *rate* (through an increase in the accounting bias).

The implications of these distortions for the public profile of drug firms can be represented by a controversy between Siegfried and Tiemann (1974, 1975) and Cocks (1975a). Siegfried and Tiemann attempted to show that Harberger's 1954 monopoly welfare loss estimate of 0.1 percent of U.S.

national income can be attributed to a few industries; the purpose was to show that, though the monopoly loss is small, it can be isolated in a few industries and hence antitrust policy is not unreasonably expensive. By manipulating the standard welfare cost triangle methodology to use readily observable data, and by assuming constant costs, linear demand curves, and uniform demand elasticities across industries, they estimate welfare cost and share of welfare cost attributable to each of 125 IRS-defined industries in the U.S. mining and manufacturing sectors. (These industries are at approximately the three–digit SIC level.) After confirming Harberger's aggregate estimate, they find that five industries (drugs, plastics, petroleum, office and computing machinery, and motor vehicles) cause 67 percent of total monopoly welfare loss; motor vehicles alone account for 44 percent. The drug industry alone accounts for just under 5 percent.

Cocks (1975a) responded by arguing that Siegfried and Tiemann's estimates failed to account for R & D capital by using accounting data that distort measures of static welfare cost. Cocks changes Siegfried and Tiemann's welfare loss measure to one that takes account of R & D assets and the associated depreciation expense. By doing so, he claims to demonstrate that the measured welfare cost is more than 90 percent biased for pharmaceuticals; the implication is that monopoly in the drug industry is very slight. This estimate would vary, of course, with different assumptions as to depreciation rates and the methodology used in capitalizng R & D.

Interestingly, Cocks' results are generally consistent with what had gradually become the accepted measure of accounting bias. Comanor and Wilson, in their original article, stated that "industries with high advertising outlays . . . earn, on average, at a profit rate which exceeds that of other industries by nearly four percentage points" (p. 437). Ayanian's and Clarkson's estimates of the accounting bias attributable to intangible capital are consistent with this estimate (Ayanian estimates 4.01 percentage points difference at a 9 percent depreciation rate; Clarkson estimates about a 7 percentage point decline). Given this unusual agreement between the estimates of Comanor and Wilson, Ayanian, and Clarkson, Cocks' estimate that Siegfried and Tiemann's attribution of monpoloy profits is more than 90 percent biased is believable. Siegfried and Tiemann (1975) offer only tangential objections to Cocks' argument.

Given the state of the literature at this point, no conclusions come out definitively, other than that some degree of bias is present in rate of return estimates. By Clarkson's estimates, approximately half of the difference between drug industry rates of return and average rates can be attributed to bias, as compared to Cocks' estimate of over 90 percent. The issue of causality remains unresolved; everyone has opinions, but no definitive evidence has surfaced in the literature, as to whether advertising causes high profits, or vice versa; the existence of such a relationship, dealt a serious blow by Ayanian's regressions, is still vehemently defended by its supporters (see, for example, Mann et al., [1974]).

On this last point, a recent paper by Hornbrook (1978) finds that promotional intensity has a negative effect on market domination. The implication is that promotion has a pro-competitive effect. This finding is consistent with that of Telser (1975) because it suggests that promotion acts as a means of entry more effectively than as a barrier to entry.

Consumer Rationality: Loyalty versus Penetration

Two articles in a book of readings edited by Goldschmid, Mann, and Weston (1974) raise the possibility that the argument over the effect of advertising is really an argument about the nature of consumers. Brozen sees consumers as rational, using advertising as a substitute for search and personal experience. He cites evidence for this, showing that elimination of a prohibition on advertising on eyeglass prices (Benham, 1972) lowered average prices of glasses by making search less expensive. In contrast to the view espoused by Bain, that advertising creates consumer loyalty, protecting the market shares of the existing products, Brozen contends that the primary effect of advertising is to create consumer disloyalty, by making comparison easier.

On the other hand, Mann sees consumers as less willing to make decisions and more reliant on advertising information. Further, consumers are concerned with "image" and are willing to pay a price for it.

Evidence on Brozen's price-reducing view of advertising has been addressed by Cady (1976), Fletcher (1966), and Scheidell (1973). Cady looks at the question of whether prohibitions on advertising by pharmacists of prescription drug prices benefits pharmacists (by higher prices), or consumers (lower prices or better service). He identifies three possible cases: "legalized cartel," where higher prices but not higher service occur in states with regulation than without; "professional control," with higher prices and more services in states with regulation; or "cost-shifting," where service levels are higher in regulated states, but prices are higher in unregulated states. Looking at market research data on 1,900 pharmacies nationwide, he finds (pp. 9, 11) that

> no significant differences exist between the proportion of pharmacies in regulated and the proportion in unregulated states that offer delivery service, prescription credit accounts, or prescription waiting areas . . . that prescription drug prices are signficantly higher in regulated as compared to unregulated states, . . . and hence the regulation of prescription drug advertising presents a legalized cartel situation.

Scheidell's analysis (1973) is a theoretical description of adjustment of demand lags as affected by advertising. He argues as follows (p. 541):

> Thus, a lag in the market's reaction to a price change can be due to a lag in the consumer's awareness . . . of the change or a lag in the consumer's evaluation of the implications of the change . . . for him, or both . . . Given these factors, informative and persuasive advertising can increase the market's reaction speed by increasing the speed with which consumers become aware of the price change and also by increasing the speed of their subjective evaluation of the price change . . . advertising will reduce the positive pricing bias caused by demand lags and thus lead to a lower price, if the earlier realization of a potential revenue increase generated by a price reduction is not offset by the increased cost of advertising.

Telser's article in Helms (1975), a shortened version of his study in the *Journal of Law and Economics* (Telser et al., 1975), is a definitive statement of this view. It is based, moreover, on the most exhaustive study available of the empirical evidence on sales and promotional expenditures for different therapeutic classes in the pharmaceutical industry. Telser found that there was a positive correlation between promotional intensity and entry into the various therapeutic classes and a negative correlation with the four-firm concentration rate. These findings provide solid empirical support for the views of Brozen, mentioned above, to the effect that advertising is essentially procompetitive through the creation of consumer disloyalty.

Economies of Scale in Advertising

The issue of economies of scale in advertising was first mentioned by Kaldor (1950). Comanor and Wilson argue that if economies of scale exist in advertising, the barrier to entry will be even greater. Schmalensee (1972) investigated the question and found that economies of scale were not significant in advertising. By 1974 even Mann (p. 140) conceded that "neither existing evidence nor theoretical argumentation provide much reason to believe that the minimum efficient size of the firm is increased by advertising, either in general or in any particular industry." Hence the argument that economies of scale tend to lead to heavier concentration of industries that advertise intensively (which was popular during the 1960s as a theoretical possibility) has essentially died out.

PATENTS

Another significant barrier to entry that has been discussed at some length in the literature is patents. As mentioned earlier, it has been argued that drugs are relatively inexpensive to duplicate, once invented; hence in the absence of artificial barriers to entry, competitors would duplicate technical innovations easily, driving down prices and eliminating the returns to the R & D that produced the innovation [See, for example, Joseph Cooper (1969, 1976); Vernon (1971); Measday (1977); Schifrin (1967).] The argument has been disputed. One question that has been seriously argued is whether this barrier to substitution is desirable or not. On the one hand, it is argued that patents and the returns they make possible are a necessary incentive to research and the fair return to inventiveness; on the other hand, it has been argued that drug research is largely imitative and meaningless, and patents simply enable false product differentiation to occur and so create monopolies within therapeutic submarkets. Patents are generally grouped together with brand-name marketing as ways that firms discourage potential competition by legally enforced devices.

The literature that discusses drug industry patents may be grouped into three sections: those writings that oppose patent protection outright; those that support patent protection; and those that talk in terms of optimal patent life. This classification may be roughly correlated with the importance attached to incentives to drug industry research. The first group generally believes that drug industry research is trivial, imitative, and performed largely in nonindustry laboratories. The second group takes a favorable view of industry research, pointing to the significant innovations arising from industry labs and arguing that the supply of innovation is positively linked to the returns it receives. The third group tends to look on patents as a social optimizing device and to ask what patent life will be such as to bring forth the supply of innovation desired by society—that is, which equates the supply and demand for innovation at different prices. This third group might be called the marginalist position.

Historical Trend

As compared to the articles on promotion, there is less of a clear time trend in the thinking about patents. With promotion, it generally became clear that much of the link between advertising and profits could be explained by spurious correlation because of accounting practices; that the link between advertising and firm size could not be shown to exist; and that the entry-barrier view relied upon an assumption of consumer irrationality. On the other hand, the two sides in the patent discussion have largely talked past each other, and no clear conclusion can be said to have been reached. Most of the articles critical of drug research and of patents were published in the mid to late 1960s; but the position is certainly still alive, as seen in Measday's study (1977). The position that patents are necessary to induce innovation is very ancient, dating back at least to Ricardo, and was certainly not new to drug industry critics. The "marginalist" position also cannot be reasonably dated.

Studies Arguing That Patents Lead to Monopoly Positions

Steele (1964), Comanor (1964, 1979) and Schifrin (1964, 1967) are most often linked with an attack on drug industry patents and research.

The substance of Steele's attack on patents as an entry barrier may be found in his 1964 article (p. 221):

Holders of patents (or sometimes merely of patent applications) may legally exercise restrictions on output and maintain prices at levels that are extremely high relative to production campaigns which contribute materially to the already grave imperfections of market information. By this means, small sellers of generic name drugs are deprived of the physician's attention, and cannot obtain any significant share of the prescription market, even though they may be selling at prices which are a small fraction of their larger rivals'.

As a result, he advocates two policy measures: "the abolition of the patent privilege as it applies to drug products, and the expansion of the powers of the Food and Drug Administration" (pp. 221–22).

This argument is founded on several of Steele's ideas. First, he feels that much research in the drug industry serves no real purpose, other than to research around other patents. If patents were eliminated, this unnecessary research would be eliminated. Since most research of a fundamental nature is highly risky and does not occur in drug firms, but rather in government-funded or university laboratories, the amount of basic research is not likely to be hurt.

One cannot really appraise Steele's assertions without looking at the evidence. The fact is, new drugs have been overwhelmingly developed by industry laboratories, not those of government and academe,* and the degree of dependence on industry has actually increased during recent years that have shown an explosion in government funding for health research. It is certainly true that there has been cross fertilization in both directions between the researchers of industry and those of the National Institutes of Health and the universities. The historical record, however, does not support the idea that industry leaves basic research to government and academe and simply gets a free ride on the discoveries of these

---

*See Chapter 7 for an extended discussion of the contribution of industry to new drug development.

nonprofit sectors. The annual surveys of the National Science Foundation have shown the pharmaceutical industry at or near the top, not only in the ratio of company-funded R & D to sales but in the ratio of basic research to total R & D.

Experience in the industry, or as a close observer of the industry, would disabuse any academic scholar of the notion that companies can assure a commercial success for an indifferent product (one that is marginally if at all superior to a cheaper existing drug) simply by a lavish application of advertising and detailing. Normally, the company abandons such a compound before completing clinical trials. The marketing history of this industry is replete with Edsels, whose sponsors were sincerely convinced that they were superior products but that simply could not make it in a skeptical market of prescribers.

Schifrin (1967) takes a position that is somewhat less clear–cut. After praising the drug industry's research efforts (for example, from 1948 to 1963), he points out that 5,386 new drugs were introduced, of which 618 were new chemical entities ("the drug industry is the most research-conscious of all nondefense industries" [p. 898]). He argues that advertising (which, he asserts, has twice the industry budget of R & D) and trade names have contributed to isolation of therapeutic markets and product differentiation. The problem he sees is to eliminate "unnecessarily high profits" without eliminating the incentive for R & D. Schifrin (1967, p. 914) argues that a reduction in patent length to three years would accomplish this:

> It is doubtful that the continuation and advancement of drug research would be impaired by such modification of drug patents. The industry is characterized by rapid product turnover and obsolescence; studies have shown that the greatest portion of sales of any product is likely to occur in the first few years after its introduction. Company price policies explicitly include these considerations, and most, if not all companies, estimate quite conservatively the market life of their products, taking three years as the average period to recoup outlays and earn a profit.

In Schifrin's testimony (1967) before a congressional committee, he makes an additional point of some interest. Profits per se, he argues (p. 900), are not necessary to induce innovative research:

> "Profits, of course, are the residual between revenues and costs. Thus you have profits only when all your costs are met. Research is part of your cost. Thus, the high profit exists after the research outlay has already been accounted for."

Schifrin's comments on the "residual" nature of profits betray the flaws of a static approach and a confusion between absolute profits and the rate of profitability. It is true that for any given year, a company's net earnings are reported *after* deduction for R & D and other expenses. It is also true that the fact that R & D is treated as a current expense, although being by nature an investment means that the *rate* of return of the research-intensive firm or industry is overstated.

To be fair to Schifrin, it should be remembered that these comments were made in 1967, well before any of the various studies had appeared demonstrating the distortion caused in the accounting rate of return of R & D-intensive industries owing to the universal (and justifiable) practice of treating research investment as an expense. He simply assumed that the conventional corporate accounting data on profitability (as in the Federal Trade Commission's (FTC) *Quarterly Financial Report*) provided an adequate basis for making interindustry profitability comparisons. It was not until five years later that the FTC itself confirmed the need to recognize differences in R & D by industry in collecting Line of Business data.

Now that the FTC has issued the first of its Line of Business reports, it is possible to judge the accuracy of Schifrin's assertion that the pharmaceutical industry budgets twice as much on advertising as on R & D. This first report reveals that the 12 firms in the Ethical Drugs sample spent 3.6 times as much on R & D as on advertising. The most comprehensive survey of total promotional expenditure of the industry, including detailing as well as advertising, was that of David Schwartzman (1976a) who arrived at a total of $721.8 million for 1972. This exceeds the $600.7 million that (according to the Pharmaceutical Manufacturers' Association annual survey) the industry expended on domestic R & D for human-use drugs in 1972, but by nowhere near the ratio so often asserted by some industry critics.

William Comanor (1964), although unsympathetic to industry research, takes a rather forgiving attitude toward the patent system (p. 380): "It has strengthened and encouraged the high degree of chemical product differentiation which is the primary form taken by technical change within the pharmaceutical industry." On the other hand, the high level of R & D costs, together with heavy promotional expenditures, serve as a barrier to entry, according to Comanor. He concluded, moreover, that the drug industry had more incentive to innovate in the introduction of new products than in the reduction of costs because "where producer rivalry is high and the effective life of individual products is short, firms are unwilling to invest large amounts toward reducing production costs . . . By the time new techniques are developed . . . demand for the product may have dropped to a relatively low level" (pp. 377–8).

In his 1966 article, Comanor compares the contribution of the domestic drug industry's R & D to that of nonindustry laboratories and of foreign laboratories. He concludes that the U.S. industry has not concentrated on major innovations but rather on drugs that have frequent use and that hence have "doctor confidence." The industry, he argues, emphasizes modifications (not all of which are important) and the translation of new discoveries into marketable goods—which also involves the requisite testing. It is therefore not fair to compare the industry and nonindustry laboratories by the same criteria. They are complementary and do not draw resources from each other; the industry laboratories concentrate on applied research and on development, which they perform very efficiently. On the basis of this analysis, Comanor concludes that compulsory patent licensing could be introduced safely. Although it might reduce total research expenditure, it need not reduce the introduction of the "most important new products."

The conclusions of Comanor's 1966 article, favoring compulsory patent licensing, hardly follow logically from the assumption that government and industry research are different but complementary. The problem clearly lies with Comanor's additional assumptions. He seems to see a conflict between the significance of a compound and the frequency of its use by doctors. To be sure, volume of sales may not be a reliable criterion for determining medical significance—since it does not encompass the case of the truly significant drug for the relatively rare condition. However, it would be equally misguided to assume a reverse relationship between sales volume and medical significance.

Second, the evidence indicates that Comanor was mistaken in suggesting that the most important discoveries come from nonindustry laboratories. The origin of new chemical entities introduced in different periods has been the subject of research by Jerome Schnee (1973). He finds that for the period 1935–49, 52 percent of drug discoveries came from industry, that for the period 1950–62, the industry share rose to 69 percent, while for the period 1963–70 the ratio rose to 82 percent.* Annual tabulations on new drug introductions as published by Paul de Haen seem to confirm a continuation of this situation. Of the 23 new single-entity compounds introduced in the United States in 1978, he reports that 20 were discovered by companies, with the remaining 3, including one from France, coming from academic institutions.

It is certainly true, however, that compounds that were considered by their developers to have been important advances are subsequently evaluated by the market as being of only marginal value. It is difficult to follow the logic of Comanor's suggestion that a weakening of patent protection (through compulsory licensing) would affect merely the marginal drugs but not the incentives to introduce the "most important products." Certainly, commercial potential is not now the sole criterion for R & D selection—

---

*Chapter 7 explores this issue in detail.

otherwise, there would be few if any introductions of cancer drugs or of vaccines, which are almost uniformly unprofitable. A further weakening of patent incentives would appear logically to reduce still further the ability and disposition of manufacturers to introduce drugs for relatively rare conditions (that is, the "orphan diseases").

Walker (1971) presents the same arguments against the industry, somewhat more fully documented. Perhaps his most determined assertion is that patents establish the exclusivity of a product, thereby limiting competition. His documentation is more complete than the others, and the catalog of (alleged) sins is more thorough.

Baily (1972) has prepared a model that implies that there are a limited number of research opportunities, thus presenting a problem comparable to the classical case of fisheries or of commonly owned land. The individual's marginal cost calculation as to the optimum level of research expenditure may differ from that of society as a whole. If the former is higher, this may lead to an overinvestment in R & D. While this conclusion (which his model suggests) might imply that patent incentives might safely be reduced, Baily (p. 83, 84) seems to warn against too ready an acceptance of this conclusion, however, by pointing out that "the patent system is not Pareto optimal efficient in any case," and, the hypothesis that research opportunities are limited is "at present not proven."

Baily's model has been admired and elaborated on by other econometricians. He demonstrated a correlation between the level of patents, the level of R & D, and a company's earnings. He also provided a useful reminder that the adverse effect, to an industry's earnings, of the decline in new product introductions is partly offset by the increased market life and earnings from older products that would otherwise have been displaced.

Studies Arguing That Patents Induce Innovations

The standard argument in favor of patents is that they are necessary to induce innovation. Since information is costly to produce, but relatively inexpensive to reproduce, it is argued, patents are necessary to ensure that producers of new information receive the returns of their production; from a social viewpoint, innovation is considered desirable, and patents provide the necessary incentive to induce innovation.

Two of the studies in this category present the standard argument in a standard way. Forman (1969) and Jucker (1972) point to the necessity for returns to induce innovation. They warn that compulsory licensing and other such proposals are certain to reduce the rewards, argue that drug firms have produced many useful innovations, and contend that adoption of these proposals will stop the flow of useful innovations. These arguments may be useful or correct, but they represent no new thinking on the subject.

Whitney (1968, p. 838) adopts a similar viewpoint in attacking drug industry critics and asks whether those critics are referring to "rational businessmen, or some new types who will step-up research activity, the more its rewards are restricted."

Cocks (1975a) argues that R & D is an important element of competition in pharmaceuticals rather than a way of reducing competition. Though some resource misallocation may result from patents and R & D, the misallocation is relatively short-lived, whereas the procompetitive effect of substantial innovation is long term and determines the basic nature of the industry. Arguing empirically that "there is a fundamental relationship between the incentives for innovation that yield new drug products, as well as between the institutionalization of R & D that is the basis for price competition, and the temporary firm advantages that may be experienced through the market power of new drugs," he feels that policies aimed at eliminating that temporary market power would also eliminate R & D, and thereby increase the market power of existing drugs.

Empirical support for Cocks' conclusions on the procompetitive effect of patents has been provided in the work of Bernard Kemp (1975). Particularly in the case of diuretics, but also for a number of other drug classes, Kemp found that the introduction of a patented "breakthrough" drug, like Diuril, was soon followed by a number of "follow-on" compounds, with special features applicable to particular subclasses of patients. Since these were often at lower prices, this process, in which the breakthrough drug's market share was eroded, was accompanied by a wider range of therapeutic choice for physicians and lower average prices. Far from being a barrier to entry—except for the same identical compound—the successful patented drug appears to attract competitors. There are even some observers who consider that the information revealed in the original patent (for example, for Diuril—chlorothiazide) provides a shortcut for competing researchers seeking a compound with much the same effect yet sufficiently distinct to be patented.

The Kemp studies seem to challenge many of the assumptions accepted by earlier participants in the debate over drug patents. They have made it clear that competition is not postponed until after patent expiration but is quite lively long before that point. His work also does much to remove the pejorative sting from the term "me-too drug."

Faust (1971) presents the research director's viewpoint on all of this. He describes the project selection process and emphasizes the "exploratory," "opportunistic," and "serendipitous" nature of drug research. His other article (1973) is similarly descriptive.

Feldstein (1969, p. 243), after citing Schifrin's argument that there is no need for high profits to finance research, offers an interesting finding:

the higher the equilibrium price elasticity of demand, the lower will be the ration of research expenditures to total sales revenue. Thus, government policies to increase demand elasticity may also decrease research. For example, the proposal to require a compulsory licensing of patents after a short period of exclusive use would tend to decrease the ratio of research expenditures to sales in two ways. First, the impact of research on a company's sales would be diminished by the requirement to share the information through licensing. Second, the presence of many firms producing the same product would increase the elasticity of quantity with respect to price.

SUMMARY AND AREAS FOR FUTURE RESEARCH

The relationship between advertising and profitability has not been firmly established (see Figure 5.1). No one has been able to provide a rigorous quantitative demonstration as to the direction of causality. Profit rates and advertising intensity may be linked only indirectly; each may depend on an underlying phenomenon such as innovation.

There does, however, appear to be agreement that the association between high profits and high advertising intensity has been exaggerated. This happened because early measurements of the advertising-profit relationship failed to consider the upward bias in reported profit rates that occurs when advertising is treated as an expense rather than what it really is: namely, an investment. There also appears to be strong empirical support that advertising, rather than being a barrier to entry, is a stimulant. Finally, the idea that there are significant economies of scale in advertising has been discredited.

As for patents, the dichotomy between the traditional and dynamic views of their role is stark. The argument that patents are barriers to innovation has been strongly challenged by the more recent view that patents are a prerequisite to innovation, which itself is the flywheel of the process causing markets to be both product and price competitive. Therefore, if there were no patents, there would be little innovation and in the long run less competition of all sorts. Some parties to the debate argue that if patent protection were reduced or other actions were taken to reduce rewards from innovation, prices on existing products probably would be lower. A key question, therefore, is how the welfare gains from lower prices on existing products compare with projected losses from less innovation, which would consist of the sum of the following:

• Foregone net benefits from new drugs that would not have been developed in the absence of patents

FIGURE 5.1. Path Chart of Advertising as Barrier to Entry

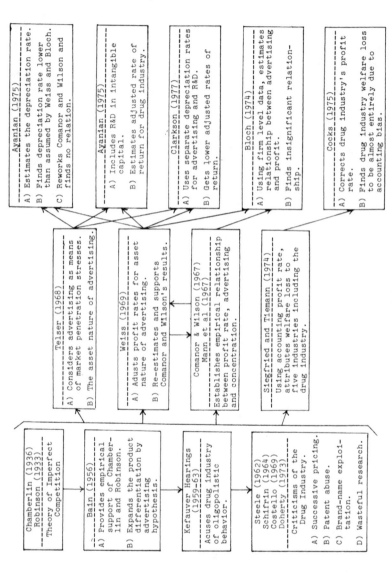

Source: Compiled by the authors.

• Foregone price reductions on old drugs that would have occurred as a competitive response to the introduction of new drugs. (The extent of price reductions in excess of those resulting from cost-reducing innovations pertaining to old products depends heavily on the degree to which new drugs represent an improvement over competing existing drugs.)

There are five other significant unresolved issues pertaining to entry barriers and competition in the pharmaceutical industry:

Ayanian presents the argument that entry barriers raised by advertising are irrelevant if established firms have to bear their own entry costs, even though there were no other firms in the market. He assumes that entry capital does not depreciate. Does the level of entry costs in the drug industry, or in the therapeutic submarkets, depend on the number of firms already in that market? Does entry capital depreciate at a slower rate than other kinds of capital?

Both Ayanian and Clarkson find that eliminating accounting biases moves drug industry profit rather closer to the manufacturing average. However, both find that a significant gap remains. What is the explanation for this remaining gap? Can firm or industry-level risk explain it; are there remaining accounting biases; can it be attributed to some noncompetitive element in industrial structure; or is there some other explanation?

Drugs are often only one form of treatment available to a doctor in treating a disease. The doctors must choose among alternative therapies. Obviously, drugs almost always will be cheaper than the hospitalization and/or surgery they seek to displace. If all sectors experienced the same rate of inflation, one would expect this displacement effect to lead to an enlargement of the drug share of total health costs. Instead, the share of drugs, for all health care and for inpatient care, has been declining. Is this solely due to the greater inflation-resistance of drug prices? Or are there other factors?

What is the impact on the price of drugs on R & D expenditures? How long does it take for a new drug to recover the R & D expenditures made to bring it to the market?

What is the average life of a drug product? What are average annual and lifetime sales?

6

PROFITABILITY IN THE PHARMACEUTICAL INDUSTRY

INTRODUCTION AND HISTORICAL BACKGROUND

Among the controversial characteristics of the drug industry, its high profit rate has not only attracted the most attention from the industry critics but is also often has served as primary proof of its alleged monopolistic practices. Cooper, in his introduction to *The Proceedings of the Second Seminar on Economics of Pharmaceutical Innovation* (1976, p. 16) states: "I believe that practically all the attacks upon the drug industry stem from feelings about profits. That includes safety, efficacy, the brand name issue, molecular modifications, and others." The consistency of the high accounting rate of return has caused the industry to undergo repeated scrutiny from the government and the economics profession. A good example of the type of charges frequently leveled at the drug industry is provided in Measday's discussion of profitability in *The Structure of American Industry* (1977). Using FTC and company annual reports for the period 1958 to 1975, Measday claims (p. 275):

> During the entire period, the annual rates of return for all manufacturing averaged 11.0 percent, compared to 18.1 percent for the drug industry and 19.7 percent for the 12 large companies. Furthermore, . . . there has been relatively less variation in drug industry profits than in all manufacturing. The industry's profits after taxes rose in every year from 1958 ($343 million) to 1975 ($1.6 billion), including those years in which net manufacturing income as a whole declined. Few, if any, other industries in the economy can match this record.

Underlying such charges is the simple economic theory that in order to achieve efficient allocation of resources, no sector should earn above "normal" rates of return on the resource. The occurrence of such abnormal returns should attract more of the resource into the sector, and thus bring down the rate through competition. The constancy of a high rate of return then implies presence of entry barriers. Society stands to lose from less production in that sector, in the form of higher prices and unavailability of the final good.

Although this thesis concerning economic rates of return is widely accepted, many economists have shown that accounting measures of the rate of return can lead to incorrect conclusions under close examination. Furthermore, some industries suffer this deficiency more than others. The drug industry has been a notable example of this measurement bias.

The high profit rate in the drug industry has been attributed by the industry to the alleged high-risk nature of its products, which is not incorporated into the usual accounting measures. Standard economic theory specifies that riskiness in an investment has to be compensated with higher rates; but the theory encounters an obstacle in the determination of how much higher the rate of return should be, given the alleged risk. The standard practice that the "residual" high profit is allocated to the risk factor is often not sufficient to dispel the allegation of "extranormal" profit.

The bias created by the accounting method has far-reaching consequences. The observed rate of return has been the cornerstone of many studies on the industry structure, performance, and conduct. As has already been seen in Chapter 5, many empirical works have been challenged as being unacceptable because of the inappropriateness of accounting profit rate data for economic purposes.

Thus we feel the rate of return in the pharmaceutical industry requires separate attention for its importance in evaluating a number of assertions frequently made about the industry. Because of the nature of the subject material, this chapter is necessarily somewhat technical.

APPROACH OF THE CHAPTER

We initially intend to clarify the nature of the accounting bias and relate it to the drug industry in particular. We then present the various methods of correcting this bias and their respective results. In addition, we explore the difference between accounting and economic measures by considering their theoretical determinants. Among these determinants, some interesting implications can be derived concerning the growth of the drug industry. Finally we consider the elusive risk factor embedded in the rate of return and related policy implications.

BIAS OF THE ACCOUNTING MEASURES

The rate of return can be measured on many levels and is influenced by many factors. On each of these levels (industry, firm, and product) different sets of variables affect the difference between the accounting and economic measures. Although there is a consensus that the accounting rate of return is upwardly biased, the studies are far from similar in their perspective and approach.

In this section we attempt to focus on the major theme that underlies all of them: the asset nature of advertising and R & D expenditures.

Source of Bias

Although this problem is not new to accountants and businessmen, its appearance in the economic literature, again, is a by-product of a controversial issue in the field of industrial organization: the relationship between profitability and advertising intensity. Since the development of the issue has been dealt with quite extensively elsewhere in this book, we merely quote Telser (1968, p. 167) who points attention to this matter:

> Alas the figures are fallacious, because they cling to old-fashioned accounting conventions that define capital as consisting only of investments in tangible items such as plant, equipment, and inventories. However, the true capital of a company includes expenditures that yield a return long after the initial outlays. Advertising expenditures together with research and development have this property.

Weiss (1969, p. 421) expresses the accounting bias systematically with the following notation:

π_t = accounting profits (net income after tax) in year t. The adjective "accounting" means that intangibles are "expensed," that is, written off as current expenses.

π^*_t = "true" profits in year t. "True" means that intangibles are "capitalized," that is, added to assets and depreciated over their expected lives.

E_t = accounting equity at the end of year t.

E^*_t = "true" equity at the end of year t.

A_t = investment in advertising in year t. A_o refers to such investment in a base year from which growth is measured.

r = annual percentage rate of growth in A.

λ = the ratio between year-end net value of an intangible investment and its value at the start of the year. The annual depreciation rate is therefore $(1 - \lambda)$.

Assuming that advertising grows at a constant rate of r, the present advertising expense becomes:

$$A_t = A_o (1 + r)^t$$

The current depreciation charge comes to:

$$(1 - \lambda)A_o[(1 + r)^t + \lambda(1 + r)^{t-1} + \ldots \lambda^i (1 + r)^{t-i+} \ldots]$$

Since the relationship between the "true" and accounting measure is:

$\pi_{t^*} = \pi_t + A_t -$ (current depreciation charges on intangibles), the bias

can be expressed as the second right-hand side term in:

$$\pi_{t^*} = \pi_t + A_o (1 + r)^t (\lambda r/1 + r - \lambda).$$

Several points can be drawn from the above equation, which is applicable not just to advertising but to the other main form of intangible capital as well—research and development expenditures. When advertisement or R & D spending does not grow, $r = 0$, there is no bias. The same result occurs when there is instant depreciation, $\lambda = 0$. If, on the other hand, there is either fast growth in investment or slow depreciation of intangible capital in the industry, the bias in the accounting profit can be substantial.

Many authors bring forth and discuss this bias in different contexts (see Bloch, 1974; Solomon, 1970; Stauffer, 1971; and Ayanian, 1975a); but the nature and the existence of the bias are accepted by all who have looked at the issue.

Two features of the pharmaceutical industry suggest *a priori* that the accounting rates of return may be significantly biased upward. First, the industry's intangible capital assets—R & D and advertising—are high relative to total assets and are expensed in the year incurred rather than capitalized and depreciated. Second, there is a long time lag between the investment and the return on the investment.

Given this lag, the lack of discounting creates another form of bias. Mund (1970, p. 131) states the problem clearly:

> Profitability analysis in the drug industry is also misleading for another reason. Even if R & D expenses could be better matched with drug sales, conventional financial statements would fail to take into account the differences in the time value of money in matching past expenditures with current revenue. In many industries, the distortions caused by this practice are small, because time differences between expenditures and current revenue are not great. But, in the drug industry, the distortions are significant because of the long period of time which elapses between R & D investment and the attainment of a saleable product and then its final obsolescence.

The rigorous presentation of the bias in the drug industry profit rate came about with the appearance of three articles in Helms, *Drug Development and Marketing*, (1975), by Stauffer, Ayanian (1975b), and Schwartzman. Both

Stauffer and Ayanian had developed their methodology in previous expositions on a more generalized level (Ayanian, 1975a; Stauffer, 1971). Ayanian (1975b, p. 82) addressing the accounting bias in the drug industry, describes the nature of advertising and R & D (ARD) expenditures as assets:

> The key to the bias is the fact that ARD expenditures are in reality investments that yield revenues to the firm over a number of years. These expenditures are investments in an intangible asset: knowledge. This knowledge is comprised of consumers' knowledge of the firm's products, that is, its reputation or goodwill, and the firm's knowledge of technological processes.

Stauffer (1975, p. 101) elaborates on the necessity of treating R & D as an asset by pointing out that *all* R & D spending should be treated as an asset, not just the cost of successful R & D projects:

> On the other hand, unsuccessful exploration or R & D is an unwelcome but integral part of the process of obtaining successes, whether they be producing wells or new products. Therefore, one may cogently argue that all exploration or R & D outlays in a given period must be charged against the future income streams generated by the fraction of the expenditures that are successful.

Stauffer (1975, p. 100) also deals in depth with the distorting effect of the time lag between R & D investment and the time when a return on that investment begins:

> The second source of potential discrepancy in rate of return measurement for a pharmaceutical firm is more subtle and elusive but nonetheless real and rather large. There are significant time lags between the expenditure of an R & D dollar and the first sales receipts generated by a new product. Such lags obviously entail potentially important financial opportunity costs, yet they do not appear explicitly in any firm's accounts . . . The conventional accounting procedures . . . applied to pharmaceuticals in no way recognize this time lag effect, so that the firm's profitability is overstated. The error is proportional in some sense to the length of time that is ignored.

The implication of Stauffer's analysis is important. Simply put, if pharmaceutical manufacturer accounting profits, for example, as reported by the Federal Trade Commission, stayed approximately level while the time lag between drug development and drug marketing increased, then, ceteris paribus, the appropriate conclusion to draw about the state of the industry would be that the true rate of return was declining.

Schwartzman (1975, p. 63), focusing on the distinction between the accounting and the expected rate of return, highlights the need to distinguish between the two:

The expected rate of return is forward looking, as the name suggests, and thus is the relevant criterion for investment decisions, while the accounting rate is a measure of the success of past investments. The accounting rate frequently is used as a measure of the expected rate, and the distinction is not always made. In the drug industry the resulting error is likely to be large because of the long R & D period for a new drug and the consequent long lag of income behind investment.

The above authors are bringing the concept of drug life cycle into the measurement of profit. The true economic rate of return has to be based on the expenditure and revenue throughout the economic life of the drug products. It is clear, then, that any of the factors, such as patent life, rate of innovation, stringency of the government regulation on the new drug, and substitution by further new drug innovations, play an important role in determining the true rate.

Corrected Rates of Return

All the studies mentioned above reach the conclusion that the real economic rate of return on drugs is lower than the one shown by the accounting measure. This general finding can properly be considered robust as it has been confirmed by numerous other studies as well.

Friedman and Friedman (1972), in their challenge to the use of accounting rate of return as a measure of monopoly power, correct for the R & D expenditure and inflation rates. They calculate rates of return for three drug companies and compare them to the rates for total manufacturing (p. 57):

> For the various adjustments shown, the rate of return for total manufacturing in the 1967–70 period is reduced by an amount varying from 0.3 to 2.0 percentage points, while the reduction in the rate of return for the three drug companies ranges from 5.8 to 11.0 points. Expressed differently, the spread in rate of return as between the drug firms and total manufacturing is 11.7 percentage points before adjustment, and the effect of the adjustments shown is to narrow this spread to between 3.7 and 7.2 percentage points.

On the general level (cross-industries) Bloch (1974) and Ayanian (1975a) recalculate rates of return for 40 food manufacturing and 39 heavy advertising firms, respectively. It suffices to say that Bloch finds the new rates of return all to be lower than or equal to the old ones. Ayanian shows a similar result in his 39 firms with varying differences among the firms. It should be noted, for the interest of this report, Pfizer's corrected rate of

TABLE 6.1. Accounting and Estimated Corrected Rates of Return for Six Drug Firms, 1973 (in percents)

Firm	Accounting Rate of Return	When ARD Depreciation Rate is 13 Percent	When ARD Depreciation Rate is 9 Percent
Abbott Laboratories	14.12	11.47	11.20
Eli Lilly and Company	21.30	16.45	16.00
Pfizer	15.90	13.62	13.34
Richardson-Merrell	13.91	12.19	12.06
G. D. Searle and Company	21.94	17.72	17.23
Upjohn Company	19.03	12.89	12.32
Six-firm average	17.70	14.06	13.69

Source: R. Ayanian, "The Profit Rates and Economic Performance of Drug Firms," in *Drug Development and Marketing*, ed. R. Helms (Washington, D.C.: American Enterprise Institute for Public Policy Research, 1975), p. 89.

return, 13.85, was only .04 lower than the uncorrected one, whereas Sterling Drug showed a drop of 7.8 percentage points.

When Ayanian (1975b) applies the same methodology for six drug firms, including Pfizer, he reaches the results shown in Table 6.1. Pfizer this time shows a significant drop of 2.28 percentage points in its rate of return. The reason for the change is simply that Ayanian this time includes R & D expenditure, while in the former study he included only advertising.

Stauffer (1975) also estimates corrected rates of return for six drug firms, and the results are shown in Table 6.2. The discrepancies between the two rates vary from 0.2 to 8.2 points for the five firms that have positive error. One firm, on the other hand, has its accounting rate lower than the corrected one. Stauffer (1975, p. 111) comments on his results:

> Even though detailed calculations are necessary for each example, certain general relationships between real and accounting rates of return can be isolated:
>
> 1. The error is positive if the growth rate is less than the firm's accounting rate of return, and conversely.
>
> 2. The error is approximately proportional to the ratio of annual R & D outlays to the firm's net assets.
>
> 3. The error is reduced in such measure as the firm's compound rate of growth over any period is close to its book rate of return for that same period.

The theoretical assumptions underlying these points will be discussed more thoroughly in the next section of this chapter.

TABLE 6.2. Estimated Financial Rates of Return

Firm	Period	Accounting Return on Investment (percent)	Corrected or Economic (percent)	Discrepancy (percentage points)
A	1963–72	17.5	15.0	+2.5
B	1953–72	20.1	16.4	+3.7
C	1955–72	9.8	12.1	−2.3
D	1953–72	29.4	21.2	+8.2
E	1959–72	20.4	16.3	+4.1
F	1958–72	13.3	13.1	+0.2

Source: T. Stauffer, "Profitability Measures in the Pharmaceutical Industry," in *Drug Development and Marketing*, ed. R. Helms (Washington, D.C: American Enterprise Institute for Public Policy Research, 1975), p. 110.

For the period of 1950 to 1970, Bloch (1976) determines the internal rate of return for drug R & D expenditures to be 28 percent, with a 15 percent true after-tax rate of return on sales. Bloch suspects this internal rate of return reflects the fast growth of the drug industry during the 1950s and early 1960s. Bloch also adjusts the 1969 after-tax rate of return for four firms: Schering; Smith, Kline and French; Parke Davis; and Upjohn. Their respective corrected rates of return are found to be 16.1, 14.2, 7.6, and 10.5. Bloch (1976, p. 155) comments on these results:

> Reported profit rates in the range of those reported by Smith, Kline and French and Schering are more typical among major pharmaceutical firms than are reported profit rates such as that reported by Parke Davis. Hence, it is likely that the true profitability of major pharmaceutical firms is above the average of firms in other industries. However, the magnitude of the difference in profitability is clearly not as large as a casual inspection of reported rates of return would indicate.

Underlying Bloch's estimated rates of return is a regression equation from which he derives both the economic life span of R & D expenditure and the depreciation profile of the expenditure. His method of regressing current sales on past sales and R & D expenditures is susceptible to many measurement errors. For one thing, with the limited number of degrees of freedom, all of the Durbin-Watson (D-W) statistics lie in the "inclusive region." Furthermore, the use of the regular D-W is not only inappropriate in the case of the lagged dependent variable but also underestimates the degree of autocorrelation (Johnston, 1972). Nevertheless the results of the regression show that 96 percent of the R & D expenditure is expended in the first 13 years, an assumption close to those of other authors (Clymer, 1970; and Friedman and Friedman, 1972).

We can find the corrected rate of return for a more recent period in Clarkson's works (Clarkson, 1977a and b). Adjusting for both promotional and R & D expenditures, Clarkson finds the rate of return on net worth for the pharmaceutical manufacturers to be consistently around 11 percent from 1965 to 1972, then dropping to 9.36 percent in 1974 (results are shown in Table 6.3). Then with the same methodology, rates of return are calculated for interindustry comparison over the period 1959–73 with a sample of 69 firms representing 11 industries (see Table 6.4). Clarkson's central finding is that there is a significant upward bias for R & D and promotion-intensive industries. He comments specifically on the pharmaceutical industry (1977b, p. 23):

> The pharmaceutical industry experiences the largest decline in its rate of return. Its average corrected rate of return is 5.4 percentage points less than its average accounting return.
>
> Despite a 5.4 point drop, pharmaceutical industry profits are the highest under the corrected calculations, as they are under conventional calculations. But the corrected calculations do bring the difference between average returns for the drug industry and for all eleven industries down from 7.1 to 3.3 percentage points.

Despite the fact that the variations in the actual measurements of true profit rate are numerous, the results are close enough to be generalized with two exceptions. The drug industry corrected rates of return (ROR) on the industry level cluster around 13 percent for the 1960s and early 1970s (shown in Table 6.5). This compares with approximately 10 percent, as an average of other manufacturing industries. The consensus has to be qualified by noting that the industry averages are derived from few firms whose market shares are sometimes not being considered; therefore, there are potential differences when different firm data are used. Also, the rate of return studies done to date do not consider the impact of other influences such as inflation.

The exception to these rates of return is Schwartzman's (1975a) findings on the rate of return to R & D expenditure in particular. His study, however, is different from the others in two respects. First, his objective is to measure expected return rather than historical return. Second, he measures *only* the return on R & D. Nonetheless, the resulting 3.3 percent is so much lower than the other estimates of firm returns that the question inevitably arises: "Why is the gap so large?" If Schwartzman's results were confirmed by others, the clear implication would be that something has been happening in recent years that has considerably dimmed the industry's future prospects for earning an acceptable return from R & D. Two possibilities have been discussed in depth. One is the effect of FDA

TABLE 6.3. Pharmaceutical Manufacturers' Rates of Return on Net Worth and Assets Based on Book Value (millions of constant 1973 dollars)

Year	Uncorrected Profits	Advertising and Promotion Outlays	Research and Development Capital	Corrected Profits	Net Worth Uncorrected	Net Worth Corrected	Rate of Return on Net Worth (percent) Uncorrected	Rate of Return on Net Worth (percent) Corrected
1965	53.4	79.5	44.8	96.4	321.1	864.4	16.33	11.15
1966	61.7	90.1	48.3	108.4	336.6	941.2	18.32	11.51
1967	66.3	103.1	50.4	120.1	387.5	1,064.7	17.11	11.30
1968	82.9	111.3	55.8	141.8	451.9	1,206.2	18.35	11.75
1969	93.2	119.5	64.3	156.9	513.7	1,350.8	18.14	11.61
1970	97.9	124.0	70.9	165.4	571.1	1,493.9	17.15	11.07
1971	98.9	167.4	78.3	183.9	627.1	1,665.5	15.78	11.04
1972	122.2	170.1	81.2	205.3	669.4	1,844.1	17.47	11.14
1973	129.7	179.4	96.1	209.5	730.2	1,969.5	17.76	10.64
1974	119.6	163.7	109.7	189.5	713.6	1,024.6	16.76	9.36

Note: Advertising and promotion are depreciated for 3 years; basic research accumulates for 11 years and development accumulates for 6 years; basic research is depreciated for 15 years and development is depreciated for 10 years.

Source: K. Clarkson, *Intangible Capital and Rates of Returns* (Washington, D.C.: American Enterprise Institute for Public Policy Research, 1977), pp. 47 and 49.

TABLE 6.4. Average Accounting and Corrected Rates of Return on Net Worth, 1959–73 (in percentages)

Industry	Accounting Rates of Return	Corrected Rates of Return	Difference
Pharmaceuticals	18.3	12.9	−5.4
Electrical machinery	13.3	10.1	−3.2
Foods	11.8	10.6	−1.2
Petroleum	11.2	10.8	−0.4
Chemicals	10.6	9.1	−1.5
Paper	10.5	10.1	−0.4
Office machinery	10.5	9.9	−0.6
Motor vehicles	10.5	9.2	−1.3
Rubber products	10.1	8.7	−1.4
Aerospace	9.2	7.4	−1.8
Ferrous metals	7.6	7.3	−0.3
Average	11.2	9.6	−1.6
Variance	7.5	2.5	

Source: K. Clarkson, *Intangible Capital and Rates of Return* (Washington, D. C.: American Enterprise Institute for Public Policy Research, 1977), p. 64.

regulation and the other is the "knowledge-depletion" hypothesis that alleges that, despite the explosion of new knowledge about basic biochemical processes, the stock of profitable new drug development opportunities has temporarily run out. These issues will be dealt with in Chapter 8 in detail.

Relationship between Accounting Bias and Industry Growth Rate

The bias in the accounting rate of return is significantly affected by the growth rate of an industry's capital. Solomon (1970), for example, shows that the accounting measure has zero bias when the growth rate of the company equals its true rate of return.* He offers an intuitive example. Let us say we have

$$b_t = \frac{F_t - d_t}{B_t}$$

---

*The true rate of return, r, is defined as the rate at which the net cash flows from investment have a present value equal to the original investment outlay.

TABLE 6.5 Summary of Corrected Rates of Return (ROR)

Author	Period	Number of Firms	Drug Industry ROR (percent)	Other Manufacturing ROR (percent)	Comments
Friedman and Friedman (1962)	1967–70	6	12.9	9.2	With 5 percent inflation rate and tax effect
Weiss (1969)	1963–64		13.1		
Stauffer (1975)	1953–72	6	15.6		
Ayanian (1975b)	1973	6	13.69		Estimates the depreciation rate
Schwartzman (1975a)	1973		3.3		Only on R & D return not for the firm
Bloch (1976)	1969	4	13.6		Advertising is not included
Clarkson (1977a)	1959–73	8	12.9	9.6	

Source: Compiled by the authors.

where

b_t = accounting rate of return
F_t = cash flow
d_t = depreciation and expenses outlays
B_t = net book value.

We also have

$$g_t = \frac{I_t - d_t}{B_t}$$

where

g_t = growth rate of capital
I_t = new investment.

By definition, the condition r = g (the true rate of return equals the growth rate) means all net cash flow is reinvested; since $F_t = I_t$, the condition g = b holds because of the previous two equations. The result is: if g = r, then g = b, thus b = r. Hence, the accounting rate of return is an unbiased and accurate measure of the true rate of return if the industry grows steadily at a rate equal to the rate of return (r or b).

However, Stauffer (1971) shows this to be a very special case. That is, even if g = r, the accounting measure equals the true, economic one only when the depreciation schedule is equivalent to the time rate of change of the present value of the future income stream. He concludes (p. 442): "Since depreciation schedules and lifetimes are in large measure arbitrary, being established by convention or through conformity with standards specified by fiscal authorities, it would be purely fortuitous if the two rates of return were identical in actual cases."

A result of the above exercise is that the accounting bias may be negative or positive depending on the true rate of return and the growth rate. This can be easily shown by Bloch's (1976, p. 156) equation for the bias:

$$\text{Bias} = \pi/E - (\pi + \Delta R^*)/(E + R^*)$$

where

π = accounting profit
E = stockholder's equity
R^* = value of R & D asset
ΔR^* = net investment in R & D asset.

With some manipulation it can be expressed as:

$$\text{Bias} = \left(\frac{\pi}{E} - \frac{\Delta R^*}{R^*} \right) \left(\frac{R^*/E}{1 + R^*/E} \right)$$

Solomon's point can be seen here: When the rate of return (π/E), equals the growth rate, $(\Delta R^*/R^*)$, the bias disappears. Similarly, when the growth rate is greater than the rate of return, the bias will be negative or downward, and vice versa; that is, when the growth rate is less than the true rate of return, the bias will be positive or upward.

The above discussion is more than a trivial exercise. The fact that there is positive accounting bias in the drug industry means that the industry growth rate is less than its rate of return. After reviewing works of Stauffer (1975) and Ayanian (1975b), Baily brings out this point emphatically (Helms, 1975, p. 127):

Now, a general finding that comes out of Professor Ayanian's paper, and also Stauffer's, is that either we have π/E, the accounting rate of return, greater than π^*/E^*, the true rate of return, which in turn is greater than the growth rate expressed as $P/(1 + P)$, or else we have the opposite set of inequalities:

$$\frac{\pi}{E} \leq \frac{\pi^*}{E^*} \leq \frac{P}{1 + P}$$

the inequalities can have only one sequence, or its exact opposite.

Therefore, for most cases in the drug industry, a finding that a true rate of return . . . is less than the accounting rate of return is equivalent to a finding that the growth rate in their capital is less than their rate of growth.*†

Baily thinks most of the industries plow back their profits and wonders why the growth rate of capital in the drug industry is less than its profit rate (Helms, 1975, p. 128):

Does that mean that the drug industry is not doing well in terms of growth? Apparently right now it is not. There is something atypical in the finding that, for pharmaceuticals, the accounting rate of return is higher than the true rate. This could mean that the data we are looking at are unusual for that industry because it is going through a transition phase.

If this is actually the case, we may expect the divergence between accounting and true measures of rates of return to widen since many economists consider the drug R & D atmosphere to be deteriorating (for example, Clymer, 1970).

RISK PREMIUM

High Risk and High Profit

In spite of all the corrections performed upon the accounting rate of return, the drug industry still ranks high among other industries. However, there is another economic theory justifying the persistent high profit rate: the theory of risk premium. Simply put, this theory states that the greater the risk, the greater the profit potential has to be before investors will be

---

*The true rate of return is defined here to be the rate of return computed after capitalizing advertising and R & D spending. Thus, it is different from Solomon's definition.

†P is the growth rate of capital. The term $1 + P$ in the denominator is an adjustment from continuous compounding to a straight annual rate of return.

willing to commit their capital. Risk in this context means the degree to which a hazard—for example, loss of capital—is not fully insurable. Accordingly, if any industry is unusually risky, higher than average profits are not inconsistent with a high degree of competition.

Measurement of Risk

The simplicity of the theory is matched by the difficulty of observing uncertainty, since its perception is quite subjective and random. Friedman and Friedman (1972, p. 55) express their feeling on the subject in their study of rates of return: "To recognize the relevance of such risk rewards is one thing; to quantify them, quite another. The record is full of unsuccessful efforts which suggest that the struggle has strong similarities to the long history of attempts to square the circle."

The size of the risk premium and the actual degree of riskiness are not at all apparent on the first glance. The risk premium is an empirical question; presumably, only the market itself offers a way to evaluate the size of the premium, and hence it is hard to tell if the actual return is that which the market decrees to be the appropriate risk premium or is high for some other reason. The degree of risk also should include the firms that entered and failed; excluding them would bias upwardly the mean rate of return. Brozen (in Clarkson, 1977a) has argued the drug industry has high entry and high failure; so the observed mean rate of return is distorted for this reason.

A wide variety of measures of uncertainty have been proposed, but the one most commonly used is the variance of net income. Cootner and Holland (1970) use the standard deviation of an individual company's rate of return around the industry mean for the measurement of uncertainty. Their regression of rate of return on this uncertainty measurement produced significant correlation, confirming the hypothesis that dispersion of company rates of return is a determinant of the return on investment.

There is some discussion on whether to use the intertemporal or interspatial (Fisher and Hall, 1969; Rodney Smith 1974) variation in measuring the uncertainty. The former measure supposedly reflects the uncertainty of predicting a company's future rate of return. However, Conrad and Plotkin (1968) assert the superiority of the latter measure because some portion of the intertemporal variation is predictable; also in their study they find it to be insignificant. The question may not be so clearly settled when we note that Conrad and Plotkin use both of the measures in step-wise fashion in their regression. The fact that the intertemporal variables become insignificant when interspatial ones are added may very possibly be the result of severe multicollinearity.

Nevertheless, Conrad and Plotkin (1968) show a strong relationship between the degree of uncertainty and rates of return; and in their empirical findings the drug industry has the highest variance and second highest rate of return. This result was brought out in the Senate hearings on *Competitive Problems in the Drug Industry* (1968d) to justify the high rate of return in the industry.

Mueller, in the same hearing, claims that the findings of Conrad and Plotkin really show the relative market power in the drug industry; a noncompetitive industry inherently has wide dispersion in rates of return because of entry barriers caused by product differentiation and advertising.

The controversy is a typical cause-and-effect problem in the uses of econometric analysis. Many economists tend to ignore the fact that single-equation regression is extremely inadequate in making any "causal" statement; at best a high R^2 or F shows some statistical correlation. In any attempt to explain the variation in the dependent variable, one at least has to strive for a "full specification," that is, including all relevant independent variables. In this light we can see that the simple regression between rates of return and uncertainty (a one-independent-variable case although more than one form of it is included) is insufficient in identifying the "cause" of high rates of return in the drug industry. The misuse of the regression technique provokes this type of controversy where no one can be sure what the relationship means.

POLICY IMPLICATIONS

According to formal welfare economics, if higher than average profits cannot be explained by higher than average risks, constraints that dampen the degree of price competition are assumed to exist. Specifically, if an industry such as pharmaceuticals shows persistently above average profits, the presumption is that it has been successful in erecting barriers to price competition that should be removed. Such barriers are deemed contrary to the public interest, on grounds that resource allocation does not reach a state of Pareto optimality unless there is sufficient price competition to drive prices down to marginal costs and profits down to a rate of return equivalent to the average for the economy as a whole.

If this chain of reasoning holds up under scrutiny, then in view of the drug industry's superior profit record, it is difficult to avoid the conclusion that anticompetitive elements are present in force. Thus, an evaluation of the industry's economic behavior inevitably must rest on analysis of the appropriateness of using the rubric of formal welfare economics as the measure for determining compliance with desired performance.

Worchester and Nesse (1978, p. 79) highlight the inappropriateness of using the formal conditions of the theory of economic efficiency as a standard of evaluation:

> Under the formal requirements, a firm makes the most if the added cost of producing a little more (the marginal cost) is exactly equal to the price for which it sells. But the presence or absence of this equality is difficult if not impossible to observe. So students of market structure substitute high profits, scarcity of firms in a market, and barriers to entry. This substitution leads away from the evaluation of feasible alternatives to a proliferation of suspected market failures based upon real and imagined discrepancies from the formal idealized model that cannot be attained under any circumstances. Concentration on formal market failures obscures perception of the performances of the actual system that may approximate or even better that expected of the formal model.... The plain fact is that none of the alternatives among which a choice can be made meet the highly abstract tests of formal welfare economics.

With regard to profits, Worcester and Nesse (pp. 84-85) argue:

> Just as high profit rates are highly unreliable guides to a wasteful use of resources, ... low profits are not in themselves a reliable indicator of efficiency. The difficulty is that the facts of life include indivisibilities, ignorance, moral hazard (the inclination to take personal advantage at the expense of others by sloth, carelessness when insured, and worse), risk-aversion, and the desire for new experiences, for prestige, for influence, and for approval. The costly tools used to accommodate these unruly facts of life are the same ones that stand accused as building blocks of inefficiency: "monopoly" in formal welfare theory.

The most important real–world element neglected in the formal theory of competition is the element of change—for example, the creation of *new* products and *new* processes; changes in the nature and scope of markets; changes in the methods by which products are paid for; and so on. To the extent that these kinds of changes are occurring within an industry and outside, its prices can never reach equilibrium because the equilibrium point itself is always changing. Put another way, if there is a significant amount of innovative activity in an industry, and if the factors affecting demand for its products are changing significantly, there is no reason to expect that its rate of return should match the average for all manufacturing. Thus, it would seem inappropriate to infer lack of competitiveness from the mere fact that an industry's return is above average.

Before a positive finding of inadequate competition could be reached, other factors would have to be considered. One of the most important of these is the extent to which an industry's return is higher because some of the companies have developed better products. If, through innovation, a company comes up with a product sufficiently superior to other alternatives that consumers voluntarily act *as if* it were the only product on the market, the innovating company would temporarily enjoy a quasi–monopoly position. That circumstance, however, is not necessarily inconsistent with a competitive environment, that is, one where there are continuing downward pressures pushing the prices on *existing* products toward marginal costs.

If an industry is judged according to the austere, abstract criteria of classic welfare economics, it will show up well only if its primary if not exclusive basis for competition is price. But there are other forms of competiton and it is an open question as to which type is most desirable from the standpoint of the consumer. Specifically, Grabowski and Vernon (1979, P. 29) have pointed out the industry's heavy reliance on product-based competition and the implications this has for evaluating its performance:

> A number of studies using the structure-conduct-performance paradigm have pointed to the high profit rate and wide price disparities between closely substitutable products as strong evidence for high entry barriers and market power in the ethical drug industry. Some recent studies, using a much more microeconomic and dynamic methodological approach, have directly challenged this conclusion. In particular they point to a rapid rate of innovation in the industry as a key element of dynamic competition that positively influences consumer welfare, both by providing therapeutic advance over existing products and by introducing a dynamic form of price competition to this industry. Futhermore they offer evidence to support the position that promotional activities are a complementary activity to diffusion of innovation and the entry of new firms into particular therapeutic markets and therefore "facilitate" rather than erect barriers to entry.

Comanor (1979, p. 66) takes issue with Grabowski and Vernon's point that the rapid pace of new product introduction in the pharmaceutical industry has led to much improved consumer welfare:

> Although consumer welfare may be improved by the rapid pace of product innovation, it may also be reduced by prices that exceed costs because of limited competitive pressures. In the best of circumstances rapid innovation would not be at the expense of effective price competition. However, such circumstances are not always encountered, and the dilemma imposed by the Schumpeterian hypothesis is that rapid innovation may indeed be at the expense of substantial price competition.

SUMMARY AND AREAS FOR FUTURE RESEARCH

When measuring the profit rate in the drug industry, the upward bias caused by the accounting method has been clearly established by economists (see Figure 6.1) The high level of promotional and R & D expenditures in the industry easily prove the bias to be significant. The task of searching for the "true" rate of return is more complicated since both a fair amount of industry knowledge and a sound methodology are required. The problem is vastly complicated if not made impossible by the fact that the drug industry is relatively dynamic, and therefore the true rate of return is likely to change significantly over time. It is thus inevitable that different researchers reach different sets of numbers.

No studies on the industry's rate of return have been done for the period since the full impact of the 1962 amendments began to be felt, that is, from the late 1960s to the present (early 1980s). An update of this sort would be useful in assessing the validity of the claim that the real rate of return has been declining. Inclusion of adjustments for the impact of inflation on measured rates of return would also have considerable appeal in this regard.

A positive accounting bias in terms of the industry growth rate means that drug company managements are diverting cash flow from pharmaceuticals to other areas. Yet some economists maintain that R & D expenditures continue to increase. These contradictory indications need to be reconciled. Specifically, understanding of the industry would be enhanced if the following questions were addressed in depth:

What has been happening to expected rates of return from pharmaceutical R & D? Since the expected rate of return serves as the basis for investment decision making, an analysis of this issue would yield important insights into whether incentives to engage in R & D are changing and, if so, how.

What has been happening to R & D in constant dollar terms relative to sales in constant dollar terms? The pattern of real R & D spending needs to be revealed before anything definitive can be said about the trend in R & D.

Given the already developed methodology, it seems the issue of profit rates can be explored in further depth with respect to its relationship to other characteristics of the industry instead of stopping short at the mere correction of profit rates. In particular, it would be of interest to measure the relationship between rates of return and new product introductions, that is, innovation.

Although the risk factor in drug R & D is well accepted, its quantification presents difficulties; the variation of the net income is only partially

FIGURE 6.1 Path Chart of Drug Industry Profit Rate

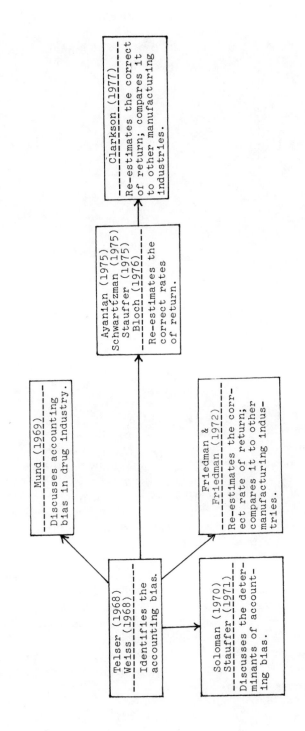

Source: Compiled by the authors.

101

FIGURE 6.2. Impact of R & D Gestation Lags

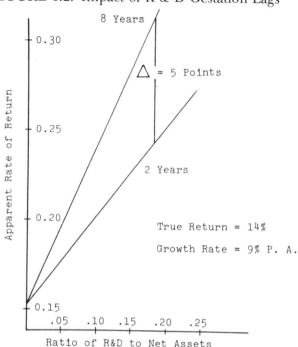

caused by the expected risk. The treatment of risk premium as the residual portion from the normal rate of return is quite simplistic. There is also a distinct difference between uncertainty on the product and firm level. Some methods of risk reduction are known to be at the disposal of the firm, such as product diversification, larger number of research projects, international operations. Unless these factors are taken into consideration, it is doubtful that the size of the risk premium can be determined independently.

As discussed in detail in Chapter 4, today's product competition generates in the future both a stream of new products and downward pressures on prices for existing products. But product competition today means that price competition today is less than it might be otherwise. Thus the basic question policy makers must answer is this: under which circumstance is the consumer better off—lower prices today or a stream of new products and lower prices on old products tomorrow?

There is also a crucial subsidiary question. Is the cash flow from single-source drugs sufficient to finance R & D by itself? If not, then government efforts to increase price competition among multi-source drugs will on balance produce a benefit to the consumer (lower prices) only at a substantial risk that discounted future losses in the form of fewer new drugs and foregone price cuts on old drugs will be far greater.

7

INNOVATION IN THE
PHARMACEUTICAL INDUSTRY

INTRODUCTION AND
HISTORICAL BACKGROUND

The importance of technological innovation has to be perceived on a level more general than that of any particular industry. Product innovations have been the cornerstone of the success and well-being of any economic system, in particular, a capitalistic economy. To this end, the free market system has been considered by many to be the system most conducive to technical innovations. On the other hand, the importance of technical innovation to our economy has been recognized only recently. Edward Denison (1962) surprised many economists when he estimated that 42 percent of the rise in output per worker between 1929 and 1957 could be attributed to work force education, 36 percent to the advance of scientific and technological knowledge, and only 9 percent to increase in capital intensity. Increasing productivity, which results from technological knowledge, has been recognized as an essential bulwark against inflation and recession. Thus the rate of technological change and innovation in an industry is a crucial indicator as to its performance and contribution to the society. A healthy rate of innovation signifies rising productivity, output, employment, and strong trade surpluses internationally.

The drug industry has largely shown these healthy signs since the 1950s with one recent exception: the decreasing rate of new drug innovation. The phenomenon has understandably created some alarm since the industry considers innovation to be the main support to its economic activities. It is also argued that the slow rate of innovation causes welfare losses to society.

In order for an appropriate response to be developed, it becomes crucial to decide what has been causing the slowdown in the rate of drug innovation. Is it normal market forces or some outside intervention? It is to this question that a great portion of the recent literature we have surveyed is devoted.

Although the question cannot be answered with quantitative precision, a consensus seems to have emerged in the literature that the 1962 amendments to the Food, Drug, and Cosmetic Act played a major but not necessarily exclusive role. Other factors hypothesized as contributing to the well-documented decreasing rate of drug innovation are depletion of research opportunity, and decreasing returns to scale in the industry.

APPROACH OF THE CHAPTER

This chapter and the following one should be read together as they both deal with the issue of what has been happening to the rate of pharmaceutical innovation and why. In this chapter we describe what the recent trends in drug innovation have been and briefly sketch how the drug innovation process works. This latter step is necessary because it is impossible to understand the economics of the industry without first having some insight into its central activity—innovation.

Of the three factors hypothesized as causing a decline in the rate of drug innovation, the issue of how returns vary according to firm size differs importantly from the other two. First, unlike the "research opportunity depletion" theory or the effects of government regulation, the trend toward a fewer number of large companies can be viewed *either* as a cause of the decline in new drug introduction (decreasing returns to scale) *or* as an effect of changes in the drug development environment. Second, the issue of economies of scale in the drug industry is generally considered to have been settled. Simply put, the decreasing return to scale hypothesis has been disproved, and the contrary hypothesis—economies of scale—has been confirmed. In this chapter we trace the intellectual history of the development of this consensus. Discussion of the knowledge depletion hypothesis and the effects of government regulation will be left to Chapter 8.

THE ENVIRONMENT OF DRUG INNOVATION

The enormous amount of uncertainty and delay between input and output makes any long-term drug production plan close to guesswork. This is especially true when the importance of the product makes it susceptible to many social and political factors upon which the industry has marginal, if any, influence. Consequently, the supply side of the industry can be analyzed only on the general level of its "environment," rather than on a set of precise, definite conditions.

Decreasing Rate of Innovation

Whatever the causes, the decrease in the rate of drug innovation has been observed by many analysts beginning in the mid–1960s—about the time that the 1962 amendments took their effect. Specifically, there is little dispute about the fact that there is a drastic difference between the numbers of new drugs introduced before and after the early 1960s. Schnee and Caglarcan (1976) found that compared with the peak era of 1951 to 1960, the recent annual average rate of new product introductions had declined by one-half. These products can be classified into four categories: new chemical entities, duplicate products, compound products, and alternate dosage forms. Table 7.1 shows the rate of introduction from 1950 to 1974.

Schnee and Caglarcan point out that the decline in new product introductions is in a sense understated because a significant proportion of the recent new drug introductions were in the cancer drug therapy area where there are only narrow uses for them. Put another way, if the results in Table 7.1 were expressed in terms of prescription volume rather than numbers of new products, the decline from the mid-1960s would be even more dramatic.

The thesis that the decline has been mainly in the "me-too" drugs is not obvious from Table 7.1. Wardell and Lasagna (1975a) investigated the kinds of declines in introduction for 15 drugs for the period 1963 to 1974. For new chemical entities (NCE) administered to man, they find the following (p. 157):

> Each of the three-year periods following the Kefauver-Harris amendments shows a substantially higher number of such NCEs than the period following; the average rate for the initial three-year period was 75 per year. A plateau seems to have been reached by 1966. For the last three complete years, 1971-1973, the average rate was 46 per year, which is 60 percent less than the earlier period.

Concerning the fate of NCE applications, their study also shows a drastic decline in the percentage of NCE applications with approved New Drug Application; about 6 percent of all NCE applications filed from 1962 through 1966 made it all the way through the testing and regulatory review process to approval for marketing. The mean number of the years from filing of applications to approval also shows an increasing trend since 1963.

It also has become apparent that the U.S. drug companies are shifting their initial research efforts abroad where new drug regulations are not so

TABLE 7.1. New Product Introductions in the Ethical
Pharmaceutical Industry, 1950–74

Year	Total New Products	New Single Chemicals	Duplicate Products	Compounded Products	New Dosage Forms
1950	326	28	100	198	118
1951	321	35	74	212	120
1952	314	35	77	202	170
1953	353	48	79	226	97
1954	380	38	87	255	108
1955	403	31	90	282	96
1956	401	42	79	280	66
1957	400	51	88	261	96
1958	370	44	73	253	109
1959	315	63	49	203	104
1960	306	45	62	199	98
1961	260	39	32	189	106
1962	250	27	43	180	84
1963	199	16	34	149	52
1964	157	17	29	111	41
1965	112	23	18	71	22
1966	80	12	15	53	26
1967	82	25	25	32	14
1968	87	11	26	50	21
1969	62	9	22	31	12
1970	105	16	50	39	23
1971	83	14	40	29	30
1972	64	11	35	18	30
1973	74	19	37	18	17
1974	83	18	42	23	26
Total	5,587	717	1,306	3,564	1,686

Sources: Paul de Haen, Ten Year New Product Survey, 1950–1960, in Paul de Haen, *Nonproprietary Name Index*, Vol. 6 (New York: Paul de Haen, Inc., 1967); and Paul de Haen, *New Products Parade, 1973–74* (New York: Paul de Haen, Inc., 1975).

rigid, and therefore the time and cost of introducing a new drug is not as great. This shift arising from differences in the "tightness" of national drug regulatory authorities leads to the question of whether the United States is behind other countries in introducing new useful drugs. Schnee and Caglarcan (1976, p. 37) conclude:

There are substantial international differences in the availability, use, and knowledge of new drug products. When the pattern of new drug introductions in the U.S. was compared with the pattern in England, a significant U.S. drug lag was found. However, the gap between the two countries has been narrowed considerably in the last few years.

Grabowski et al. (1976, p. 77) have also performed a comparative analysis of U.S. innovative performance and conclude:

A principal finding that emerged from this analysis is the U.S. "productivity"—defined as a number of NCEs discovered and introduced in the U.S. per dollar of R & D expenditure—declined by about sixfold between 1960-1961 and 1966-1970. The corresponding decrease in the U.K. was about threefold. Clearly, some worldwide phenomenon, which might be labelled a "depletion of research opportunities," seems to hold for pharmaceutical R & D. However, there is also strong support for the hypothesis that an additional factor is at work in the U.S. industry.

The decrease in productivity per dollar of R & D expenditure is also evident in Baily's (1972) study on cost and return in the pharmaceutical industry of the 1954–69 period.

Nevertheless, according to Brand (1974), from 1963 to 1972, output per man-hour in the industry still has risen at an average annual rate of 4.2 percent, which is substantially higher than that for other manufacturing industries. Recognizing the decreasing rate of drug innovation, Brand thought that as of 1974 the industry still had a strong position for the time being but expresses concern for a longer term (p. 12):

The decline in the number of new pharmaceutical products has had no determinable impact on overall output and productivity trends, which have largely been sustained by the continued strong growth of established products and by gains in the efficiency of manufacturing them. Over the long term, however, the introduction of newly synthetized drugs spurs output growth and helps maintain high rates of capacity utilization. Hence, the declining number presages possible problems.

Changing Environment

Research and development take place in the private sector because the innovative products bring back at least a normal rate of return on the resources committed. Scherer (1970) describes the innovative process as four separate functions: invention, entrepreneurship, investment, and development. He explains (p. 380):

Invention then is the act of insight by which a new and promising technical possibility is recognized and worked out (at least mentally and perhaps also physically) in its essential, most rudimentary form. Development is the lengthy sequence of detail-oriented technical activities, including trial-and-error testing, through which the original concept is modified and perfected until it is ready for commercial utilization. The entrepreneurial function involves deciding to go forward with the effort, organizing it, and obtaining financial support for it. Investment is the act of risking funds for the venture.

It is in the environment surrounding these functions that the drug industry has been finding some sharp changes. Most noticeably, they are in terms of risk, cost, and time lag. Speaking of the postamendment period, Schnee and Caglarcan (1976, p. 37) state:

There have been sharp increases in the cost, duration, and risks of drug development during the last decade. The cost to develop one new pharmaceutical product now approximates $12.0 million, which is more than ten times greater than the comparable cost for the pre-1962 period. Similarly, the probability of developing a successful product is close to one-fourth of the pre-1962 success rate.

Clymer (1970, p. 110), from the perspective of an R & D manager, agrees:

The time needed is now so great, in fact, that it exceeds the period for which we have data to show just what to expect of the innovative process in a changed and still changing milieu. In the last decade, this time has increased three- or fourfold and has been coupled with an even greater increase in costs and financial risk.

Many other economists observe in particular the severe cost increase in the drug industry. Grabowski et al. (1976) also note that industry R & D expenditures have increased severalfold, while the introduction of NCEs has significantly declined. Sarett (1974) suggests that over the period 1962 to 1972, the development cost per NCE has risen from $1.2 to $11.5 million. Schwartzman (1976a) includes the cost of research on drugs that do not reach the market and comes up with a cost of $24 million per new drug. In the most recent and most empirical analysis of the cost of drug development, Hansen (1979) finds that the total estimated cost per NCE as of 1976 amounted to $54 million. This study cannot be directly compared with the previous studies because Hansen takes into account inflation, the investment cost associated with time, as well as the direct accounting costs.

THE DRUG INNOVATION PROCESS

Early commentators on the pharmaceutical industry (Steele, 1964) emphasized the distinction between basic and applied research and further inferred that the contribution of the drug industry to significant innovations was minor. When, however, the drug R & D process is subjected to careful analysis, there may be a reasonable alternative explanation of the industry's role in drug innovation.

An understanding of the controversies surrounding drug innovation depends heavily on some appreciation of how the process of drug discovery and development works. Factors at every stage of the drug development process serve as a form of feedback to the decisions to research potential new drugs and improve old ones.

Historically, successful pharmaceutical discoveries have occurred in one of two ways: either serendipitously by a fortuitous clinical observation or through a reiterative process where feedback from efforts to apply basic new knowledge of life processes expands that knowledge, thus improving the prospects that it will be successfully applied.

In contrast to physics, where much progress has taken place by the application of breakthroughs in theory, the key to progress in drug therapy has been empirical chemical compound processing and clinical observation. Specifically each of the traditional pathways to pharmaceutical discovery and development—the serendipity route and the repeated cycling of information from laboratory to clinic and back—is critically dependent on tests of pharmacologic activity in man. Together these approaches have accounted for the great majority of drugs currently in use. Oates (1975, pp. 187–89) lists some of the major drugs whose usefulness was recognized initially in clinical studies as follows: the antihypertensive actions of the Beta blockers; methyldopa, and hydralizine, the antigout action of allopurinol; the antiinflammatory actions of steroids; and all the major psychotherapeutic drugs.

Drug Therapy

Among those who have examined the issue of the contributions of the pharmaceutical industry to progress in drug therapy there appears to be agreement on two findings: perhaps because of its emphasis on clinical investigation the industry's contribution has been disportionately large; and its contribution has grown over time.

Caglarcan (1977, pp. 23–27), who did a summary and synthesis of the literature on the relative contribution of various sources of drug development, reports as follows:

> The available data indicate that pharmaceutical industry sources have discovered 92 percent of all new drugs introduced in the United States between 1940 and 1975. The remaining 8 percent originated in university or government laboratories. Although industry research laboratories have been responsible for the majority of new drugs, this ratio depends on the disease involved. For example, while the pharmaceutical industry originated 100 percent of some types of arthritis drugs, only 45 percent of anticoagulants came from industry research laboratories.

Similarly Schnee (1973) studied a separate sample of 68 pharmaceutical innovations put on the market during the 1935-1962 period and concluded that the pharmaceutical industry accounted for 46 percent of the discoveries; and external sources (mainly foreign firms, universities, hospitals, research institutes, and individuals) were responsible for approximately 54 percent of the innovations.

The relative share of the pharmaceutical industry has increased in recent years. For example, when Schnee divided the 1935–1962 period into two distinct segments, he found that the importance of pharmaceutical industry R & D has increased over time.

The proportion of discoveries by drug industry sources in 1950-1962 was 62 percent, compared with 54 percent for the 1935-1949 period. Schnee and Caglarcan (1978, p. 99) indicate that external sources continued to decline in importance during the 1960s. Pharmaceutical industry R & D laboratories originated 89 percent of the innovations marketed between 1963 and 1970.

Schwartzman (1975a, pp. 9-19) has also examined this issue and concluded that industrial sources are more important than other originators of pharmaceuticals. He reports that for the 1950-1969 period, the proportion of new chemical entities discovered and introduced by the pharmaceutical industry was 86 percent and for 1960-69 it was 91 percent. A Food and Drug Administration compilation also corroborates the pharmaceutical industry's role as the major originator in the discovery of new drugs. The FDA results essentially are similar to those of others mentioned above. According to this FDA report, the industry was the source of 86 percent of important new drugs introduced in the 1960-1969 period. Another list by the same government agency indicates that the industry's share increased from 69 percent for the 1950-1962 period to 82 percent for the 1963-1970 period.

The Nature of the Drug Innovation Process and the Regulatory Interface

The nature of the pharmaceutical innovation process and its interface with the regulatory process has been described as shown in Figure 7.1 and Table 7.2. As is clear by inspection of Table 7.2, the Food and Drug Administration gets involved at a very early stage of investigation. Specifically, if animal toxicology and pharmacologic tests on a particular compound are satisfactory, an investigational drug application (IND) is sent to the FDA. Once the drug's sponsor has obtained the agency's approval, clinical tests are begun. These tests are divided into three phases: Phase I where the compound is tested for safety on a few healthy human volunteers; Phase II where the compound is tested on a few patients to determine efficacy as well as side effects; Phase III where the compound is tested on a much larger number of patients for safety and efficacy. If the results from testing the compound remain favorable, the manufacturer files a new drug application (NDA) to obtain approval for marketing. The NDA is then reviewed by the FDA to determine whether the tests are sufficiently indicative of safety and efficacy to permit marketing.

Whatever its other effects, the involvement of the regulatory agency in the drug development process may slow down the all-important feedback process from clinic to lab and back again. The net result could be a decline in the probability that successful new compounds will be developed and an increase in the time and cost of development. Specifically, Hansen (1979) concludes that of the drugs that have received IND approval since enactment of the 1962 amendments (that is, have received approval for testing in man), not more than one out of eight will receive approval for marketing. He further reports that the average clinical development time for new pharmaceuticals is on the order of six or seven years and the preclinical research prior to development extends several years earlier. The clear implication of this is that the financial resources required to "stay in the drug development game" are considerable.

Wardell and Lasagna (1975a, pp. 161-62) give this example of the survival rate from 1968 to 1974:

> . . . it is obvious that the percentage of approvals of all NCEs administered to man is low: 29 out of 649 applications, or 4.5 percent overall. This is, to be sure, an underestimate, since presumably some of the NCE's still pending will ultimately be approved. Nevertheless the number approved out of those INDs filed since 1968, is, as we have shown, vanishingly small (less than 1 percent).

FIGURE 7.1 Time Pattern of the Development of an NCE

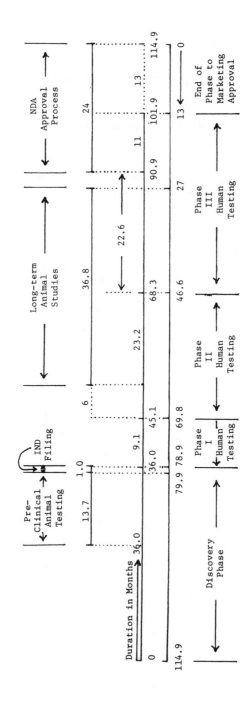

Source: R. W. Hansen, "The Pharmaceutical Development Process: Estimate of Current Development Costs and Times and the Effects of Regulatory Changes," Working Paper No. GPB 77-10, pp. 1–60, Center for Government Policy and Business of the Graduate School of Management, University of Rochester, August 1977.

112

TABLE 7.2. Typical Stages of the Drug Development Process

1. *Discovery phase*
Basic research synthesis of new chemicals and early studies of chemical properties. Identification of a specific new chemical entity (NCE) worthy of further testing.

2. *Preclinical animal testing*
Short-term animal toxicity testing for evidence of safety in the short-run in preparation for human testing.

3. *IND filing*
A request is made for authorization to begin human testing by filing a notice of claimed investigational exemption for new drug (IND).

4. *Phase I human testing*
Dosage administered to healthy volunteers for evidence of toxicity in humans.

5. *Phase II human testing*
Used on humans with the particular pathological condition to evaluate therapeutic value of the NCE.

6. *Phase III human testing*
Large-scale tests on humans over a longer period to uncover unanticipated side-effects.

7. *Long-term animal studies*
To determine the effects of prolonged exposures and the effects on subsequent generations. Such studies are typically conducted concurrently with other studies.

8. *New drug application (NDA)*
Application for commercial marketing of the new drug. Review of evidence by the FDA. Approval was received for NCEs representing about one out of eight of the original NCEs for which an IND was granted in the sample reported by Hansen.

Source: John R. Virts and J. Fred Weston, "Returns to Research and Development in the U.S. Pharmaceutical Industry," *Managerial and Decision Economics* 1 (1980): 103–11.

Hansen's (1979) estimates of pharmaceutical development costs and times permit the construction of a sensitivity analysis showing the relative impact on costs of changes in drug development times and research project attrition rates. Using a sample of cost data for 8 percent of the NCEs and development time data for 10 percent of the NCEs introduced by the 25 U.S. firms surveyed, he finds that the discovery costs and testing expenditures per marketed new chemical entity, capitalized at an 8 percent rate to the point of marketing approval, is $54 million in 1976 dollars. This figure is obtained as follows (figures in millions of dollars):

	(1) Average actual cash outlays per NCE entering clinical trials	(2) Cash outlays per NCE marketed (based on an attrition rate of 7 out of 8)	(3) Cash outlays per marketed NCE capitalized to point of marketing approval at a rate of 8 percent
Discovery cost	2.10	16.08	30.4
Average cost per NCE entering clinical trials	1.87	14.90	23.6
Totals	3.97	30.98	54.0

Hansen's analysis yields several important conclusions: In order for a pharmaceutical manufacturer to generate any true economic profit from a new chemical entity, that NCE must produce a return of approximately $54 million (in 1976 dollars) over and above the direct costs of production and marketing. Regulatory changes that affect the attrition rate (or conversely the probability of individual project success) can have a very significant impact on the economic viability of new drug development— even more than regulations that increase the time taken to review the information on a drug after it has been developed. Specifically, extensive FDA involvement in the early stages of clinical research could have especially adverse consequences to the extent that it hampers the ability to follow up efficiently on promising but unexpected leads. Bloom (1976, p. 365) expresses concern that this may be what is happening:

> In a drug research project at the pre-feasibility stage, the rate of discovery is importantly determined by how efficiently key clinical tests of validity can be accomplished. Delay in meaningful clinical feedback to the laboratory team will inevitably bog down the entire process, because it leaves the scientist without a meaningful indication of how his work is measuring up. He

ason for excessive prescribing is obvious: drug companies need
nake money. This must account, in large part, for drug advertise-
medical journals and the large investments made by the phar-
al industry in attempts to sell doctors on their products."

above allegations need further close examination. The over-
n of advertising is a familiar occurrence in most of the advertising-
industries; but the determination of whether there is an over-
n or not is mostly subjective since it has scanty theoretical basis.
nt is: to the extent they can measure it, a firm spends on
nal activity until the cost of the last unit (of some form of
n) brings back equal amounts of revenue. An efficient firm does
ingly overspend on promotion.

second allegation, concerning the incompleteness of detailmen's
ion, is also a product of short-sighted firms. A firm wishing to
a sound reputation seldom indulges in overselling the product
accuracy of the information may cause permanent damage to the
age.

prescription has its roots in the relationship between the
and the patient. Melmon et al. explain (1975, p. 11): "Although
ician tends to over-prescribe for subjective and frequently
reasons (his wish to be or to appear to be effective, decisive and
the patient may also irrationally demand prescriptions. We are a
at believes in the magic of technology: surely "miracle drugs" exist
ife's inevitable woes." Whatever the solution to the problem is, the
ustry should not be held entirely responsible for it.

he other hand, we also find economists providing justification for
promotional expenses. Schwartzman (1976, p. 192) also tests the
s that firm size does not influence the level of promotional
re from the same equation:

$$c = 6.98 + .127 \ln S + .113 \ln N.$$
$$(t = 1.6) \qquad (t = 4.2) \quad R^2 = .30$$

promotional intensity
firm size
number of innovations.

nfluence of firm size is only marginally significant. However, the
y between firm size and number of innovations makes it difficult
et the econometric results.

is, therefore, unable to select for follow-up those la
are demonstrably relevant to clinical therapy. The
at the pre-feasibility stage.

Nevertheless, a host of valuable new drugs fo
degenerative diseases were successfully discovered
period in precisely this manner. Why has this not
satisfactory rate? One highly significant change t
years—with this country at the forefront—is that
one of the new forms of scientific innovation in w
of discovery is importantly subject to governmer
order to take the necessary steps to seek clinica
finding, approval must be obtained from both F
mechanisms prior to undertaking the first tests
impact of this has been so great that in many inst
research resources are not rate–determining in
clinical results are.

If Bloom's hypothesis is true, then the sc
tunities phenomenon may to some extent be a
structure rather than a circumstance whose o
relation between regulation and innovation.
the relative impact of regulation and other fac
& D can ever be quantified precisely, empirica
regulation on research project success prob
useful in determining where the burden of p

Promotional Activities

The role of promotional activities is imp
of the costs and risks involved in bringing n
There are generally two types of criticisms on
penditures. First is the familiar entry barr
industry spends on advertising their produc
entry barrier of the industry. Since the topic
discussed, we basically ignore it here. The
industry's promotional expenditures are lar

The description "wasteful," in the crit
saturating the physicians, giving incomplete
unnecessary drug uses. Doctors are said to
materials and the attention of detailmen
However, according to the Sainsbury Rep
physicians consider the detailmen to be a so
the other hand, the physicians do not trust t
detailmen. And the third case is expressed k

"On
sales
men
mac

satur
inter
satur
The
prom
prom
not k

infor
main
where
firm's

physic
the p
irratio
helpfu
society
even fo
drug i

the lar
hypoth
expend

In

where

Pr
S
N

Th
collinea
to inter

In the midst of the hostile reaction toward drug promotion, Peltzman (1975b) reminds us of the value of information coming from the promotional activities. We should note, however, that the value of information can not justify the activities without considering the efficiency of alternative methods of information diffusion. It has been suggested that government take over the role of the information diffuser. As Melmon et al. (1975, p. 7) point out, there is a need for a centralized information source where all uses and misuses of pharmaceutical products are recorded: "We probably need a central clearinghouse for reports both of efficacy and adverse drug reactions, but before such an effort would be effective we must train people to obtain useful information."

There is a sound economic reason why a central source of information may be more efficient: Information has the characteristic of being a public good. While a central information source may lead to greater efficiency in information diffusion, it is not clear that the source must be publicly or governmentally owned.

DETERMINANTS OF DRUG INNOVATION

To understand how pharmaceutical R & D is affected by environmental change, it is necessary to understand not only how the process works, but also what determines how much is spent on R & D. All the factors that are embedded in the stages of production have causal linkages to the decision to invest in future R & D. This investment behavior in the drug industry is a subject of great interest, since all involved parties are interested in knowing how the industry is adapting to the new R & D environment.

Although the factors influencing R & D expenditures are numerous, there is a scarcity of rigorous empirical work on the subject. The one we have selected is Grabowski's (1968) study of chemical, drug, and petroleum industries.

The model employed by Grabowski is the following (pp. 292–305):

$$R_{i,t}/S_{i,t} = b_o + b_1 P_1 + b_2 D_i + b_3 (I_{i,t-1}/S_{i,t})$$

Where

$R_{i,t}$ = the level of R & D expenditures of the *ith* firm in the *tth* period
$S_{i,t}$ = the level of sales of the *ith* firm in the *tth* period
$I_{i,t-1}$ = the sum of after tax profits plus depreciation and depletion expenses of the *ith* firm in the t−1 period

P_i = the number of patents received per scientist and engineer employed by the *ith* firm in a prior four-year period (1955–59)

D = the index of diversification of the *ith* firm.

The model uses 1959–62 data for the ten drug firms. The resulting parameters are all significant:

$b_1 = .54$
$(.12)$

$b_2 = .41$
$(.07)$

$b_3 = .26$
$(.05)$

with the $R^2 = .86$ (numbers in parentheses are standard errors).

Among the results of the three variables, those of the productivity variable, P, and the profit variable, I, conform to the hypothesis that the investment decision process in the drug industry depends highly on the past technological success and rate of return. The role of diversification has less consensus. Comanor (1965) considers the diversification process "not helpful" to the firms, but Grabowski's result shows that, nevertheless, large R & D expenditures are related to it.

If Grabowski's model is correct, the recent declining rate of drug innovation should be causing a curtailment of R & D spending in the United States. To some extent this had been happening. Schnee and Caglarcan (1976) show that spending on R & D deflated by the GNP implicit price deflator increased at an annual rate of only 5 percent between 1965 and 1974. Furthermore, almost all of the increase took place before 1970. By contrast, over the same period, R & D spending by U.S. companies abroad tripled with about three-fourths of the increase occurring after 1970.

Although there has been some curtailment of R & D spending, it has not been sharp. Furthermore, only a small number of firms have eliminated their large-scale R & D operations. How can these observations be reconciled with the Grabowski thesis that R & D investment depends highly on past technological success and rate of return? Schwartzman (1976a) presents four reasons.

● Firms may expect to do better than average on the basis of their past records or on the basis of specific research projects already under way.

• Firms must maintain research staffs and programs if they hope to produce a breakthrough that will inaugurate another stream of innovations.

• Firms may be willing to gamble in hopes of beating the high odds against finding another drug like Valium.

• Although it has not been tested empirically in the literature, another possibility may be that drug firms have diversified their R & D effort into nonpharmaceutical activities.

MARKET STRUCTURE AND INNOVATION

With the decreasing rate of drug innovation, both industry management and observers are concerned with the changing structure of the industry. It may well be that we are witnessing a transitional period of the industry, and our understanding of it may influence its future course.

Three questions arise in connection with the problem of innovational efficiency at the firm level: Is the decreasing rate of innovation a simple phenomenon of decreasing returns to scale? How have firms responded to the changing R & D environment? What changes are required for firm survival?

The Relationship between Innovation and Firm Size

The thesis that larger firms are not only better equipped for fast technological innovation but actually do achieve increasing return to scale is mainly promoted by two of the most well-known economists of this century: Joseph A. Schumpeter and John Kenneth Galbraith. Schumpeter, in his prophetic work, *Capitalism, Socialism, and Democracy* (1950) stresses the role of innovation and the kind of market structure most conducive to it (p. 106):

> What we have got to accept is that the large–scale establishment of unit of control has come to be the most powerful engine of economic progress. In this respect, perfect competition is not only impossible but inferior, and has no title to being set up as a model of ideal efficiency.

Galbraith (1952, p. 91) continues to support this thesis by arguing "the modern industry of few large firms is an almost perfect instrument for inducing technical change."

There are several reasons why large firms are considered to be more adapted to a high rate of technological innovation. The obvious one is the prohibitive cost of R & D; only large firms have the resources to engage in large-scale R & D activities. Second, since risk is an integral part of R & D, larger firms can diversify and absorb the risk better than the smaller firms. Third, economies of scale in conducting the R & D accrue to the large firms through the use of equipment, specialty personnel, and other infrastructures within the firm. Finally, return to technical innovation is larger for firms with high output level, especially in the case of process innovation.

Against this impressive array of arguments there do exist some disadvantages of being "large." The most often mentioned is the "sluggishness" of decision making of large firms. Supposedly this is a result of the cumbersome bureaucratic structure, such as getting a consensus among too many people, passing of responsibilities through the levels of management, creating unnecessary positions, stifling creative young personnel by the seniority system, and so on. Large firms are also alleged to shy away from imaginative ideas because of the security consciousness of the employee.

The settlement of the two opposing hypotheses is obviously not to be expected at the theoretical level. There are so many different firms and industries that no conclusive statement can be made without some form of empirical examination.

Early studies tended to cast doubt on the Schumpeterian thesis. In his study of the petroleum, chemical, and steel industries, Mansfield (1968) found that only in the chemical industry did an increase in R & D expenditures result in a more than proportional increase in inventive output. Furthermore, he concludes (p. 199):

> When a firm's expenditures on research and development are held constant, increases in size of firm seem to be associated in most industries with decreases in inventive output. Thus, the evidence suggests that the productivity of a research and development effort of a given scale is lower in the largest firms than in medium-size and small ones.

The pharmaceutical industry, with its heavy privately sponsored R & D activities, also quickly became a prime candidate for such research. As early as 1965, Comanor (1965) attempted to resolve the empirical question of R & D economies of scale in the drug industry with 1955–60 data from 57 firms. While finding a positive relationship between research and development and product output, Comanor determined that the marginal productivity of professional research personnel is inversely related to size of firm.

The techniques involved in the study deserve some attention because subsequent works, supporting or opposing Comanor's results, follow his approach. His principal regression equation is:

$$Y/S = a_o + a_1 R/S + a_2 R^2/S + a_3 S + a_4 I + a_5 D$$

where:

Y = sales in the first two years of new single entities introduced in 1955–60

S = firm size, measured by the mean value of annual prescription and hospital sales during 1955–60.

R = number of professional research personnel

D = measure of diversification*

I = interacton variable, product of S and R

and the division of Y and R by S is due to heteroscedasticity problems. The estimated equation is (p. 185):

$$Y = 0.422 - 4.671 \ R/S + 0.547 \ R^2/S + 0.0000344S -$$
$$\quad (3.1) \quad\quad (3.6) \quad\quad\quad (5.1) \quad\quad\quad\quad (3.7)$$

$$0.000000128RS - 0.13D$$
$$(4.0) \quad\quad\quad\quad (3.2)$$

$R^2 = 0.40$; t-values are in parentheses.

As can be seen from the t-values, all parameters are significant. The quadratic equation shows that the research effort, in terms of professional personnel, does increase sales from new outputs more than proportionally. However, the coefficient on the interaction variable is negative.

When the derivative of the above equation (after being multiplied by S) is taken with respect to R, the S (firm size) becomes a negative influence on the marginal product of research effort:

$$Y = 0.422S - (4.671 + 0.000000128S^2) \ R + 0.547R^2 + 0.0000344S^2 -$$
$$0.130DS$$

and

$$\frac{\partial Y}{\partial R} = -4.671 - 0.000000128S^2 + 2\,(0.547)R$$

This is the first empirical evidence that there may be diseconomies of scale in pharmaceutical firm expansion.

The next major empirical work on the relationship between firm size and innovative output supported the Comanor conclusion. Mansfield, Rapoport, Schnee, Wagner, and Hamburger devoted a full chapter of their

---

*The diversification measure here is not comparable to the same term used in Grabowski's study (1976) discussed earlier. Comanor examines diversification of output among various pharmaceutical markets while Grabowski considers a firm's output across Standard Industrial Classification product classifications.

study to examining the relationship between drug innovation and firm size (Mansfield et al., 1971). Instead of using sales of new drugs as output, Mansfield et al. matched the list of pharmaceutical innovations produced by the American Medical Association's Commission on the Cost of Medical Care (1964) with data compiled by Paul de Haen (1967a,b) to determine the identity of the firms.

The number of innovations were then regressed against the firm sizes of 58 pharmaceutical companies through a quadratic equation. This was done for two periods, 1935–49, and 1950–62. Although the dependent variable was weighted medically and economically, the results were similar. Regardless of whether innovations were unweighted, economically weighted, or medically weighted, the coefficients in front of the variable measuring firm size (S^2) were consistently negative.

Considerable controversy, however, developed over the significance of the S^2 coefficients. Schwartzman, in a later study, highlighted the unweighted 1950–62 equation and charged that the conclusion of Mansfield et al. was wrong because of the insignificant S^2 coefficient. Specifically, even though the 1935–49 equations confirm the decreasing return hypothesis, the rest of the equations did embody weak S^2 coefficients. The unweighted equation's S^2 coefficient was only significant at the 40 percent level (two-tail test), a result most statisticians will abandon. In the remaining two equations the coefficients are significant at the 20 percent level.

Studies done for periods including years subsequent to enactment of the 1962 drug amendments were unanimous in reaching conclusions opposite to what was found for earlier periods. Simply put, the central finding was that larger firms did indeed enjoy economies of scale in their R & D operations. Using 12 international drug firms, Angilley (1973) regressed innovative output on pharmaceutical sales and then on R & D expenditures for the period 1958–70. After employing the double-log transformation, Angilley found the coefficients on R & D expenditure to be around 2.3, suggesting the existence of economies of scale with respect to R & D expenditure. However, the double-log specification is not used for the firm size equations; consequently we are not able to comment easily on the economies of scale question with respect to firm size.

Armed with 1965–70 period data, Vernon and Gusen (1974) challenge the Comanor study with the hypothesis that the amendments actually have favored the large firms by creating economies of scale; the larger firms are able to face the stringent new FDA regulations better than the smaller ones. Taking the direct route, Vernon and Gusen run the same specification used by Comanor, but with the new data, and achieve the following result (p. 296):

$$Y/S = 0.4 - 9.6\ R/S - .02\ R^2/S + .000002S$$
$$\quad\quad\quad (.92)\quad\quad (.52)\quad\quad (2.9)$$

$$+ \quad .0000000009 \ RS + .02D$$
$$\quad (.9) \qquad\qquad\qquad (.09) \qquad\qquad R^2 = .20$$

All but the S variable have become insignificant. Vernon and Gusen also improve Comanor's model by replacing sales of new drugs as the dependent variable with the number of new chemical entities. The result is the following:

$$CE = .35 + .0043 \ R - .000019 \ R^2$$
$$\qquad\quad (1.75) \qquad (4.27)$$

$$+ .000000076 \ R \ S$$
$$(3.40) \qquad\qquad\qquad R^2 = .38$$

where

$CE =$ number of NCE
$R =$ number of R & D personnel
$S =$ firm size measured by sales of ethical drugs

The crucial coefficient of R S is significantly positive now. Using the Comanor analysis, this means firm size varies positively with drug productivity. Checking for marketing productivity Vernon and Gusen have the following findings:

$$\log (Y/CE) = -7.11 + .744 \ \log S + .579 \ \log M$$
$$\qquad\qquad\qquad (4.57) \qquad\qquad (2.86)$$

$$R^2 = .56$$

where

$Y =$ sales of NCE by firm
$M =$ industry sales in the therapeutic class into which the NCE was introduced.

S actually represents promotional intensity, P, because they have a .93 correlation coefficient between them, causing severe multicollinearity. Vernon and Gusen confidently conclude (p. 301): "Our results indicate that larger pharmaceutical manufacturers appear to have decided advantages over smaller ones in accomplishing technical change."

There is a reason why the word "appear" is used in the conclusion. The sign of R^2 (the square of the number of R & D personnel) changed from a positive one in Comanor's study to a negative marginal productivity of research effort. Cocks offers the explanation in his dissertation that this could happen because the industry during this period was in the process of adjustment from a period of disequilibrium. Vernon and Gusen recognize the problem by calculating the "net effect" between marginal productivity and increasing firm size. Nevertheless, a negative marginal productivity flies in the face of economic theory. It should also be pointed out that the coefficient on the S variable in the marketing productivity equation is positive but less than one, meaning promotional activity increases sales per NCE less than proportionally: a case of diminishing returns. Although Vernon and Gusen nullify the result of Comanor's study, the model they present is also far from perfect.

Schwartzman (1976a) provides further evidence for firm size economies of scale in the postamendment period with a battery of regressions to test the hypothesis that:

- Firm size increases research personnel more than proportionally.
- Firm size increases publications more than proportionally.
- Laboratory employment increases the number of NCEs more than proportionally.
- Firm size increases the number of NCEs more than proportionally.

Schwartzman's (1976a, p. 94) main methodology can be shown by an example, such as the firm size and NCE equation:

$$\ln N = 9.75 - .32 \ln S + .49 \, (\ln S)^2$$
$$(t = -.29) \quad (t = 2.51)$$

$$R^2 = .59$$

where

$N =$ number of NCEs, 1965–70
$S =$ firm size measured by sales of ethical drugs

and the numbers in the parentheses are the t-values. If we take the differential of the equation we have:

$$d \ln N = -.32 d\ln S + 2(.49) \ln S \, d\ln S$$

Calculating the elasticity of N with respect to S we have:

$$d \ln N / d \ln S = -.32 + 2 \, (.49) \ln S$$

Thus he finds the elasticity to be positive, which indicates that the number of NCEs with respect to firm size increases as firm size increases. An important footnote to his results is the size of the coefficient of the log variable, for example 2(.49) or .98 in the above equations: If it is less than one, the elasticity increases at a decreasing rate; and if it is greater than one, the elasticity increases at an increasing rate.

In summary, it is likely that for the past decade, there has been a transition in the drug R & D environment through regulation such that larger drug firms may have an advantage in the productivity of research efforts.

Firm Reponse to the Changing R & D Environment

Grabowski et al. (1976) confirm the trend toward firm concentration by showing the increasing concentration in the recent innovational output (shown in Table 7.3) in the drug industry. Innovational output is measured as new chemical entity sales during the first three full years after product innovation.

Both the number of new chemical entities and number of firms having an NCE have decreased post-1962. Meanwhile, the four-firm concentration of the NCEs has steadily increased. In their later publication Grabowski and Vernon (1977a, p. 364) caution us about this situation:

> Consequently, the supply of new drugs has not only declined, but it has also become more concentrated over time in the larger multinational firms better able to deal with this more stringent environment. Given the rapid spread of

TABLE 7.3 Concentration of Innovational Output in the U.S. Ethical Drug Industry

Period	Total Number of NCEs	Number of Firms Having an NCE	Concentration Ratio Innovational Output		
			4-Firm	8-Firm	20-Firm
1957–61	233	51	.462	.712	.931
1962–66	93	34	.546	.789	.976
1967–71	76	23	.610	.815	.978

Source: Henry G. Grabowski, John M. Vernon, and Lacy G. Thomas, "The Effects of Regulatory Policy on the Incentives to Innovate: An International Comparative Analysis," in *Impact of Public Policy on Drug Innovation and Pricing,* ed. S. A. Mitchell and E. A. Link (Washington, D.C.: The American University, 1976), p. 72.

health and safety regulations controls throughout all sectors of the economy, further attention to the adverse effects of regulation on industry competitive structure would seem highly desirable. They constitute a potentially important source of long–run indirect costs to society that must be weighed against the benefits of these new regulatory controls.

It should be made clear that although the economies of scale question has been settled in the literature, the argument that the 1962 amendments are encouraging "concentration" in the drug industry needs another "logical step," namely, that the amendments are responsible for the changing environment. This issue will be dealt with directly in the next chapter.

Prerequisites for Firm Survival

Facing this new environment, how are firms, small and large, going to respond? Stauffer (1976) has addressed the problem of firm survival under uncertainty of R & D success. He starts from the position that the viability of the business of investing in research and development to develop new therapy depends ultimately on the ability of a research-intensive pharmaceutical manufacturer constantly to replenish its portfolio of drugs, given its budgetary constraints. This ability is a function of: the probability that a particular drug development project will be successful, the number of R & D projects that can be funded, and the net payout of each successful venture.

The basic equation for calculating the expected return of a specific project is as follows:

$$EV = pX - b = (pX/b - 1)b,$$

where:

EV = expected value of a particular research project
p = probability of success
X = *net* payout discounted at opportunity cost of capital
b = cost of a particular research project.

Stauffer points out that as p decreases, the minimum number of projects that must be undertaken in order to make it a "fair game" for the firm has to increase. This means, however, that firms with large budgets have better chances in the long run. The only other way is to increase the payout, X, for the projects, but this is not always under the firm's control (given the present market structure in the drug industry).

TABLE 7.4. Minimum Exploration/R & D Budget

Project Success Probability	0.05	0.10	0.20	0.40
Case One: EV = 1.2				
PR = 0.9	140	67	30	12
PR = 0.8	98	47	21	8
Case Two: EV = 1.5				
PR = 0.9	77	36	17	7
PR = 0.8	54	25	12	5

Notes: PR = probability of firm's survival.
"Budget" measured in multiples of the cost of a single exploration/research project.
EV = ratio of the expected net payment to the cost of an individual R & D project or exploration program.
Source: Thomas R. Stauffer, "Discovery Risk, Profitability Performance and Survival Risk in a Pharmaceutical Firm," in *The Proceedings of the Second Seminar on Economics of Pharmaceutical Innovation,* ed. Joseph D. Cooper (Washington, D. C.: The American University, 1976).

A particularly noteworthy aspect of Stauffer's calculations is the startlingly high amount by which a firm has to increase its R & D budget just to keep its probability of survival constant in the face of a declining probability of success on particular projects. For example, as Stauffer shows in his table presenting the relationship between project success probability and R & D budgets, a decline in success probabilities from 0.40 to 0.05 requires a more than tenfold increase in the budget if a firm wishes to maintain a 90 percent chance of keeping its R & D program viable (see Table 7.4).

The mathematics underlying these calculations constitute what is known as the "Gambler's Ruin" problem (Feller, 1966, p. 179ff.). Essentially, the reason why the risk of exhaustion of finanical resources is so sensitive to changes in project success probabilities is that a decline in the latter greatly increases the financial resources required to weather a streak of bad luck.

It should be noted, however, that Stauffer's calculations overstate the degree to which a decline in success probabilities increases the risk of exhaustion of financial resources as far as pharmaceutical manufacturers are concerned. This is because Stauffer's calculations assume that the budget for a research project is the same whether it is successful or not. Such is not the case with the drug industry because as a research project progresses, the sponsor constantly gains additional information as to its eventual outcome. The information received during the research process enables a company to decide what to do about a project well before the full

FIGURE 7.2. Path Chart of Market Structure and Innovation

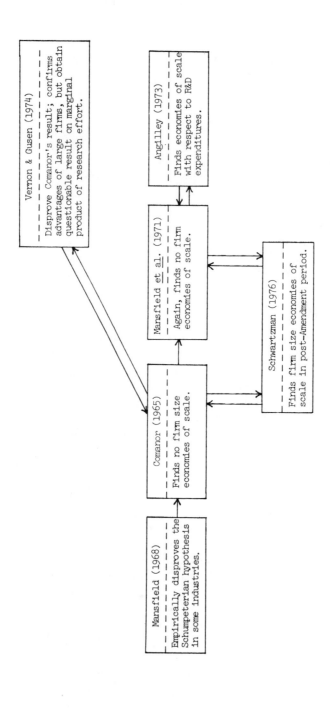

Source: Compiled by the authors.

cost of an unsuccessful project will end up being equivalent to some fraction of the cost of a successful project rather than the whole.

Despite this caveat, the effects of changes that reduce project success probabilities and increase drug approval times are still substantial and should be of utmost concern to those concerned with the economic viability of drug development and the industry's competitiveness. Stauffer (1976, p. 113) specifies the consequences to the pharmaceutical industry as follows:

> If ever-higher R & D expenditures are necessary to introduce a new drug, competition in the industry will be reduced. This will be reflected in rising concentration ratios in the industry, and the heightening of the barriers against entry of new firms into the industry. Another phenomenon associated with this higher risk is that there will be even greater "phantom" profits reported by the surviving firms (i.e., the spread between reported profits and true economic profits will widen).

For firms facing declining success probability with a moderate budget, there are four alternatives: retrenchment, expansion, mergers, or overseas operations. Stauffer (1976, pp. 121–22) explains them:

> First of all, the firms which cannot expand their R & D sufficiently to maintain a reasonable probability for survival simply must retrench. Second, those firms which have great confidence in their own innovative capability might accept the risk—might "bite the bullet" so to speak—and expand their R & D levels up to a high enough level of expenditure so that they reach or exceed the critical mass. The third alternative is merger as a risk-reduction strategy—and the fourth, which we cannot pursue here, is shifting the emphasis of their operations overseas into a different regulatory environment—if, indeed, it is the regulatory controls which are at fault.

SUMMARY AND AREAS FOR FUTURE RESEARCH

There seems to be little disagreement in the literature that the pharmaceutical industry is undergoing some structural change (see Figure 7.2). The immediate and observable effect is the decreasing rate of NCE introduction; but the consensus disappears when the questions on a deeper level are brought forth. The effect of governmental actions resulting from the 1962 amendments has gone through rigorous analyses and is held partially responsible for the rising cost, risk, and time requirement of drug R & D. The unsolved question is about the remaining factors that are also causing a decline in drug innovation. The depletion of research opportunity is known to be one of these factors, but its effect can be only inconclusively determined.

The question of whether large firms are adapting themselves to the new environment better than small ones in view of the stringent government actions has been resolved along the lines of economies of scale. The array of empirical studies seems to point out that the large firms may have some advantages in coping with the increased risk, costs, and length of the R & D period. The results encourage the thesis that the stringent environment may be conducive to increasing seller concentration.

8

EFFECTS OF GOVERNMENT REGULATION

INTRODUCTION AND HISTORICAL BACKGROUND

Since their passage in 1962, the Kefauver amendments have been the subject of continuing controversy. At the heart of the issue has been the behavior of the pharmaceutical industry in adjusting to the amendments; its behavior with respect to innovation and R & D investment has caused much concern and discussion among economists, medical specialists, and industry representatives. A number of writers have attributed declining rates of growth of innovation and of domestic R & D expenditure to the disincentives embodied in the 1962 amendments. Other writers have argued that other important factors can be linked to R & D and innovation; that the declining growth rates are not themselves cause for concern; and that the amendments have yielded net benefits to consumers. This chapter will review briefly the evidence and arguments and conclude by suggesting a few areas that remain unexamined in this discussion.

Trends in the Drug Industry

The trend in FDA approval of NCEs has been clearly downward over the past three decades (note Table 7.1). The 1950s in general were characterized by widely fluctuating FDA approval rates around a comparatively high average. Toward the end of the decade, a slight downward trend can be perceived; for example, for the four years ending in 1961 (the year before the imposition of the 1962 amendments), an annual average of 55 NCEs were approved, compared to an average of 63 per year for the preceding four years. This end-of-the-decade decline can probably be attributed to a decline in the number of drugs tested, since no changes in

FDA policy are apparent for that period. However, the decline occurring at the end of the 1950s is slight compared to that experienced just after the 1962 amendments were imposed. The break in the statistics is sharp and immediately apparent: The four years after 1962 saw an average of 23 NCEs per year. The downward trend has continued into the 1970s; since 1968, for example, in no year have even 20 NCEs been approved.

The trend is just as clear in a related series entitled "NCEs excluding salts," defined as "excludes salts or esters of previously marketed drugs." Again taking four-year averages starting in 1954, the series falls from an average of 44.25 in 1954–57 to an average of 42.75 in 1958–61; however, in 1962–65 the decline is quite dramatic, to an average of 18.75 per year.

On the other hand, the decline has been almost as steep over the last two decades in other major Western countries. Over the period 1960–73, for example, the number of NCEs marketed in the United States fell from 44 in 1960 to 17 in 1973, with a low point of 9 in 1972. In England, NCEs marketed were 54 in 1960 and 22 in 1973, with a low of 15 in 1971; in France, the number fell from 59 in 1960 to a low of 15 in 1973; and Germany, after marketing 49 in 1961 (the only one of the four to market more NCEs in 1961 than in 1960), fell to 24 in 1973, with a low of 15 in 1971. It is clear that, for whatever reason, the United States has been part of a general decline in new drug marketing in the major trading countries. [Data are from Commissioner Alexander Schmidt's testimony to U.S. Senate Subcommittee on Health of the Committee on Labor and Public Welfare (1974, p. 3051).]

Finally, let us look at the behavior of NCEs in the United States that are deemed "important" by the FDA. Four separate data series on the number of important therapeutic advances have been presented by FDA spokesmen at different times. Significantly, none of the four shows a clear downward trend at any time over the last three decades. However, the FDA has not made it clear how it defines these drugs, and other writers have disputed these figures (see, for example, Teeling-Smith in Joseph Cooper, 1976).

Competing Explanations for Declining Drug Innovations

The sharp break in new drug introductions after 1962 points immediate attention to the 1962 amendments as a potential explanation. As will be detailed later, a persuasive body of evidence has been assembled by economists and industry representatives that this is an important explanation for the decline in NCEs. The regulations have raised costs in several ways. First, a large additional amount of testing must be undertaken, which of course is costly. This testing occurs both before the submission of the

NDA and during FDA's review. Second, the delays arising from FDA involvement in early clinical research and the time taken by the bureaucratic process within the FDA necessarily extends the time between drug development and marketing. In investment terms, the attractiveness of the undertaking is reduced by raising the initial costs and by postponing the realization of returns.

The major alternative hypothesis is that medical or pharmacologic knowledge has reached certain barriers that must be overcome. In the meantime, until those barriers are removed, the pace of advance is necessarily slowed. This hypothesis is that there is a "depletion" of research opportunities. Again, there is reasonably good evidence that this factor has contributed to a reduced flow of NCEs.

Finally, it has been argued that the reduced flow of NCEs is simply a demonstration that the FDA has reduced the number of ineffective drugs that previously had been reaching the market. The principal evidence for this thesis is subjective evidence produced by the FDA in its own defense. Though there is little doubt that the FDA has made some contribution in this respect, the evidence that this has been the principal factor is not compelling.

These arguments are presented as alternatives. However, there is little reason to think that only one of these arguments explains the whole of the decline. It seems reasonable to assume that each of them has contributed to the decline.

APPROACH TO THE CHAPTER

In the next section we will review and critique the evidence that has been presented for each of the three competing explanations for the decline in the rate of innovation. The effects of other forms of regulation on the pharmaceutical industry will also be explored.

REVIEW OF COMPETING EXPLANATIONS

Regulation and Innovation

It is one thing to argue, as most of the writers cited have done, that regulation has contributed to the decline in annual new chemical entities; this is something that regulation critics and advocates can agree on. However, it is something else to argue that the disincentive effects alone account for all of the decline, with almost no effect coming from depleted research opportunities, more careful screening of drugs, or other possible causes; and furthermore, that the amendments account for a net loss to society of $400 million annually. This is the position taken by Sam Peltzman (1973), whose analysis of the effects of regulation remains the central reference in this literature. Since it was in fact the intent of the amendments to reduce the flow of NCEs, Peltzman's emphasis on the welfare effects is crucial to the argument.

Peltzman (1973)

Peltzman first estimates the effects of the amendments on the size of the flow. He views the annual flow of new drugs as an attempt to close gradually the gap between the number of drugs firms desire to market (a function of the expected size of the market and price) and the number of drugs on the market. Estimating a distributed-lag model using pre-1962 data, he then inserts the post-1962 values of his exogenous variables to predict the "expected" values for the post-1962 flow of new chemical entities. The actual values are less than half the expected values. Because his model presumably accounts for all the market behavior affecting drug development, he concludes that only "extramarket" forces, such as the amendment, could have reduced the flow below its predicted value (pp. 1055–057: "I conclude from these data that (a) the 1962 amendments significantly reduced the flow of NCE's and, what is perhaps more interesting, (b) *all* of the observed difference between pre- and post-1962 NCE flows can be attributed to the 1962 amendments."

His second conclusion, that *all* of the drop is due to the amendments, is an implication of the assumptions built into his model, and not necessarily of the data alone. His model, on which his predictions are based, is entirely a demand-side model, that is, it assumes that the supply of drugs expands to meet the quantity of drugs demanded, and only demand variables enter his predictive equation. Therefore he excludes any effect on the rate of innovation that may occur on the supply side of the market; in particular, he excludes the possibility that a depletion of research opportunities has reduced the flow of NCEs, and he attributes whatever effects this may have to the amendments. This assumption will also necessarily tend to increase the magnitude of the welfare effects he attributes to the amendments.

The welfare cost of the amendments is estimated in two stages. First he estimates the gross cost of the amendments in reducing the flow of drugs that would otherwise yield net benefits to consumers; second, he estimates the gain to consumers from the reduction in waste on ineffectiv' drugs. Underlying both steps is a view of the amendments as a way :o reduce information costs about safety and efficacy to consumers. The first stage in the estimation procedure depends directly on this view.

To the extent that they are successful in this, the effective price of drug therapy is reduced to consumers, thereby shifting out more rapidly the demand curve for those drugs that are actually marketed postamendments, as compared to the level or rate of movement that would have been attained in the absence of the amendments. On the other hand, if the regulators keep drugs off the market that would yield net benefits, the demand for drugs is necessarily less than it otherwise would be. The effect of the amendments is therefore what he measures as the current level of demand as compared to what he predicts as the level of demand that would have been attained without the amendments. On this basis, Peltzman estimates the annual gross loss in consumers' surplus to be $42 million; assuming that drugs are nondepreciating, he uses a 10 percent discount rate to derive a net present value loss per year of $420 million.

Clearly, there are a number of critical assumptions present. First, if supply factors, such as a decline in research opportunities, were taken into account, the net loss attributable to the amendments would be less, perhaps substantially. Second, he assumes drugs do not depreciate; clearly this is inadequate. Assuming any kind of depreciation rate—and, given the patent life of 17 years a depreciation rate of 5.8 percent annually is a reasonable minimum—the loss would clearly be reduced.

To estimate the gross benefits of the amendments, he makes an explicit assumption about the degree to which the postamendment demand curve is shifted out when benefits are received. He says (p. 1076):

> If the amendments have been dealing effectively with what was once an important problem, we should see the difference between pre- and post–amendment new-drug demand narrowing over time, since the pre-amendment consumers would have been abandoning the ineffective drugs that the amendments now screen out.

On this basis, he estimates the annual preamendment waste from ineffective drugs at only $0.4 million, as compared to his estimate of $43 million in annual benefits from new NCEs foregone as a result of the amendment.

Since the benefits from an innovation are likely to grow over time, the first-year benefits of $43 million from NCEs introduced in a given year are likely to grow to $63 million by the fourth year after introduction. Assuming a perpetual life for the drug with this initial pattern of growth, he estimates a net consumer loss from the amendments of $400 million annually; assuming a 15-year life with all depreciation at the end of the life, the comparable figure is $330 million annually. He concludes (p. 1089):

> The 1962 drug amendments sought to reduce consumer waste on ineffective drugs. This goal appears to have been attained, but the costs in the process

seem clearly to have outweighed the benefits. It was shown that the amendments have produced a substantial decline in drug innovation since 1962. This could have produced net benefits if the impact of the decline had been highly selective against ineffective drugs and pre-amendment expenditures on ineffective drugs had been substantial. Neither condition is consistent with the data.

Five problems may be identified with Peltzman's work. First, as pointed out by McGuire, Nelson, and Spavins (1975), Peltzman's use of aggregate demand curves distorts the welfare effects when individual consumers are moving their own demands in a direction possibly opposite to that of the aggregate curves. This suggests that Peltzman may well have underestimated gains from an increase in consumer information. The problem here, as opposed to the usual consumers' surplus situation, is that each consumer faces a different degree of misinformation or distortion, some of which may be substantial; the usual consumers' surplus model requires a uniform market distortion, such as a tax. Because Peltzman can look only at the aggregate, and not at the gains for individuals, his estimate is unreliable—it could be biased in either direction.

Second, as Grabowski argues, no supply-side effects are permitted in the model; instead, they are all captured in his dummy variable representing the amendments. Whatever supply effects may be occurring are incorrectly captured there. As Grabowski, Vernon, and Thomas (1976) show, these supply effects may be substantial.

Third, Peltzman uses NCEs only in his estimates and does not estimate the demand for "other new drugs," defined as "new combinations of previously marketed chemical entities and duplicates of chemical entities marketed under a new brand name" (p. 1053). This exclusion would seem to reduce both his cost and benefit estimates.

Fourth, Peltzman assumes no depreciation of drugs. The closest he comes, by way of creating a "lower bound" for his loss estimate, is to assume zero depreciation for 15 years, followed by instantaneous decay of economic value. This would be reasonable only in the unlikely case of a drug maintaining full value until patent expiration. However, as Reekie (1978, 1979) and Teeling-Smith (1975) have shown, most drugs of significant innovational content tend to decline in price and profitability over time. Hence his estimates of benefits foregone by drug regulation may be too large.

Finally, there is the doubt voiced both by Grabowski (1976) and McGuire, Nelson, and Spavins (1975) about using consumers' surplus analysis in a situation where the nature of the demand curve and of the "consumer" has been questioned. Grabowski (1976, p. 70-71) says on this point:

A different set of issues concerns Peltzman's use of consumer-surplus methodology to estimate the value of gains or losses to consumers from the reduced flow of NCEs. Although this is a standard approach in cost-benefit analysis, its applicability has been questioned for markets like ethical drugs where consumers have a limited role in selecting the final products consumed. Specifically, it has been argued that doctors will be much less price sensitive than patients. In addition, many drugs are paid for through third-party payment schemes, and this can also serve to distort the drug valuation imputed from estimated market demand curves. These factors influence Peltzman's measure of benefits and costs in a qualitatively similar fashion, which means they may not change the final outcome. They do, however, introduce uncertainties about his calculated values of benefits and costs.

Baily (1972)

Martin Baily attempted to measure the effect of the amendments on new drug development, though he did not attempt a measurement of the net consumer benefits from the amendment. Also included in Baily's model was an indirect measurement of depletion of research opportunities. Baily uses a production function model of new drug development in which the number of new drugs introduced in a given year (as a proportion of total R & D expenditures that become effective in that year) is a function of the depletion of research opportunities and the presence of FDA regulation. His data are NCEs introduced per year from 1954 to 1969.

Both variables of interest are statistically significant and of the expected sign. His equation is highly significant for a time series model ($R^2 = .95$) with very little evidence of autocorrelation. Of interest here is his strong finding with respect to the effect of the amendments. The regulatory variable in his model shows a large quantitative effect on the number of NCEs developed per R & D dollar. For example, he finds that the R & D investment required to produce an NCE has risen sharply, as a result of the regulatory control, after correcting for the full effect of a change in R & D effort on the number of research opportunities.

Grabowski (1976, p. 26) points to two problems with Baily's work. First, he argues that Baily's choice of variables leaves much room for measurement error:

A potential problem in the Baily analysis is that both the effects of regulation and the effects of research depletion are measured by proxy variables, and are therefore subject to considerable measurement error.... It is quite possible that the effects of regulation and research depletion may be confounded when they are measured by these aggregate proxy variables.

Though it may be possible, the strong significance of the equation makes significant measurement error unlikely. Measurement error would tend to bias the coefficients toward zero and the standard errors upward. There is no evidence of this being a significant problem. On the other hand, there is no assurance that the variables measure exactly what Baily says they measure. The depletion variable in particular, a lagged seven-year moving average of all NCEs introduced, leaves itself open to many possible interpretations. Similarly, the time-dependent dummy variable (=0 pre-1962, =1 after) could be strongly correlated with the decline in research opportunities that may have occurred in the early 1960s. As a result, Grabowski is correct in saying that the effects of the two alternative hypotheses could easily be confounded in Baily's equation.

Grabowski's second objection to Baily arises from an experiment he performed in another article (Grabowski, Vernon, and Thomas, 1976). In that article he updates Baily's estimates by adding an additional five years of data to the 15-year period used by Baily. This reestimation yields a sharp decline in the significance of the depletion variable and a relatively slight decline in the explanatory power of the equation. Grabowski concludes (1976, p. 27):

> The proxy variable employed by Baily for research depletion thus turns out to be unstable when his analysis is extended forward in time. Given the poor statistical performance of this variable and the elusive nature of the concept itself, the development of alternative means of separating regulatory from non-regulatory factors would seem desirable.

This argument seems reasonable. There are two ways to rationalize Grabowski's result. First, multicollinearity may be present between Baily's two independent variables, which may account for the erratic performance of the equation. Second, the behavior would be consistent with the depletion hypothesis if the depletion of opportunities "bottomed out" in the last five years of data, adding a region of low variability in that variable. Since either explanation is possible, even assuming that no measurement error is present, Baily's model does not give useful or reliable results. Furthermore, even if Baily's results and Grabowski's extrapolation of them could be relied upon as providing certain evidence of the effect of regulation, it could not be concluded that the decline in NCEs was bad in welfare terms, since there is no welfare cost analysis comparable to Peltzman's.

Wardell (1973)

An alternative form of evidence to the econometric analysis of Baily and Peltzman is the international comparison used by Wardell (1973, 1974a, 1974b), Wardell and Lasagna (1975b), and Grabowski, Vernon, and

Thomas (1976). All of these writers use the United Kingdom as a comparison with the United States, because the United Kingdom has a somewhat less stringent regulatory system than the United States. The main differences are these: first, the United Kingdom has no proof-of-efficacy standard, which was the major facet of the 1962 amendments in the United States; second, the United States requires an IND filing before human testing, while the United Kingdom does not; third, the major review authority in the United Kingdom is in the hands of independent medical experts, whereas in the United States the authority lies with career civil servants with greater incentive to err on the side of conservatism; and finally, the United States relies entirely on a preapproval screening, whereas the United Kingdom places more reliance on post marketing surveillance (Wardell and Lasagna, 1975b).

Wardell (1973) explores the nature of what he calls the "drug lag" in the United States. Over the period 1962-71 he finds that, in nine therapeutic categories together, the total number of new chemical entities in the United States was about two-thirds the number in Britain. Furthermore, Britain tended to have earlier introductions of major new drugs. In his second article (1974a), Wardell attempts to get some measure of the therapeutic importance of these differences. He finds for a few of the drugs available in the United Kingdom but not in the United States that they are widely prescribed in Britain and are sometimes the best available drug; and that American doctors would generally like to have these drugs available to them. Wardell concludes in his third article (1974b) that the United States has not avoided drug toxicity but has lost in not having those drugs available sooner. Adverse drug reactions in the United Kingdom have not been greater from new drugs than from the old ones (however, he does not compare adverse reaction rates for all drugs between the United States and the United Kingdom). He believes the United States has lost on balance from its more conservative approach. In a final article in Helm's book (1975), he updates his analysis to account for recent changes in the two countries; the two countries have tended to move closer together in regulatory approach.

Grabowski, Vernon, and Thomas (1976)

Grabowski, Vernon, and Thomas attempt to distinguish between the regulatory and depletion hypotheses through comparison of the United States and the United Kingdom. Their operating assumption is that

> while the depletion explanation should have affected the industries in both countries, the increased regulatory tightness that began in the U.S. in 1962 was not duplicated in the U.K. Hence we should be able to use the U.K. industry as our "control group" in our attempt to identify the effect of regulation on the U.S. industry (p. 56).

Also, they argue that the number of NCEs in the United Kingdom is probably reduced by the effects of regulatory tightness in the United States, since U.S. firms control a major share of the U.K. market. On the other hand, they believe that *discoveries* (as opposed to introductions) in the United Kingdom should be unaffected by U.S. developments.

Hence in their analysis they compare U.S. and U.K. discoveries per R & D dollar. They find that the average productivity of an R & D dollar has declined almost sixfold in the United States over the period of 1960-61 to 1966–67, as compared to a threefold decline in the United Kingdom. They conclude from this (p. 65):

> One interpretation is that the more rapid U.S. decline is attributable to the increased stringency of the regulation that took place in the U.S. beginning in 1962. If we assume that the 3 to 1 U.K. decline is a result of the depletion of research opportunities, then the depletion effect only in the U.S. would have led to a decline in the U.S. index (of innovational productivity, 1966-67 = 100) from about 600 to about 200. The additional U.S. decline from 200 to 100 would then imply a very rough measure of the regulation effect. This halving of productivity in the U.S. due to regulation (from 200 to 100) of course implies a doubling of cost per NCE discovered.

They also rerun Baily's model with additional data and compare the effects of the regulatory and depletion variable in the United States and the United Kingdom. They find that depletion declines to insignificance in the U.S. market but remains important in the United Kingdom. This latter result has already been discussed.

There are two other points that may be made about the Grabowski et al. study. As pointed out in an article by Sarett (1974), one of the effects of the regulations has been to cause a reallocation of R & D expenditures away from research and toward development. Assuming this to be true, it makes it quite likely that, even if nothing else had happened due to regulation, the *discovery* productivity per R & D dollar would have declined in the United States. Discoveries, it seems reasonable to suppose, depend on the amount of research dollars, whereas introductions would depend on the number of discoveries and the amount of development dollars. In other words, development dollars should not affect discoveries; reallocating funds from research to development, holding constant the overall R & D budget, will reduce the discovery productivity of an R & D dollar. This may explain a part of the effect Grabowski, Vernon, and Thomas (GVT) capture.

Kendall (1974)

Kendall updates Baily's work by improving his measure of regulation. Baily measured regulatory impact by a simple dummy variable discriminating between pre-1962 and post-1962. Kendall substitutes for this the mean approval time for NCEs over the period 1954-72. This is an extension of Baily's original time period, which was 1954–69. Kendall finds that the time extension alone reduces the significance of the research depletion variable, consistently with GVT's result above, and causes a reduction in the cost increase of 20 NCEs from 144 percent to 121 percent of the pre-1962 level. The improvement of the regulatory variable *and* the time extension restore significance to the depletion variable and result in an intermediate figure of a 132 percent increase in the R & D cost of 20 NCEs from 1961-72. Kendall points out that he believes a serious fault with his own, Baily's, and Peltzman's work is that they "do not allow complete consideration of the possibility of cyclical phenomena in the introduction of NCE's . . . the model will not allow a continuing downward trend in the number of NCE's introduced" (p. 6). The problem is simply that the idea of research opportunity depletion, however logically plausible it may be, is extremely difficult to define in an empirically useful way.

Kendall also estimates a model in which rate of return for drug firms is related to a weighted sum of NCEs introduced over a single patent period (17 years) and number of duplicate drugs. He finds a strong positive relationship with the first and strong negative relationship with the second. He then varies the patent life implied in the weighted sum and finds that the rate of return falls when the "patent life" is shortened.

It is not clear why anyone would introduce a product (a duplicate) that reduces his rate of return, lowers its profits by $7 million, and lowers its sales by $31 million. This result is meaningless to us and indicates serious problems with either his model or his data, since firms clearly do introduce duplicates. Since his "risk premium" is based on this result, it is unclear what the "premium" really means. Kendall's own evaluation is that "the reliability of these results is not high" (p. 2).

Lasagna (1972)

Lasagna notes the estimates of high costs of developing NCEs and the decline in the rate of introduction over the past ten years. He points to two possible explanations of this decline—depletion and regulation—and states that he finds the latter more plausible. He feels that high costs and long delays are generally greater in the United States than elsewhere, and believes a priori that the FDA will necessarily deter development of drugs for exotic diseases with small markets. He feels the FDA has gone further than necessary to protect the public, and he makes several proposals that he feels would safely expedite NDAs: clear requirements for approval; professionally developed guidelines for testing; regular conferences between the FDA and drug companies and the medical community; limiting the amount of necessary evidence to a "reasonable" number of experiments; more postmarketing monitoring for adverse effects; outside advisors to the FDA; elimination of the present bias that a new drug must be better than all competitors and realization that there are different dimensions of usefulness for a drug; and less emphasis on large-scale tests. He concludes (1972b, p. 77):

> Most people would accept the fundamental validity of the role of a regulatory agency in modern medicine . . . . But one can criticize the concept that a drug regulatory agency will perform best if it delays as long as possible the introduction of new drugs from the market or removes drugs from the market on the basis of unjustified political pressures, whim or caprice. The FDA should rather act in such a way as to maximize public benefit . . . . It may be politically expedient, for the short haul, to disregard the health of the U.S. drug industry, but its destruction would be a gigantic tragedy—and not just for its shareholders.

He feels that, to some extent, adverse drug reactions are the fault of the prescribing doctor rather than the drug and urges more information be provided to doctors and more regulation of their quality (though his critique of the effects of regulation of drugs is not a strong recommendation for regulation of doctors).

Sarett (1974)

Finally, an interesting paper by Lewis Sarett, the president of Merck, Sharpe, and Dohme Research Laboratories, gives some insight into the effects of regulation on the individual firm, as well as the industry. Sarett argues that the major impact of the FDA has been to greatly increase the development times for new drugs. This has had several effects: average development costs per drug are rising at a 30 percent annual rate; it has concentrated R & D into the major companies; it has caused the ratio of development costs to research costs to rise; it has caused a decline in "me-too" drugs, which he defends; it has resulted in fewer research projects undertaken; greater efficiency in research—use of project team organization, more emphasis on more important diseases, and so on—has resulted; and it has forced more emphasis on less-risky, short-term-use drugs.

Innovation and Depletion of Research Opportunities

In this section we will review briefly the evidence for the view that a decline in research opportunities has taken place since the "Golden Age" of drug research in the 1950s. Lasagna puts this view persuasively (1972b, p. 50):

Why these changes? One view... is that the fantastic output of the pharmaceutical industry preempted many additional contributions by tackling successfully the "easier" development problems, and that post-"Golden Age" research is necessarily less productive because the nuts left to crack are tougher ones.

The evidence for this view is really of two major types. First, there is the international evidence that the decline in the number of drug innovations in the United States has been matched by a similar decline in Great Britain, the only other country with comparable data. Second, there is the fact that some degree of significance has been consistently present in econometric work done by Baily and others. Both of these kinds of evidence have been questioned. In addition to them, the fact that research output had shown some decline in the years before 1962 (though it is clear that 1962 had a major effect on the time series) is sometimes cited as evidence of declining opportunities.

However reasonable the idea of declining research opportunities may be, it clearly is not meant to be the only alternative to the regulatory explanation. Rather, it has served as a proxy for whatever other non-regulatory factors may exist. to the extent that "depletion" is found to be an important element of recent innovative behavior, it is necessary to look behind the simple meaning of the word for the true nonregulatory effects that have caused the decline.

The international evidence presented by Grabowski, Vernon, and Thomas (1976) has already been discussed. Basically, they found that R & D "productivity" has declined more in the United States than in the United Kingdom. They feel that the additional decline in the United States is the result of regulation, but this accounts for only one-third of the total decline. The remaining two-thirds of the U.S. decline is matched by a similar decline in Britain, an effect that Grabowski states is "consistent with the hypothesis of a worldwide depletion of research opportunities" (1976, p. 36).

The problem with this form of evidence is that, once again, it is very hard to distinguish the "echo" effects of regulation from a true depletion effect. It has been argued (Grabowski, 1976) that the decline of innovation can really be attributed to the U.S. regulatory climate, since the U.S. firms constitute a large share of the British market and account for much of the total new product innovation in Britain. Grabowski says (1976, p. 38):

Before the 1962 amendments, the prevalent strategy of U.S. firms apparently was to introduce their products first into the the U.S. market and then introduce them (with a lag) into foreign countries. Moreover, these new products were often manufactured here and exported abroad in the earlier stages of the product life cycle. However, as the U.S. regulatory climate became more stringent and the number of NCEs cleared in the United States declined sharply, the stock of U.S. new product innovations available for subsequent introductions abroad also declined. Hence, one might expect that a corresponding decline would take place (somewhat lagged in time) in the innovational performance of U.S. firms abroad. This is precisely what is observed in the United Kingdom over the decade 1962-1971.

This may be true; however, one would also expect to see other effects of the regulation. For example, U.S. firms would tend to shift their own research and innovational activity abroad as a result of the amendment. There is in fact evidence that U.S. firms have shifted research activity abroad and have tended to make Britain, instead of the United States, the site of first human testing. In fact, it might be expected that U.S. firms would tend to introduce the innovations in Britain (and other countries) first, since the testing requirements are less stringent; in this case one might see an increase in introductions in the United Kingdom as a result of U.S. regulatory stringency—unless there were also a decline in available opportunities.

Furthermore, even if U.S. introductions into the British market have declined, this creates strong incentives for British firms to expand their own innovational activity, since, as Peltzman has shown, innovation often acts as a means of market penetration. As a result, there is no clear reason that the number of British introductions should have declined if U.S. firms had shifted activity abroad and British firms took advantage of the opportunity to expand their research output. There is substantial evidence that both of these effects have occurred, to some extent. Therefore, the concurrent decline in U.K. and U.S. introductions should not have occurred if there were not also some other, nonregulatory effects. In short, if no depletion were occurring, it is not established that British innovations would have declined as U.S. innovations fell. There is room for further investigation here.

The other form of evidence on the depletion hypothesis is the econometric evidence developed by Baily, and extended by Kendall and Grabowski, Vernon, and Thomas. Baily (1972) created a proxy to measure the necessarily elusive depletion effect. His proxy was a seven-year moving average of past total new drug introductions in the United States. He justifies this proxy choice as follows (p. 75): "The research project is formulated six to seven years before introduction; thus, if a large number of new drugs were introduced in the period prior to this, we would expect some reduction in the number of directions for fruitful R & D."

This is a respectable attempt at a definition of research depletion, but it seems to be agreed by the authors in this area that it is imperfect. The concept of declining research opportunities is necessarily slippery and hard to define. Though Kendall and GVT have used the same definition, a variety of measures should be tried before it is concluded that depletion either is or is not present.

The results that Baily, Kendall, and GVT have found, running the same equation over different time periods (and in one case, a changed definition of regulatory stringency), have varied mysteriously in significance. The outcome of these conflicting results is, of course, unknown. Of particular interest is the fact that the improved definition of regulatory stringency used by Kendall restored significance to the depletion variable. This may indicate a fundamental strength of hypothesis, or it may indicate multicollinearity in Kendall's equation. The subject should be explored further.

The final evidence that some nonregulatory effects may be contributing to the recent decline in research output is the fact that the decline apparently started before the change in regulatory policy. It is possible to argue that this is an anticipatory effect, given the start of the Kefauver hearings in the late 1950s, but the more likely anticipatory effect is to step up R & D to try to get drugs approved before additional regulatory requirements are imposed.

In conclusion, the evidence for a depletion effect reducing research output is of uncertain reliability. It seems both a priori plausible and consistent with the evidence that some depletion has occurred. However, all of the evidence can be questioned and no certain conclusions reached. However, the evidence for a regulatory effect does not seem to lead to a firm assurance that *all* of the decline has been caused by regulation; in fact, the evidence seems to indicate that regulation caused a substantial but by no means exclusive effect. Depletion can be seen as the residual for all remaining effects.

Effective Control of Ineffective Drugs

The remaining possible explanation for the decline in research output is that the FDA has effectively clamped down on drug firms that insist upon marketing ineffective drugs. Their more stringent controls have prevented a large number of drugs from reaching the marketplace. This is, after all, the original intent of the 1962 amendments.

It is possible that this argument could be confused with the argument presented earlier that regulation has slowed innovation by raising costs. They are, however, different and distinct arguments. The earlier argument is that regulation has prevented many effective drugs from being discovered or introduced because of the increase in costs. The hypothesis considered here is that effective drugs have not slowed, but many of the ineffective or duplicative drugs have been eliminated; this argument has been embraced by the FDA.

This view of drug regulation was presented by Henry Simmons (1974). He argues that duplicates and combinations of already existing drugs are wasteful and dangerous, and they are the ones that have been discouraged. He states (p. 101)

The relevant question has never been *how many* new drugs are marketed each year, but rather how many *significant, useful* and *unique* therapeutic entities are developed . . . this has in this country remained relatively stable. The major change that has occurred during the past decade is that the percentage of significant drugs approved has increased by over 300 percent while the number of "me-too" drugs has declined.

His response to the drug-lag argument is interesting. He argues that cross-country drug introductions depend more on marketability, costs, and information in the importing country than on regulatory barriers. The United States is therefore not the only country with a drug lag—all countries have a lag, in terms of the number of new drugs introduced abroad that are not introduced at home until later; many drugs are simply never exported, for a variety of reasons. Furthermore, there are many drugs that the United States has had for a substantial time that only recently (1974) have been introduced in other countries. Hence there is no need to worry about a U.S. drug lag due to regulation.

Much of the evidence for Simmons' assertion that "significant, useful and unique" drugs have remained in steady flow comes from expert evaluations of approved drugs. There have been lists of drugs meeting criteria of significance published by the FDA, as well as private rankings. The FDA lists display moderate variability on a year-to-year basis, but the differences between rankings remain relatively steady over the years 1950-70, indicating that differing criteria standards have been employed on a consistent basis. Three of the four FDA lists show little change in important therapeutic advances annually since the early 1950s; the fourth shows a moderate decline, from 12.3 annually on the average from 1950 to 1962, to 9.1 annually thereafter to 1970. Even this one does not seem to be of crisis proportions. On this basis, Simmons' assertion holds up reasonably well.

Peltzman has looked at this question as in integral part of his 1973 study, which compares the growth rates of sales of new drugs before and after the 1962 amendments. He assumes that if consumers learn a drug is ineffective, its market share should decline over time. If a drug is found by consumers to be effective, its market share will grow over time. On this basis, he finds that a relatively small percentage of NCEs were ineffective drugs. The growth rates of sales of new drugs remain approximately constant after the amendments are imposed. This tends to refute the argument that only ineffective drugs have declined. One problem with this argument is that it looks only at effectiveness of drugs and not at the number of duplicates or combinations, which have also been affected by the FDA's post–1962 policies.

In conclusion, the strength of this argument is mixed. The principal evidence for it comes from the FDA itself; this would be cause to be skeptical of the evidence if the same attitude were also applied to information given out by the industry. Reasonably persuasive evidence against this hypothesis has been given by an independent analyst. The success of FDA regulation in eliminating exclusively ineffective or duplicate drugs has probably not been a significant part of the total decline in drug approvals.

IMPACTS OF OTHER FORMS
OF GOVERNMENT REGULATION

Government regulatory activities affect the economics of the pharmaceutical industry in numerous other ways beyond the FDA's regulation of research, development, and product labeling.

The pervasiveness of government's impact and the conflicting cross-currents created by government programs are well illustrated by federal efforts affecting pharmaceutical demand. On the other hand, the federal government stimulates demand for pharmaceuticals through the Medicaid program, which provides third-party reimbursement for program participants, of whom many are elderly and therefore require an above-average number of prescriptions. In fact, Medicaid reimbursements are estimated to account for approximately 10 percent of total payments for drugs sold on an outpatient basis. On the other hand, to keep drug program expenditures down, the federal government is attempting to impose limits either on the kinds of drugs it will pay for or on how much it will pay for certain types of drugs for which it provides reimbursement.

The effects of government efforts to put a damper on the demand it stimulated initially itself are felt far beyond the pharmaceutical market. One impact of programs to reduce the growth rate of public program drug expenditures is to create a diversion of funds to nonresearch-intensive pharmaceutical manufacturers who do not have to finance R & D programs and therefore can charge lower prices. As this happens, spending on pharmaceutical R & D can be expected to decline. Grabowski (1968) points out that for every $100 reduction in research–intensive manufacturer cash flow (sales less variable costs), research and development declines by $26. These changes in the demand structure for pharmaceuticals can affect demand for health care services as a whole. For example, if, as the industry argues, there are meaningful quality differences between the products of research-oriented and nonresearch-oriented manufacturers, what impact do these differences have on demand for other health care services that may be required if drugs fail to perform as advertised? Furthermore, what effect does a diversion of resources away from R & D have on the cost–effectiveness of tomorrow's health care expenditures? These types of issues are complex, unresolved, and serve to underscore the point that government cannot do just one thing.

The vast biomedical research infrastructure funded by the federal government affects pharmaceuticals on the supply side as well as the demand side. Government funds are used both to train the scientists hired by the drug industry and to underwrite development of the biochemical

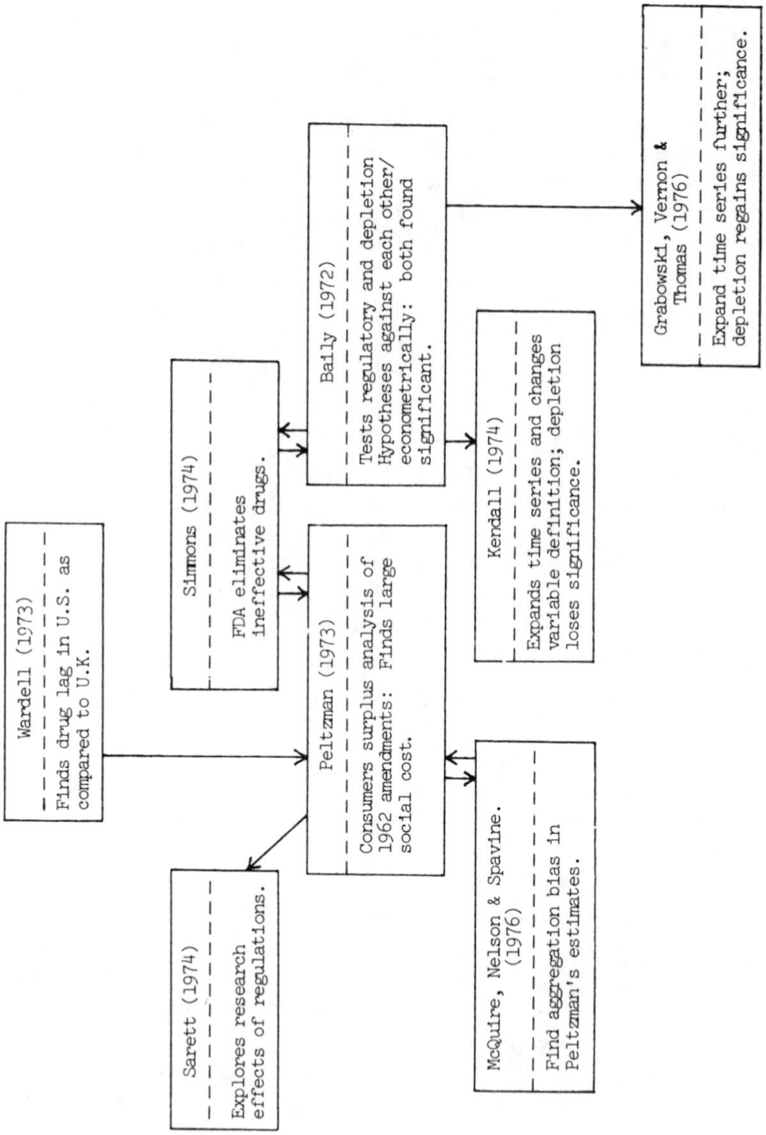

FIGURE 8.1. Path Chart on Effects of Government Regulation

knowledge from which the industry draws. The effect of these benefits on the industry's cost structure is indeterminate.

Federally conducted and/or funded biomedical research programs as well as various public health initiatives (such as antismoking, antialcohol, proexercise campaigns) also affect the demand for drugs. They do this by a variety of means such as reducing the incidence of illness, stimulating the creation of therapeutic alternatives to use of pharmaceuticals, increasing demand for certain pharmaceuticals through programs to detect chronic diseases early on in their development, and so on. To isolate and quantify the precise causes of any one particular change in the characteristics of the drug industry, it would be necessary to have a full general equilibrium model showing the interaction of all the various factors affecting its supply and demand.

SUMMARY AND AREAS FOR FUTURE RESEARCH

In summary, the collective weight of the econometric evidence makes it very likely that the regulatory practices of the FDA have had a depressing effect of some significance on innovation. This finding is supported by a near-unanimity of opinion among medical experts. On the other hand, the evidence that regulation is the only factor that has stimulated the decline is not strong.

Although measurement of its impact is elusive, FDA regulation of the research process itself may have indirectly but significantly contributed to a reduced flow of research opportunities by unnecessarily hampering the early stages of the drug development process. While a precise, definitive resolution of this issue is unlikely to be forthcoming, empirical investigation would provide useful insight into not only what the impact of alternative review processes have been, but also whether that impact has been significant.

From Hansen's (1979) analysis, it is clear that there is a strong relationship between FDA regulations and drug development times and costs. Since costs affect expected rates of return, which in turn affect decisions to engage in R & D, the following conclusions would appear appropriate:

FDA regulation is economic regulation.
Changes in the economic environment for pharmaceutical manufacturers will have important health implications. For example the FDA considers many drugs to be therapeutically equivalent despite the fact that different manufacturers have subjected their respective products to tests that vary widely in terms of comprehensiveness and stringency of standards. The results of the presumption of equivalence is a government-induced modifi-

cation of the competiveness of the products of certain manufacturers with the advantage going to nonresearch–intensive companies who can offer lower prices. Whether this policy tilt is in the public interest remains at issue until answers are obtained to the following questions:

Does a commitment to *in vivo* (in the body) tests with highly restrictive limits of acceptability make a significant difference in a drug's performance? If so, what effect does the FDA's policy of assuming therapeutic equivalence in the absence of evidence to the contrary have on current demand for other forms of health care services? Also, how do the costs of meeting this demand compare with the savings from a policy of encouraging the purchase of less expensive drugs?

What effect does a diversion of cash flow from research-intensive companies have on future relationships between the costs of health care inputs and their outcomes?

The evidence that the decline in the rate of drug innovation has definitely contributed to a loss of welfare is not satisfying. There are two reasons for this last conclusion: first, though the only study that has been done in a welfare context concludes that there has been a loss of welfare, the many problems that have been raised with the methodology of this study should be resolved before definitive conclusions should be drawn; second, the necessity of seeing the demand for drugs in the context of the demand for health inputs requires that distortions in other input markets be taken into account when drawing welfare conclusions about this input market. Accordingly, more needs to be learned about the interrelationship between pharmaceuticals and

- trends in the status of people's health.
- other health care inputs, that is the substitutability and relative costs of pharmaceuticals and other forms of therapy, for example, surgical procedures, physician services.
- publicly funded biomedical research.

9

SOME PRELIMINARY FINDINGS

DIMENSIONS OF INDUSTRY STRUCTURE

For the pharmaceutical industry as a whole, concentration ratios are relatively low. However, it has also been argued that segments of the pharmaceutical industry may be regarded as independent markets in themselves. The criteria for making such divisions would be based on cross-elasticity measures of demand and supply. When the industry is divided into submarkets, different scholars have obtained a different number of therapeutic markets. One obtained 18 markets, another study identified 10, while still another identified 69.

Measures such as the four-firm concentration ratios are static measures. A number of dynamic approaches have been suggested. One is the concept of firm turnover rate, which correlates the rank changes of firms in time. Hymer and Pashigian (1962) proposed a concept of change in market shares. This is essentially an index of the summation of the differences between the ratio of firm to industry assets at different points in time. Gort (1963) proposed another market instability measure, which is related to a correlation coefficient for market shares of leading firms between two periods.

Still another dynamic approach is the one developed by Telser (1975), which measures entry by using the proportion of sales in 1972 in a given therapeutic category by companies that were absent from the category at an earlier date. One of the main findings in the Telser study is that high concentration ratios coexist with high entry rates. A more general possibility is that instability as such creates concentration later. This is consistent with the analysis by Scherer (1970, 1980) of the stochastic determinants of market structure.

PRICING BEHAVIOR OF THE DRUG INDUSTRY

Price Index Trends

Most studies of drug prices indicate that on a deflated basis drug prices have been trending downward. Some critics have argued, however, that changing the sample coverage and weighting of the prescription drug components of a drug index to reflect actual changes in consumption patterns might show that the prices of prescription drugs have increased more than the general price level. The arguments for an increasing trend in drug prices are based on: rising average prescription prices, lags in changes in BLS (Bureau of Labor Statistics) products' weights, and relatively higher prices for new drug products.

John Firestone has been preparing price indexes based on samples of prescription drugs more comprehensive than the BLS sample and with annually revised weightings, but his results roughly parallel those of the BLS. Firestone observes also that the size of the average prescription has been increasing. According to the Firestone report for 1979, the size index was 140.2 (1967 = 100). This is 32 percent above 1969 and 68 percent above the average size in 1960. Before adjustment for size, the average charge in 1979 for new prescriptions was $7.03 or 118 percent higher than 1960. After adjustment for the increase in average prescription size, however, the change in unit price was an increase of only 30 percent. Thus drug prices dropped in absolute terms in the 1960s and increased less than the Consumer Price Index during the 1970s.

These figures adjust for prescription size but do not correct for the "trading up" effect as newer and more "expensive" products enter the market and displace older products. Thus when ulcer patients start using Tagemet instead of Tums, their average prescription price charges rise. A true price index "links" these new products at a neutral level and they do not affect the overall index until the following year. The average prescription charge index fails to do this. Thus even if one were to treat the introduction of an improved (but more expensive) new product as though it were a price increase, we would still find that the costs of unit expenditures on drugs decline in comparison with the general consumer price index. These price performance patterns are said to be inconsistent with market power. At a minimum they represent strong evidence of market performance consistent with competitive pressures for price reductions and product quality improvement.

Price Flexibility

Another issue has been the question of the degree of flexibility of drug prices. Cocks and Virts (1974) grouped the industry into ten markets. They found that prescription drug prices have not been rigid.

Primeaux and Smith (1976) obtained similar results. They tested two implications of the kinked-demand theory. First, if the drug industry were oligopolistic, price changes would be infrequent. Second, price decreases would be followed by competitors, but price increases would not. They found that the kinked-demand curve was supported by 36 percent of the price changes in duopoly market structures but only by 24 percent of the changes in the oligopoly structure. They concluded that the results of their study contradict the underpinnings of the kinked-demand theory. However, their categories of oligopoly, duploy, and monopoly for the drug industry appear to be relatively arbitrary.

Price versus Nonprice Competition

Another issue in connection with pricing relates to price versus nonprice competition. Some writers such as Steele (1962, 1964) have argued that research, innovation, advertising, and product differentiation represent formidable barriers and restrict competition. Others such as Michael Cooper (1966) have argued that the frequent changes in top-ranking firms and products in different therapeutic submarkets are evidence of competition between competing products. These forms of quality competition are simply another form of price competition.

Furthermore, Teeling-Smith (1975) and Reekie (1978) have argued that a life cycle of pricing takes place. On new significant innovations the initial price tends to be high; however, as time passes and as substitute products are developed, price tends to fall. It is argued that with marginal costs so low in the drug industry, pricing to equate the initial price to marginal cost means that the average cost would never be covered. This would inherently result in bankruptcy.

Based on detailed data for the antiinfectives market, Weston (1979) found that product competition viewed over time appears to represent the form that price competition takes in practice. He observes that the price of a drug product is its nominal price plus quality factors that include efficacy, safety, clinical evidence and experience, information communicated to physicians, and the reputation of the manufacturer. Product competition results in continuous price reductions on older products.

Generics versus Brand Name Drugs

Another issue relates the price behavior of generic drugs versus those with an established and recognized brand name. At issue is whether consumers would receive substantial savings if pharmacists followed the practice of filling prescriptions with the lowest-price generic drug even though a particular brand name drug might have been prescribed.

For several reasons, the savings that may be achieved from generic prescribing—or from substitution of brand-specified prescriptions—are substantially smaller than what one would be led to believe from a comparison of the list prices of the prestige brands with the generically labeled versions of a drug at the manufacturer's level. The savings at retail are much lower—not merely because pharmacists may fill a generic (or substituted) prescription with a relatively expensive product, but especially because they apply a larger retail margin to the cheaper product.

Another aspect is the issue of equivalency of different versions of the same drug. A review of the equivalency studies indicates that chemical equivalence is not the same as therapeutic equivalence. Other variables include manufacturing processes and quality control. Another issue is the long-run impact of reducing the returns from drugs initially introduced as unique and proprietary if their effective economic life is reduced by an emphasis on substitution of generics.

ENTRY AND STRATEGIES

Another concern is whether product differentiation in drugs gives rise to some degree of market power. On the demand side Steele (1964) argued that since doctors prescribe for patients, but do not buy, price is not a factor in the purchase of drugs. He argues that indirect demand creates inelastic demand.

On the supply side it is argued that large drug firms have no superiorities over small firms in production. It is argued that the most important economies of large size seem to lie in the area of large-scale selling and advertising. Advertising leads doctors to use brand-name products. Patents favor large firms since for a small firm the patent is simply an invitation to costly litigation. It is argued that patents simply represent another way to differentiate products by mere molecular manipulation.

Economies of Scale

The argument that large pharmaceutical companies do not have economies of scale is at best moot. While the share of total investment represented by physical plant and equipment is relatively smaller for the pharmaceutical manufacturer, there is a substantial overhead investment involved in maintaining a continuing group of scientists and specialists engaged in seeking to develop new products. Viewed in the context of the essential investment in personnel required to be an effective creator and producer of drugs, significant economies of scale on the production side do in fact exist.

Advertising

What is the role of advertising as a barrier to entry? Here there are many arguments about the relationship between advertising and profitability. However, many also argue that profitability stimulates advertising rather than the reverse. Telser (1975) further argues that it is experience with good products, not advertising, that creates brand loyalty. If a product fails to perform to anticipation, advertising will not hold the consumer. Also, Telser's analysis of advertising intensity was associated with higher entry and greater price restraint (inflation resistance). Promotion is used more to gain entry than to defend market share.

It is further argued that measures of profitability in connection with advertising fail to account for the asset nature of advertising. Expensing advertising understates true firm assets and so overstates the profit rate. Weiss (1969) reestimated Comanor and Wilson's (1967) advertising profitability regressions. He found that the positive relationship between advertising and profitability still holds up when the true rate of return is substituted for the accounting rate. However, the calculations made by Weiss use absolute profits, not profit rates. Also at issue is the life over which the advertising should be depreciated. In addition, other forms of intangible capital need to be taken into account. Studies by Ayanian (1975a, b) and Clarkson (1977a, b) find that the rates of return for drug companies are not greatly different from the economywide rates of return when all accounting adjustments are made. These previous studies used data that are now relatively old. In the meantime, the unadjusted differential in the average rate of return for drug manufacturing compared to all manufacturing in the FTC's Quarterly Financial data has been substantially reduced. More up-to-date studies would start with much smaller unadjusted accounting differences. The adjustment for expensing R & D might result in no remaining differential.

Similar issues are involved in measurement of monopoly welfare losses. Siegfried and Tieman (1974) argued that five industries including drugs cause 67 percent of total monopoly welfare losses. In response Cocks (1975a) argues that these estimates fail to account for R & D capital by using accounting data. When Cocks takes account of R & D assets and the associated depreciation expense, he finds that the measured welfare cost is more than 90 percent biased for pharmaceuticals.

The effect of advertising on profitability is influenced by the issue of whether there are economies of scale in advertising. This was argued first by Kaldor (1949) and later by Comanor and Wilson (1967). However, the study by Schmalensee (1972) found that economies of scale were not significant in advertising.

The Role of Patents

The next issue is the role of patents. One argument is that if patents were eliminated the imitative research in the drug industry would be eliminated. This argument also assumes that research of a fundamental nature does not occur in drug firms but rather in government-funded or university laboratories. However, empirical evidence establishes that new drugs have been developed primarily by industry laboratories. The annual surveys of the National Science Foundation have shown the pharmaceutical industry to be at or near the top not only in the ratio of company-funded R & D to sales but also in the ratio of basic research to total R & D.

Some have argued for compulsory patent licensing. A case for such a policy might be more persuasive if most important discoveries came from nonindustry laboratories. A related aspect is that discovery is far less costly and time-consuming than development to a marketable product—the translation of a laboratory sample into an approved medicine. Compulsory patent licensing fails to recognize that patents are necessary to insure that producers of new information receive the returns of their production. From a social viewpoint, innovation is desirable and patents provide the necessary incentives to induce innovation. Furthermore, R & D is an important element of competition in pharmaceuticals, rather than a way of reducing competition.

The procompetitive effect of substantial innovation is long term and determines the basic nature of the pharmaceutical industry. Illustrative of empirical support for the procompetitive effect of patents is the case of diuretics studied by Bernard Kemp (1975). He found that the introduction of a patented break-through drug like Diuril was soon followed by a number of follow-on compounds with special features applicable to particular subclasses of patients. The new drugs were often at lower prices so that the break-through drug's market share was eroded and was accompanied by a wider range of therapeutic choices for physicians and lower average prices for patients. This is also evidence that competition is not postponed until after patent expiration, but rather has positive and beneficial results long before that point.

PROFITABILITY IN THE DRUG INDUSTRY

Profitability in the structure-conduct-performance model is a measurement of performance. Hence this issue was raised with regard to the drug industry. The initial impression is that before correction, the reported profitability rates of drug companies are higher than the average for all industry. The difference in accounting rates of return narrows considerably in recent years. However, when corrected for the capital investment nature of R & D and advertising the differential is narrowed. Depending upon the assumptions made with regard to the depreciation rate of R & D and advertising, the differential may disappear completely.

All of the studies dealing with adjustments to accounting rates of return are dealing with average figures. Schwartzman (1975a) focuses on R & D investment because it is the major and critical investment expenditure by drug companies. He finds that the expected marginal return on R & D investment is quite low, 3.3 percent. The result is so low that skepticism of his results has been generated. However, if the Schwartzman conclusion is simply modified to indicate that the prospective returns from R & D investments have decreased and that at the margin profitability of drug industry investments may be somewhat below the all-industry average rather than above, the tenor of his conclusions seems highly plausible.

In the Virts-Weston (1980) study, a somewhat different approach is taken to the analysis of prospective returns to R & D investments by the drug industry. They begin by reviewing the Hansen (1979) estimates of the costs in 1976 dollars of bringing an NCE to marketing approval. At an 8 percent discount factor, Hansen's estimate is $54 million.

Virts-Weston then analyze the sales experience for 119 NCEs brought to the market in a recent decade. Analyzing the frequency distribution of the number of prescriptions sold, their price, the cash flows to the drug companies, as well as other factors, they calculate the patterns of present values (at the same 8 percent factor) of probable cash flows from the 119 NCEs. They find that except for a relatively small proportion of very successful products, the present value of cash flows does not reach the $54 million investment cost. They conclude that current R & D investments appear to have less favorable prospective returns than R & D investments in prior decades. Their data also suggest that the probability that an R & D investment will earn its cost of capital is now relatively low.

Virts-Weston check these results against a number of other developments in the drug industry. These include data on structural shifts in the relationship between innovation and firm size, the number of firms developing NCEs, trends in the real R & D investment rate, and the resource reallocations between pharmaceutical versus nonpharmaceutical activities by drug firms. The impacts of government policies are also related to these developments in cost-revenue relations as well as to structural shifts and resource reallocations.

INNOVATION IN THE DRUG INDUSTRY

Another important measure of industry performance is the rate of innovation. A major concern in the pharmaceutical industry in recent years has been the sharp decline in the rate of significant new product introductions. Studies indicate that the cost of developing a successful new drug has increased sharply over this period. One of the innovations in measuring the cost of developing a new chemical entity is to take the time value of the cost expenditures into account. The longer period of time required to obtain FDA approval to market a drug adds substantially to the costs involved, because of compound interest effects on costs. Thus at least a part of the lag in introducing new drugs is argued to be a result of the effects of government regulation.

An alternative theory holds that there has been a research opportunity depletion that accounts for the decline in the rate of the introduction of new drugs. However, comparisons between the United States and the United Kingdom, where regulatory approval procedures differ, suggest that opportunity depletion does not tell the whole story. In addition, R & D spending by U.S. companies abroad rather than in the United States has tripled with about three-fourths of the increase occurring after 1970.

Another explanation offered for the decline in the rate of innovation is the suggestion that the industry is subject to decreasing returns to scale. However, a number of empirical studies indicate increasing returns to scale in R & D investments by pharmaceutical companies, especially after the 1962 amendments to the Food, Drug, and Cosmetic Act. The earlier decreasing returns to scale hypothesis appears to have been disproved. There has been a trend toward a more important role in the development of new chemical entities by larger firms. It is argued that this is a result of the increased costs that are involved in the development and approval of a new drug.

EFFECTS OF GOVERNMENT REGULATION

It is generally agreed that regulation has contributed to the decline in the rate of introduction of new chemical entities. At issue is whether the disincentive effects alone account for most of the decline or only a small proportion of it. In his study of the effects of the 1962 amendments,

Peltzman (1973) concluded that the net effect of the amendment was negative. He estimated that the 1962 amendments account for a net loss to society of $400 million annually. To the extent that the 1962 amendments are successful in reducing information costs to consumers by eliminating ineffective or harmful drugs, the effective price of drug therapy to consumers is reduced; but if the regulators keep drugs off the market that would yield net benefits, this increases costs to consumers. In critiquing the Peltzman methodology, it has been argued that if a decline in research opportunities were taken into account, the net loss attributable to the amendments could be less. Additionally he assumes that drugs do not depreciate. An assumption of depreciation rate would reduce the loss. Other econometric studies of the cause of the drug lag involve arguments about choice of variables and their measurements.

Alternative approaches to the econometric analysis are the international comparative studies made by a number of writers. Here the evidence appears to be that it is a difference in review procedures in the United States as compared with other countries that may account for the difference. These international comparisons are also included in empirical studies, which try to separate the influence of opportunity depletion and the administrative procedures of the government authorities.

Several other areas in which government regulatory activities impact the economics of the pharmaceutical industry have been noted. Through the Medicaid program government accounts for approximately 10 percent of total payments for drugs sold on an outpatient basis. To keep drug expenditures down, the federal government seeks to impose limits either on the kinds of drugs it will pay for or how much it will pay for certain types of drugs.

It is noted that government policies appear to create a diversion of funds away from research-intensive pharmaceutical manufacturers to those who do not have to finance R & D programs and therefore can charge lower prices. The longer-run impact of such a policy on the rate of innovation and the cost effectiveness of health care in the future is a significant issue. Thus the analysis of the impact of government regulation needs to be placed in a longer–term framework, not just an analysis of the initial and immediate impacts on known therapies.

10

AN AGENDA FOR FUTURE RESEARCH ON THE ECONOMICS OF THE PHARMACEUTICAL INDUSTRY

This outline of some topics for future research on the economics of the pharmaceutical industry will follow the pattern of the previous chapters. These chapters were organized around the structure-conduct-performance (SCP) paradigm. However, the orientation of SCP is relatively rigid and static. The great need for understanding better the economics of the pharmaceutical industry is to employ the alternative dynamic model sketched in Chapter 1. Hence, although the sequence of topics will follow the SCP model, the emphasis will be on the type of dynamic orientation that will bring out more realistically the nature of pharmaceutical industry economics.

THE PHARMACEUTICAL INDUSTRY

The Innovation Process

The crucial determinant of success for a pharmaceutical company is its ability to bring out a succession of new products that have a significant market impact. The evidence suggests that a necessary condition for a new product to have a major market impact is that it also represents a significant breakthrough from a therapeutic standpoint. However, the converse is not true. That is, if a new product is significant from a research standpoint, it may not necessarily have a significant impact in the marketplace.

However, the relative degree of success of a firm in developing new products that are significant from an economic standpoint is a key variable. Recognition of product competition is central to an understanding of the dynamic processes taking place in the pharmaceutical industry. Analysis of the degree of innovative success relative to other companies and to its own previous history in developing new products of economic significance is the key to understanding a number of topics more generally treated in a static and mechanistic way.

Performance in the development of successful new products is the key to understanding market share patterns over time. Pricing patterns over time are also best understood in terms of the sequence of new product introductions. Profitability patterns are also best explained in relation to the performance of a firm in developing new products of economic significance.

What is important here is recognition that many of the topics studied look at results. By focusing on the rate of introduction of new products of economic significance, attention is turned to the basic causal and explanatory factors. Furthermore, the dynamic and precarious aspect of the process is highlighted. Past success in significant new product introductions is no guarantee of a similar future pattern of success. Past success that produces high market shares does not confer market power nor reflect the use of market power. To the extent that a pharmaceutical company has developed a creative team of scientists and new product groups interacting effectively with a supportive general management group, there may be continuity in its successful performance record. This is quite different, however, from the assumption that the past performance rate or the current market position provides any guarantees for the future.

Market Structure and Stability

In the past there has been a debate on whether to use overall pharmaceutical industry data for calculating market shares or whether to focus on individual therapeutic markets. To some degree at least there is a predictable tradeoff in the patterns. The higher the degree of aggregation in defining the pharmaceutical industry or its submarkets, the lower the concentration ratios are likely to be. On the other hand, the more narrowly the market or submarkets are defined, concentration ratios will rise but measures of instability of market positions will also rise. Instability in market positions is strong evidence that competitive processes are taking place. Thus, regardless of the levels of concentration measures, if accompanied by high instability, the traditional implications drawn from concentration measures have to be substantially modified.

One research area worth exploring is the extension of the Lancaster product characteristics approach to the drug industry. The Lancaster (1966) approach has been successfully used in a number of ways in connection with analysis of several other industries. It has been most successfully applied where the products have had relatively distinct quantifiable attributes. For example, in studies of automobiles, variables such as horsepower, length of the wheel base, convertible or nonconvertible, and so on, have been quantified and data developed over a period of years for different manufacturers and for different models. Whether attributes comparable to the measurable, physical characteristics of other products can be extended to drugs awaits some actual efforts to carry out the research.

It would be of interest to test the concentration level versus instability measure by comparing the results of previous studies that find a relatively small number of product markets (such as 10) versus studies that found a large number of product markets (such as 69). The research would focus on products within each of these therapeutic product of classes. A number of dimensions of analysis of the product market position of individual products could be studied. In a number of ways such a study would cut across other topics including pricing, profitability, entry, and exit. It would also have implications for government policy.

The nature of such a study might be sketched. How many years does it take for a new product to achieve a high ranking position in a given therapeutic product class? How long does it maintain a 1, 2, 3, 4, or 5 leading position? At what rate characteristically do new substitutes come into the market? To what extent are the new substitutes focused on the therapies related to the basic original therapy, or do they represent more distinct breaks in therapeutic approach? In other words, do you have new products that carve out important segments within the original market as described by Kemp (1975) for diuretics? Or alternatively, do you have relatively more distinct product developments as in the evolution from penicillins to cephalosporins? At what rate does the price of the earlier product decline as substitutes appear? To what extent is volume maintained by the older products by price reductions?

Product Entry, Exit, and Profitability Patterns

Analysis of the patterns of the introduction of new successful products and the appearance of substitutes and other forms of competition will provide insights on profitability patterns as well as analysis of entry and exits.

Preliminary data suggest that the profitability rate of individual drug companies is highly correlated with the relative rate of successful new product introductions. If this relationship can be substantiated by detailed evidence over a long period of years, the implications of profitability data are substantially altered. High profitability in a dynamic model would, therefore, be evidence of performance that is good rather than bad as implied by the structure-conduct-performance model. Furthermore, high profits could be taken as an indicator of good performance by both private and social criteria.

In the framework suggested in focusing on product entry patterns, the deficiencies outlined by Bishop in his 1952 criticism of the ceteris paribus assumptions of elasticities measurements may not be applicable. In analyzing the pattern of relationships between older products and newer products within a therapeutic product class, the dynamics of change for the products under analysis can be measured. On the other hand, the impact of the wide variety of other products in the broader pharmaceutical market is likely to be relatively random and to wash out. Furthermore, some of the problems raised by Bishop can actually be measured directly. For example, in comparing cross-elasticities between older and newer products in a therapeutic product class, if the product class is chosen narrowly, the influence of products that have been omitted but that should have been in the analysis will show up in the form of larger intercept terms or larger error terms with less statistically significant regression coefficients.

The kinds of data for analysis of product, quantity, prices, and quality differences for the pharmaceutical industry in recent years are much superior to the data generally available to economists. The data Bishop had in mind were certainly subject to the measurement problems he outlined; but the strictures set forth by Bishop in 1952 may not be applicable to quantitative studies of markets, products, prices, quantities, and qualities using the kinds of data now available for various segments of the pharmaceutical industry.

Individual measures of stability in market shares could also be tested. For example, the Hymer and Pashigian (1962) concept of changes in shares could be shifted from the level of the firm to the level of individual products. Their measure would then be an index of the summation of the differences between the ratio of an individual product's sales to the sale for a therapeutic product class over time.

The Concept of Market Power

What does market power really mean? Is there any evidence that companies in the pharmaceutical industry actually achieve market power in a dynamic context? Does the competition between newer products and older products even before patent expiration reduce the significance of patents in making possible a divergence between marginal costs and price?

If market power were defined as the existence of price in excess of marginal cost, how is marginal cost appropriately defined in a long-run sense? The costs of developing and continuing a scientific staff and other staff required for new product development may appropriately enter into a measurement of long-run marginal cost relationships under alternative price, capacity, and volume interrelationships.

The foregoing discussion of market definitions has been shown to overlap with issues in the areas of pricing, entry and exit, and profitability. This is necessarily the case because market measures are not meaningful without taking into account the dynamics of competitive processes in the pharmaceutical industry. This suggests that dividing research projects by individual topics such as pricing or profitability is inherently artificial. Nevertheless, some additional research topics will be discussed by individual areas, even though the appropriate research may require taking a number of dimensions into account simultaneously.

PRICING BEHAVIOR OF THE DRUG INDUSTRY

Price Competition

One hypothesis is that the degree of price competition varies by therapeutic class and by product. For example, when patient needs are highly specific and where there are technical problems of uniformity, purity, and bioavailability, then efficacy and quality take on greater significance. Larger price differences may be observed among drugs competing to meet therapeutic requirements of the type described.

On the other hand, when the therapeutic requirements are less specific and a family of overlapping multisource products develops (in the antibiotics and antiinfectives, for example), the price and quantity impacts of new product introductions may be larger and take place at a faster rate.

Price Dynamics

Most of the studies of pricing behavior are likely to be more productive if placed in the context of the analysis of product entry and exit over time. The pattern of new product introductions, the impact of the arrival of substitutes, and the price and quantity consequences need to be analyzed within the framework of the individual product patterns and their behavior over time.

Some broader issues are also involved. What does price competition really mean? The economist frequently has in mind the auction market for standardized agricultural and mineral products. We need to make clear why for some products like agricultural products and minerals, auction markets have been developed in which price-quantity adjustments occur almost continuously over time. In contrast, for industrial products with shorter and more highly controlled production processes and rates, there is greater flexibility. Production rates can be altered, inventory volumes can be adjusted, both of which reduce the necessity for adjustments through price changes. However, for industrial products in the sense of nonagricultural or nonbasic mineral products, the rate of product innovation and change is also higher. From a social policy standpoint, product development and competition of the kind that takes place in the drug industry may yield larger benefits to consumers than the price changes facilitated by auction markets for agricultural and mineral products.

The central point here is that auction markets perform some necessary functions for suppliers of products with the characteristics that make auction markets feasible. On the other hand, dynamic product changes over time may meet consumer needs more fully for products like pharmaceuticals than would the frequency of price change provided by auction markets. As a practical matter we do not observe auction markets for industrial products. The reasons relate to the characteristics of the products and the needs of the suppliers and users of such products. The processes of competition centered on product change in the pharmaceutical industry may represent an optimal response to the needs of users of products and efficient responses by suppliers. To evaluate the processes of competition by the auction market model may, therefore, involve serious distortions and inappropriate tests.

BARRIERS TO ENTRY AND EXIT

Advertising Barriers

The discussion of this topic in Chapter 5 focused on the impact of advertising and patents in influencing entry rates and profitability levels. With regard to advertising, further studies analyzing its role need to be made. Concern has been expressed that in some sense promotion, including the use of detail personnel as well as advertising, accounts for as much as 25 percent of sales as compared with 10 to 12 percent of sales allocated to research and development. More empirical studies of the role of promotion and advertising need to be made. Previous studies suggest that the major portion of advertising and promotion is related to new product introduction. This is evidence consistent with the finding that advertising is a stimulus to the introduction of new products and, therefore, of entry.

The issue of implications of whether there are economies of scale in promotion or advertising needs to be reassessed. If there are economies of scale in promotion and advertising, this favors larger firms—but it also reflects greater efficiency in performing some of the basic functions of a business firm, whether in the pharmaceutical industry or other industries.

Other issues are involved in connection with advertising. Does advertising increase entry costs or does it decrease entry costs? Does advertising establish entry capital for firms earlier in an industry or earlier in therapeutic submarkets? Does the size of entry capital and entry costs depend on the number of firms already in a market or submarket?

To what extent does adjusting for accounting biases move drug industry profit levels closer to the manufacturing average? Does a gap still remain? How is this gap, if it exists, explained? Is it attributable to remaining accounting biases? Is it related to other measurement defects? Such other measurement defects would include failure to include the lower average profitability of less successful firms and firms that have exited the industry. Are there biases in measuring industry profitability by the largest and relatively most successful firms? Would these biases be reduced by greater coverage for profitability measurement? Particularly, what would happen to profitability rates if the losses of firms and divisions of firms that exited the industry were taken into account?

Patent Barriers

With regard to patents, some argue that because of the protection provided this makes for monopoly positions. It is furthermore alleged that patents stimulate other firms to make minor and insignificant (from a therapeutic standpoint) modifications because of the greater profitability of such an approach.

Economists who analyze the pharmaceutical industry from a dynamic perspective challenge this line of reasoning on both conceptual and empirical grounds. Less patent protection would reduce the marginal value of productivity of new patents and would inherently reduce the rate of innovation. Previous empirical studies indicate that the higher the rate of new product introduction, the faster the decline in the prices of older products. More empirical studies along this line need to be made. If there is a relationship between the rate of new product introduction and price of older products, however, the conclusion would be that patent protection that stimulates innovation in fact reduces the prices on existing products rather than increases them. Further empirical testing will provide additional evidence.

Other

Other areas for research would include more detailed analysis of the price and sales patterns of individual drug products over time. What are average annual and lifetime sales? How do these relate to the costs of bringing a new successful drug product to the market? How are these results affected by the rate of introduction of substitute products? What implications would such studies have for the interaction of R & D expenditures and drug prices and sales volume over time?

What is the relation between drug prices and the prices of alternative therapies? Drugs will generally be less expensive than hospitalization and/or surgery for which drugs may substitute. To what extent is substitution of drugs for other therapies an important method by which the relative share of drugs versus other therapies of total health costs change over time? What are alternative explanations and interpretations of the relative share of all health care and for inpatient care costs of drugs as compared with alternative therapies?

PROFITABILITY RATES IN THE DRUG INDUSTRY

Much work has been done on seeking to adjust accounting rates of return for expensing versus capitalizing of promotional and R & D expenditures; but this is only one dimension for adjusting measured rates of return.

Other Sources of Accounting Bias

While previous studies have taken account of some potential biases in expensing versus capitalizing promotional and R & D expenditures, they have not taken into account the impact of other economic forces, for example, inflation. The impact of inflation could conceivably move accounting rates of return for the pharmaceutical industry either upward or downward. A number of other dimensions that have been referred to earlier also need to be taken into account. The data could be substantially biased toward a selection of the most successful and profitable drug companies. This may be a greater bias for the drug industry than for industry generally, because the firms omitted from the "drug industry data" may have much lower rates of profit or experience losses.

In addition, previous studies have focused on average rates of return using accounting data. More relevant is: What are the returns from new investments at the margin under current patterns of prospective revenues and costs? Average rates of return may be high or low, but rates of return on incremental investments may be in the opposite direction. The most significant forms of investment by drug companies are the research and development investments. Hence, analysis of prospective returns from R & D investments may provide more reliable measures of current profitability in the drug industry. Relevant topics would be: What has been happening to expected rates of return serves as the basis for investment decision making; an analysis of this issue would yield important insights into whether incentives to engage in research and development are changing and if so, how. What has been happening to R & D in constant dollar terms relative to sales in constant dollar terms? The patterns of real R & D spending need to be reviewed before anything definitive can be said about the trend in R & D.

Product Competition versus Price Competition

A related question is the following: Product competition generates in the future both a stream of new products and downward pressure on prices for existing products; but product competition today means that price competition today is less than it might be otherwise. Thus the basic question policy makers must answer is this: Under which circumstance is the consumer better off—lower prices today or a stream of new products and lower prices of old products tomorrow? There is also a crucial subsidiary question: Is the cash flow from single-source drugs sufficient to finance R & D by itself? If not, then government efforts to increase price competition among multisource drugs will on balance produce a benefit to the consumer (lower prices) only at a substantial risk that discounted future losses in the form of fewer new drugs and foregone price cuts on old drugs will be far greater.

To some extent there is disagreement whether the decline in the rate of new product introductions is due to opportunity depletion or government regulation. However, to what extent is the future profitability of the drug industry likely to be impacted by a slowing of the rate of new product introduction? If the average profitability of the drug industry is above that for all industry, has this been a function of its technical dynamism and high rate of new product introduction in earlier years? If the rate of new product introduction declines, is it predictable that the profitability rate of the drug industry would decline and perhaps even decline to below the average for all industry? This result would occur whether the cause of the decline is due to opportunity depletion or government regulation.

INNOVATION AND THE DRUG INDUSTRY

A number of aspects of the innovation process in the drug industry have been discussed in connection with previous research areas. Here we focus on some of the technical, empirical studies of the determinants of drug innovation. The model employed by Grabowski (1968) formulates the level of R & D expenditures of an individual drug firm as a function of cash flows per dollar of sales for the previous period, the ratio of the number of patents received per scientist and engineer employed in the prior four-year period, and an index of diversification. There is some disagreement in the literature on the logic of why diversification should be a significant variable. Also, theory suggests that it is prospective profitability rather than past productivity and profitability that should be the determinant. Additional studies in this area would be useful. Also it would be useful to check the results of such studies against other forms of indirect evidence. For example, what has been happening to R & D spending by drug companies? Has the rate of increase been changing? Has the ratio of R & D spending to sales changed in recent years? To what extent are pharmaceutical companies shifting resources from pharmaceutical investments to non-pharmaceutical investments?

The broad area of R & D economies of scale in the drug industry has not been settled. In general, Mansfield's work (Mansfield et al., 1971) suggests diseconomies of scale with respect to R & D expenditures. In his study covering 1955-60 data from 57 firms, Comanor (1965) concluded that the marginal productivity of professional research personnel is inversely related to size of firm.

However, Vernon and Gusen (1974) using 1965-70 data follow the same specification used by Comanor but with new data. They found that R & D productivity varies positively with firm size. In their marketing productivity equation the coefficient on sales as a measure of size of firms is positive, but less than one implying that promotional activity increases sales per NCE less than proportionately—a case of diminishing returns. Also, in the Vernon and Gusen study an issue arises with regard to a finding of negative marginal productivity of R & D expenditures by some inter-pretations of their results. It appears, therefore, that the empirical work in this area is not definitive and that more useful studies could be performed.

EFFECTS OF GOVERNMENT REGULATION

New Drug Introductions

One area that has been researched to a considerable degree but on which the results are not yet definitive is the area of the decline in the rate of new drug introductions in recent years. Some have ascribed the cause to the 1962 amendments. Others feel that the underlying factor is a depletion of new drug opportunities. In addition to analyzing basic causes, questions are posed with respect to effects on consumers and effects on prospective returns to drug companies.

One comprehensive study analyzing a wide range of consequences of the 1962 amendments was by Peltzman (1973). A number of alternative assumptions and methodologies potentially could have been applied. A useful follow-on study would be to take into account the questions and problems raised with respect to the Peltzman study. It would be useful to perform sensitivity studies analyzing the effects of alternative methodologies and assumptions on the quantitative results, conclusions, and implications. Without actually performing such a study, the critical issues in this area cannot be adequately assessed.

A number of studies have sought by econometric methods to separate the influences of regulation and opportunity depletion on the rate of NCE introduction. One such study was by Baily (1972), whose results meet statistical tests of significance. He finds the regulatory control effect to be large in relation to the research depletion effect. Grabowski (1976) has observed that in the Baily study both the effects of regulation and the effects of research depletion are measured by proxy variables and, therefore, subject to considerable measurement error. The direction of the bias is toward results that are less significant from a statistical standpoint, however. Also, a reestimation of the Baily study yielded somewhat different statistical results. The questions raised by the follow-on studies suggest that further work be done in the area.

Kendall (1974) updates Baily's work and changes his measure of regulation. Baily measured the regulatory impact by a dummy variable for pre-1962 and post-1962. Kendall uses the mean approval time for NCEs over the period 1954-72. Again, some changes in the statistical findings are observed.

The international comparisons of the drug-lag problem performed by Wardell and Lasagna (1975b) reveal differences in criteria and review procedures. The critical differences identified in these international comparisons suggest an assessment of how U.S. procedures could be altered and what the effects of such modifications in FDA practices would be.

Initial work has also been performed on the impact of R & D regulation on drug development costs. The Hansen study (1979) takes into account the time value of money as well as the probability of individual project success. His estimate of $54 million as the cost of bringing an NCE to market is much higher than previous estimates. It would be useful to have additional research in this area to further test the Hansen results.

Preliminary work on the effects of extra costs induced by government regulation indicates that the amounts are high in absolute terms but relatively small in the total revenues of drug companies. It is not certain of the extent to which indirect costs of regulation have been taken into account. This is an area in which further work to develop additional estimates, particularly the indirect effects of regulation on drug company costs, needs to be developed.

The Effect of Risk

One frequent argument against regulation in the drug industry is that it has reduced the rate of return in the industry to very low levels (for example, Schwartzman, 1976a). This argument does not seem to make sense, however. Why does the industry allow the return it receives on its capital to fall below its cost of capital?

The assumption usually is that the effect works directly through the demand for output and through increases in cost. Another possibility, with less ominous implications, is that the effect is indirect: The effect of the regulation has been to reduce the riskiness of drug research investment, thereby reducing the risk premium and lowering the observed rate of return. The argument rests on the idea that riskiness is conventionally and correctly measured at the firm level, not at the product level. On this basis, major drug firms are able to diversify risk at the firm level by undertaking a larger number of research projects relative to total R & D expenditures, while smaller firms have tended to move out of research altogether and concentrate on drug development. This argument was explored in Chapter 7 of this book. Since riskiness is usually compensated by a higher rate of return, a reduction in riskiness may result in a reduction in the risk premium and hence in the measured rate of return. The net effect on the quantity undertaken of the risky activity is ambiguous.

Peltzman (1974, p. 74) found that the effect of the 1962 amendments has been to reduce the variance of drug industry returns:

> The amendments have had an additional favorable effect on drug company owners, not on the level of their wealth, but on its year-to-year variability. A concomitant of reduced innovation is reduced opportunity for one firm to experience unusually large gains from innovation or losses from obsolescence. We would therefore expect the amendments to have worked to reduce the year-to-year variability of the returns to the owners of the typical drug company, and to compress the differences in returns among companies in any year. Moreover, since pre-1962 innovation tended to be cyclical, the year-to-year variability of returns to drug company owners treated as a group should also have been reduced. These anticipated effects are borne out by the data.

The net effect may well have been to reduce the risk premium to drug firms and thereby reduce the rate of return. An interesting area for future research is to reexamine attacks on drug regulation for this effect, to see the extent to which it is mitigated.

Generic Substitution and Price Regulation

Because of the increasingly high proportion of medical expenditures paid for by federal and state governments, there have been an increased number of proposals to limit drug costs by various forms of price regulation. One is the proposal of the substitution of generics when available. A number of studies would be relevant to the issues raised here. Developing systematic data on the sources of increased costs of drugs and other forms of medical care could usefully be performed. Intitial studies indicate that the government programs have resulted in increased usage representing a major source of increased outlays.

Another broad area of research would be an analysis of the impact of various forms of price regulation that have been proposed. One issue is whether price regulation programs would create a diversion of funds from research-intensive pharmaceutical manufacturers to less-research-intensive firms. The longer-run effects may, therefore, be to reduce the rate of drug innovation that would cost consumers more in the longer run.

National Health Insurance

Another research area identified has been to develop a framework to isolate and quantify the effects of individual changes on the characteristics and performance of the drug industry. This proposes a full general equilibrium model developing the interaction of the important factors affecting the supply and demand conditions facing the drug industry. Such a study would also relate to the major alternative approaches to national health insurance. Within the framework of alternative national health insurance programs, what are the likely impacts on the drug industry? What are the alternative roles that the drug industry might be called on to perform in alternative formulations of a national health insurance program?

Government Subsidization of Research

The federal government has been a heavy investor in all forms of scientific research since the Sputnik era of the late 1950s. Biomedical research has been an important part of the research funded by the government. Burger (1976) has detailed the actual substantial investment of the government in this area.

It is a common argument in economics that research often entails an externality—though society benefits greatly from an innovation, the inventor can capture only a small part of the gains. Particularly in basic research, private markets are said to fail, and this frequently justifies government support of that research. This probably is an important reason for the federal government's current role in biomedical research.

Hence the government is in the position of stimulating basic biomedical research through the National Science Foundation, the National Institutes of Health, and so on; and at the same time limiting the amount of drug-related research through the FDA. Let us assume it has been the intent of the government to adopt exactly this posture. How may it be justified?

Drugs are only one input into health; many other specifically medical inputs are present, as well as the nonmedical inputs of diet, exercise, and so on. Presumably a person maintains a higher level of health if he uses a variety of inputs instead of a single one, such as drugs. Likewise, society's interests are probably advanced by conducting research on a variety of possible therapies, rather than just one.

The experience of the 1940s and 1950s demonstrated that private enterprise is able to maintain a high level of research in drugs, and drugs are perhaps uniquely well suited to this environment. Other forms of research were less well-suited to that environment and had to be stimulated through subsidies. An externality was present in those areas. In short, the government may have found itself in a position where one health input was being developed to the relative exclusion of other inputs.

Since drugs are only one input into health, and since drug research was being emphasized while other kinds of research were being neglected, the government's policy might be interpreted as an attempt to "twist" the structure of research.

Since drugs and nondrug therapies often tend to be (perhaps imperfect) substitutes for each other, the increase in the quality of the latter resulting from government subsidization is likely to reduce the demand for drugs. One implication is that analyses such as Peltzman's, which are based on a residuals analysis by projecting preamendment behavior to the postamendment period, will necessarily overstate the demand for drugs in the later period and therefore overstate the effects of the amendments alone. Another implication is that the "depletion" that has been discussed may in fact represent a shift in social emphasis away from drugs toward other therapies; research opportunities are not depleting, they are merely showing up in an unexpected place.

The mechanism by which this resource transfer has occurred may be stated as follows. Regulation has caused resources to flow out of the drug industry (relative to the hypothesized alternative level). These have gone into the economy generally. The government taxes the whole economy to pay for research. The net result is a transfer from drugs to other research, with some efficiency loss along the way. The amounts are not necessarily equal.

It is not argued here that the government intended this form of grandiose social planning. Rather, it is argued that the existence of government research subsidization must be taken into account in analyzing the effects of drug regulation. In fact, the health market may be one of the most complex markets in the economy in terms of the various forms of government intervention. Analysis of the FDA cannot be done in isolation; it is an exercise in second-best theory.

An important area for future research, therefore, is an investigation, first, of the overall effect of government on the supply of biomedical research including drug industry research and the welfare implications of that overall impact; and second, of the interrelationships between health input markets and the effect of distortions in other factor markets on the drug market.

SUMMARY

In summary, much progress has been made in research on the pharmaceutical industry in recent years. We have a solid basis for a number of conclusions. On others, at least we have the analytics for conducting basic research studies.

However, current and prospective demographic changes suggest that issues related to the drug industry will multiply rather than diminish in the years ahead. The rising costs of various components of health care need to be analyzed in terms of the basic underlying causal factors. Broad and comprehensive models for understanding the longer-term implications of government drug price regulation and alternative approaches to national health programs need to be developed. Opportunities for fundamental research within a more realistic framework of viewing industries in a dynamic context are particularly applicable and feasible using drug industry data. Thus the research needs and research opportunities relating to the drug industry continue to be substantial.

BIBLIOGRAPHY

American Enterprise Institute for Public Policy Research. 1974. *National Health Insurance Proposals: Legislative Analysis*. Washington, D. C.: American Enterprise Institute for Public Policy Research.

———. 1976. *New Drugs: Pending Legislation*. Washington, D. C.: American Enterprise Institute for Public Policy Research.

American Medical Association, Commission on the Cost of Medical Care. 1964. *The Cost of Medical Care*, Vol. 3. Chicago: American Medical Association.

Angilley, Alan S. 1973. "Return to Scale in Research in the Ethical Pharmaceutical Industry: Some Further Empirical Evidence." *Journal of Industrial Economics* 22 (December): 81-92.

Arampulo, Angel S., and Slayman, Herman H., eds. 1969. "Quality Assurance in Drug Manufacturing." Proceedings of the Midwest Regional Training Seminar (typewritten.)

Ayanian, Robert. 1975a. "Advertising and Rate of Return." *Journal of Law and Economics* 18 (October): 479-506.

———. 1975b. "The Profit Rates and Economic Performance of Drug Firms." In *Drug Development and Marketing*, edited by Robert B. Helms, Washington, D.C.: American Enterprise Institute for Public Policy Research.

Backman, Jules. 1967. *Advertising and Competition*. New York: New York University Press.

Baily, Martin N. 1972. "Research and Development Costs and Returns: The U.S. Pharmaceutical Industry." *Journal of Political Economy* 80 (January/February): 70-85.

Bain, Joe S. 1956. *Barriers to New Competition*. Cambridge, Mass.: Harvard University Press.

———. 1959. *Industrial Organization*. New York: John Wiley.

Balter, Mitchell B. 1975. "Coping with Illness: Choices, Alternatives, and Consequences." In *Drug Development and Marketing*, edited by Robert B. Helms, pp. 27-45. Washington, D.C. American Enterprise Institute for Public Policy Research.

Battelle. 1972a. *Summary Report on Potential Impact on the Pharmaceutical Industry of*

Changes in the Health-Care Delivery Systems and Related Drug Programs and Policies for the 1970's to Pharmaceutical Manufacturers Association. Ohio: Battelle.

————. 1972b. *Final Report on Potential Impact on the Pharmaceutical Industry of Changes in the Health-Care Delivery Systems and Related Drug Programs and Policies for the 1970's to Pharmaceutical Manufacturers Association.* Ohio: Battelle.

Bauer, Raymond A., and Lawrence H. Wortzel. 1967. "Doctor's Choice: The Physician and His Sources of Information about Drugs." In *Risk Taking and Information Handling in Consumer Behavior*, edited by Donald F. Cox, Boston: Harvard University Press. pp. 152-71.

Baumol, William, and Bradford, David. 1970. "Optimal Departures from Marginal Cost Pricing." *American Economic Review* 60 (June): 265-84.

Baxter & Co. 1974. *Comparative Rates of Return for Pharmaceutical and Other Firms: A Conceptual and Empirical Analysis.* Washington, D.C.: Baxter & Co.

Benham, Lee. 1972. "The Effect of Advertising on the Price of Eyeglasses." *Journal of Law and Economics* 15 (October): 342.

Berry, William F., and Dougherty, James C. 1968. "A Close Look at Rising Medical Costs." *Monthly Labor Review* 91 (November): 1-8.

Beyer, Karl H. 1978. *Discovery Development, and Delivery of New Drugs.* New York: Spectrum Publications.

Bishop, Robert L. 1952. "Elasticities, Cross-Elasticities, and Market Relationships." *American Economic Review* 42 (December): 779–803.

Bloch, Harry. 1971. "Advertising Competition and Market Performance." Ph.D. dissertation, University of Chicago.

————. 1974. "Advertising and Profitability: A Reappraisal." *Journal of Political Economy* 82 (March/April):267-86.

————. 1976. "True Profitability Measures for Pharmaceutical Firms." In *The Proceedings of the Second Seminar on Economics of Pharmaceutical Innovation*, edited by Joseph D. Cooper, pp. 147-60. Washington, D.C.: The American University.

Bloom, Barry M. 1971. "The Rate of Contemporary Drug Discovery." *Lex et Scientia* 8 (January/March): 1-11.

————. 1976. "Socially Optimal Results from Drug Research." In *Impact of Public Policy on Drug Innovation and Pricing*, edited by S. A. Mitchell and E. A. Link, pp. 355-70. Washington, D.C.: The American University.

Bond, Ronald S., and Lean, David F. 1977. *Sales, Promotion, and Product Differentiation in Two Prescription Drug Markets.* Washington, D.C.: Federal Trade Commission.

Bottcher, Helmuth M. 1964. *Wonder Drugs: A History of Antibotics.* Translated by Einhart Kawerau. New York: Lippincott.

Brand, Horst. 1974. "Productivity in the Pharmaceutical Industry." *Monthly Labor Review* 97 (March): 9-14.

Brandenburg, Warner O. 1961. "Financial Analysis of the Pharmaceutical Industry, 1930-1959." Ph.D. dissertation, University of Illinois.

Brodie, Donald C., and Smith, William E. 1976. "Constructing a Conceptual Model of Drug Utilization Review." *Hospitals* 50 (March): 143-50.

Brownlee, Oswald H. 1979a. "Commentary" to Virts, "The Economic Regulation of Prescription Drugs." In *Issues in Pharmaceutical Economics*, edited by Robert I. Chien, pp. 211-13. Lexington, Mass.: D. C. Heath.

_____. 1979b. "The Economic Consequences of Regulating without Regard to Economic Consequences." In *Issues in Pharmaceutical Economics*, edited by Robert I. Chien, pp. 215-28. Lexington, Mass.: D. C. Heath.

_____. 1979c. "Rates of Return to Investment in the Pharmaceutical Industry: A Survey and Critical Appraisal." In *Issues in Pharmaceutical Economics*, edited by Robert I. Chien, pp. 129-41. Lexington, Mass.: D. C. Heath.

Brozen, Yale. 1969. "Significance of Profit Data for Antitrust Policy." *Antitrust Bulletin* 14 (Spring): 119-32.

_____. 1974. "Entry Barriers: Advertising and Product Differentiation." In *Industrial Concentration: The New Learning*, edited by Harvey J. Goldschmid, H. Michael Mann, and J. Fred Weston, pp. 115-37. Boston: Little, Brown.

_____. ed. 1975. *The Competitive Economy: Selected Readings.* Morristown, N.J.: General Learning Press.

Burger, Edward J., Jr. 1976. "The Current Role of the Federal Government in Drug-Related R&D: What Is It and What Should It Be?" In *Impact of Public Policy on Drug Innovation and Pricing*, edited by S. A. Mitchell and E. A. Link, pp. 383-410. Washington, D.C.: The American University.

Burns, John J. 1969. "Modern Drug Research." In *The Economics of Drug Innovation*, edited by Joseph D. Cooper, pp. 55-62. Washington, D.C.: The American University.

Cady, John F. 1976. *Restricted Advertising and Competition*. Washington, D.C.:American Enterprise Institute for Public Policy Research.

Caglarcan, Erol. 1977. "Economics of Innovation in the Pharmaceutical Industry." Ph.D. Dissertation, The George Washington University Graduate School of Arts and Sciences.

Caglarcan, Erol, and Faust, E. Richard. 1976. "Resource Allocation in Pharmaceutical Research and Development." In *Impact of Public Policy on Drug Innovation and Pricing*, edited by S. A. Mitchell and E. A. Link, pp. 331-49. Washington, D.C.: The American University.

Calesa, Edward F., and Saltzman, Edward M. 1975. "The Marketing Men's Dilemma—1976." *Medical Marketing Media* 10 (August): 15-21.

Campbell, Walter J. 1978. "The Emerging Health Care Environment: Selected Issues." In *The Pharmaceutical Industry*, edited by Cotton Lindsay, pp. 119-40. New York: John Wiley.

Campbell, Walter J., and Smith, Rodney F. 1978. "Profitability and the Pharmaceutical Industry." In *The Pharmaceutical Industry*, edited by Cotton Lindsay, pp. 105-17. New York: John Wiley.

Caplow, Theodore, and Raymond, John J. 1954. "Factors Influencing the Selection of Pharmaceutical Products." *Journal of Marketing* 19 (July) 18-23.

Chamberlin, Edwin H. 1936. *The Theory of Monopolistic Competition*. Cambridge, Mass.: Harvard University Press.

Chemical Age Survey. 1967. "Pharmaceutical Industry." *Chemical Age* 97 (July): i-iii.

Chien, Robert I. 1976. "The Effect of National Health Insurance, Maximum Allowable Cost, Anti-substitution Repeal, Volume Purchase Plans and Third-Party Payment Programs on the Economics of the Drug Industry." Paper presented at the Seminar on the Economics of the Pharmaceutical Industry, Northwestern University, Evanston, Ill. November 18-21.

————. 1979. "The Effect of National Health Insurance on the Economics of the Drug Industry." In *Issues in Pharmaceutical Economics*, edited by Robert I. Chien, pp. 229-38. Lexington, Mass.: D. C. Heath.

Choi, Eun K. 1978. "Riskiness and Risk Aversion with Many Commodities." Ph.D. dissertation, The University of Iowa.

Christensen, Dale B. 1977. "A Study of Physician Drug Prescribing Adoption and Discontinuation Behaviors." Ph.D. dissertation, University of Minnesota.

Clarke, Frank. 1973. *How Modern Medicines are Discovered*. Mt. Kisco, N.Y.: Futura.

Clarkson, Kenneth W. 1977a. *Intangible Capital and Rates of Return.* Washington, D.C.: American Enterprise Institute for Public Policy Research.

_____. 1977b. "The Use of Pharmaceutical Profitability Measures for Public Policy Actions." Paper presented at a Seminar on the Economics of the Pharmaceutical Industry, Graduate School of Management, University of California, Los Angeles, September 8-10.

_____. 1979. "The Use of Pharmaceutical Profitability Measures for Public Policy Actions." In *Issues in Pharmaceutical Economics,* edited by Robert I. Chien, pp. 105-24. Lexington, Mass.: D. C. Heath.

Clemens, Eli, W. 1958. "Price Discrimination and the Multiple Product Firm. In *Readings in Industrial Organization and Public Policy,* edited by Richard Heflebower and George W. Stocking, pp. 262-76. Homewood, Ill.: Richard D. Irwin.

Clymer, Harold A. 1970. "The Changing Costs of Pharmaceutical Innovation." In *Proceedings of the First Seminar on Economics of Pharmaceutical Innovation,* edited by Joseph D. Cooper, pp. 109-24. Washington, D. C.: The American University.

_____. 1975. "The Economic and Regulatory Climate: U.S. and Overseas Trends." In *Drug Development and Marketing,* edited by Robert D. Helms, pp. 137-54. Washington, D.C.: The American Enterprise Institute for Public Policy Research.

Cocks, Douglas L. 1973. "The Impact of the 1962 Drug Amendments on R&D Productivity in the Ethical Pharmaceutical Industry." Ph.D. dissertation, Oklahoma State University.

_____. 1974. "The Measurement of Total Factor Productivity for a Large U.S. Manufacturing Corporation." *Business Economics* 9 (September): 7-20.

_____. 1975a. "Comment on the Welfare Costs of Monopoly: An Inter-Industry Analysis." *Economic Inquiry* 13 (December): 601-06.

_____. 1975b. "Product Innovation and the Dynamic Elements of Competition in the Ethical Pharmaceutical Industry." In *Drug Development and Marketing,* edited by Robert B. Helms, pp. 225-54. Washington, D.C.: American Enterprise Institute for Public Policy Research.

_____. 1979. " 'Commentary' to Grabowski and Vernon, 'New Studies on Market Definition, Concentration, Theory of Supply, Entry, and Promotion'." In *Issues in Pharmaceutical Economics,* edited by Robert I. Chien, pp. 53-61. Lexington, Mass.: D. C. Heath.

Cocks, Douglas L., and Virts, John R. 1974. "Pricing Behavior of the Ethical Pharmaceutical Industry." *Journal of Business* 47 (July): 349-62.

Comanor, William S. 1963. "The Economics of Research and Development in the Pharmaceutical Industry." Ph.D. dissertation, Harvard University.

――――. 1964. "Research and Competitive Product Differentiation in the Pharmaceutical Industry in the United States." *Economica* 31 (November): 372-84.

――――. 1965. "Research and Technical Change in the Pharmaceutical Industry." *Review of Economics and Statistics* 47 (May): 182-90.

――――. 1966. "The Drug Industry and Medical Research: The Economics of the Kefauver Committee Investigations." *Journal of Business* 39 (January): 12-18.

――――. 1979. "Competition in the Pharmaceutical Industry." In *Issues in Pharmaceutical Economics*, edited by Robert I. Chien, p. 66. Lexington, Mass.: D. C. Heath.

Comanor, William S., and Schankerman, Mark A. 1976. "Identical Bids and Cartel Behavior." *Bell Journal of Economics* 7 (Spring): 281-86.

Comanor, William S., and Wilson, Thomas A. 1967. "Advertising, Market Structure, and Performance." *Review of Economics and Statistics* 49 (November): 423-40.

Conrad, Gordon R., and Plotkin, Irving H. 1968. "Risk/Return: U.S. Industry Pattern." *Harvard Business Review* 46 (March/April): 90-99.

Cooper, Joseph D., ed. 1969. "The Economics of Drug Innovation." In *The Proceedings of the First Seminar on Economics of Pharmaceutical Innovation*. Washington, D.C.: The American University.

――――. 1976. "Regulation, Economics and Pharmaceutical Innovation" In *The Proceedings of the Second Seminar on Economics of Pharmaceutical Innovation*. Washington, D.C.: The American University.

Cooper, Michael H. 1966. *Prices and Profits in the Pharmaceutical Industry*. New York: Pergamon.

Cooper, M. H., and Parker, J. E. S. 1968. "The Measurement and Interpretation of Profitability in the Pharmaceutical Industry." *Oxford Economic Papers* 20 (November): 435-41.

Cootner, Paul G., and Holland, Daniel M. 1970. "Rates of Return and Business Risk." *Bell Journal of Economics and Management Science*, Autumn, pp. 211-26.

Costello, Peter M. 1968. "The Tetracycline Conspiracy: Structure, Conduct and Performance in the Drug Industry." *Antitrust Law and Economics Review* 1 (Summer): 13-44.

_____. 1969. "Economics of the Ethical Drug Industry: A Reply to Whitney." *Antitrust Bulletin* 14 (Summer): 397-409.

Crout, J. R. 1976. "New Drug Regulation and Its Impact on Innovation." In *Impact of Public Policy on Drug Innovation and Pricing*, edited by S. A. Mitchell and E. A. Link, pp. 241-60. Washington, D.C.: The American University.

Dalton, James A., and Penn, David W. 1976. "The Concentration-Profitability Relationship: Is There a Critical Concentration Ratio?" *Journal of Industrial Economics* 25 (December): 133-42.

de Haen, Paul. 1967a. *Nonproprietary Name Index*. New York: Paul de Haen, Inc.

_____. 1967b. "Ten Year New Product Survey, 1950-1960," in Paul de Haen, *Nonproprietary Name Index*, Vol. 6 New York: Paul de Haen, Inc.

_____. 1975. *New Products Parade, 1973-74*. New York: Paul de Haen, Inc.

Demsetz, Harold. 1973. "The Market Concentration Doctrine," American Enterprise Institute for Public Policy Research, *AEI-Hoover Policy Study* 7 (August).

Denison, Edward F. 1962. *The Sources of Economic Growth in the United States and the Alternatives Before Us.* New York: Committee for Economic Development.

Dewey, Donald. 1976. "Industrial Concentration and the Rate of Profit: Some Neglected Theory." *Journal of Law and Economics* 19 (April): 67-78.

Doherty, Neville. 1973. "Excess Profits in the Drug Industry and Their Effect of Consumer Expenditures." *Inquiry* 10 (September): 19-28.

Duetsch, Larry L. 1973. "Research Performance in the Ethical Drug Industry." *Marquette Business Review* 17 (Fall): 129-43.

Dzurik, Andrew A. 1969. "The Pharmaceutical Industry: An Econometric Analysis of Location Patterns." Ph.D. dissertation, Cornell University.

Faust, Richard E. 1971. "Project Selection in the Pharmaceutical Industry." *Research Management* 14 (September): 46-55.

_____. 1972. "Research Planning Perspectives and Challenges." *Drug and Cosmetic Industry*, July, pp. 42-48, 113-14, 117-19.

_____. 1973. "Acquisition/Licensing Strategies for Pharmaceutical Products." *Drug and Cosmetic Industry* 113 (October): 48-52.

_____. 1974. "Assessing Research Output and Momentum." *Research Policy* 3 (July): 157-69.

Faust, Richard E., and Ackerman, George I. 1974. "Organizing and Planning for Effective Research, Program/Project Management at Hoffman-La Roche." *Research Management* 17 (January): 38-42.

Fechter, Herbert,. 1976. "Sources of Increase in Prescription Drug Expenditure, 1929-1974." Ph.D. dissertation, New York University.

Feldstein, Martin S. 1969. "Advertising, Research, and Profits in the Drug Industry." *Southern Economic Journal* 35 (January): 239-43.

Feller, William. 1966. *An Introduction to Probability Theory and Its Applications*, Vol. II. New York: John Wiley.

Firestone, John M. 1970. *Trends in Prescription Drug Prices.* Washington, D.C.: American Enterprise Institute for Public Policy Research.

————. 1979. *Firestone Report for 1979.* Washington, D.C.: Pharmaceutical Manufacturers Association, August.

Fisher, I. N., and Hall, G. R. 1969. "Risk and Corporate Rates of Return." *Quarterly Journal of Economics* 83 (February): 79-92.

Fletcher, Francis M. 1966. *Free Market Restrictions in the Retail Drug Industry.* Ann Arbor, Mich.: University Microfilms.

Forman, Howard I. 1969. "Patents, Compulsory Licensing, Prices and Innovation." *The Proceedings of the First Seminar on Economics of Pharmaceutical Innovation*, edited by Joseph D. Cooper, pp. 177-95. Washington, D.C.: The American University.

Freidland, Thomas S. 1977. "Advertising and Concentration." *Journal of Industrial Economics* 26 (December): 151-60.

Friedman, Jesse J. 1973. *R&D Intensity in the Pharmaceutical Industry.* Washington, D.C.: Economic Consultants.

Friedman, Jesse J., and Friedman, Murray N. 1972. "Relative Profitability and Monopoly Power." *Conference Board Record* 9 (December): 49-58.

Galbraith, John K. 1952. *American Capitalism: The Concept of Countervailing Power.* Boston: Houghton Mifflin.

Gauch, Ronald R. 1970. "The U.S. Food and Drug Administration, Its Commissioner and the Public Interest: A Case Study." Ph.D. dissertation, New York University.

Gibson, Robert M., and Waldo, Daniel R. 1981. "National Health Expenditures, 1980." *Health Care Financing Review* 3 (September): 1-54.

Glennie, John R. 1971. "Public Policy and the Pharmaceutical Industry: Potential Impact of Proposed Legislation." Washington, D.C.: Multimedia Communications Consultants.

Goldschmid, Harvey J.; Mann, H. Michael.; and Weston, J. Fred. 1974 *Industrial Concentration: The New Learning*. Boston: Little, Brown.

Gort, Michael. 1963. "Analysis of Stability and Change in Market Shares." *Journal of Political Economy* 71 (February): 51-61.

Grabowski, Henry G. 1967. *The Determinants and Effects of Industrial Research and Development*. Ann Arbor, Mich.: University Microfilms.

_____. 1968. "The Determinants of Industrial Research and Development: A Study of the Chemical, Drug and Petroleum Industries." *Journal of Political Economy* 76 (March/April): 292-305.

_____. 1976. *Drug Regulation and Innovation: Empirical Evidence and Policy Options*. Washington, D.C.: American Enterprise Institute for Public Policy Research.

Grabowski, Henry G., and Vernon, John M. 1977a. "Innovation and Invention: Consumer Protection Regulation in Ethical Drugs." *American Economic Review* 67 (February): 359-64.

_____. 1977b. "New Studies on Market Definition, Concentration, Theory of Supply, Entry and Promotion." Paper prepared for the Seminar on Economics of the Pharmaceutical Industry, University of California, Los Angeles, September, 8-10.

_____. 1979. "New Studies on Market Definition, Concentration, Theory of Supply, Entry and Promotion." In *Issues in Pharmaceutical Economics*, edited by Robert I. Chien, pp. 29-52. Lexington, Mass.: D. C. Heath.

Grabowski, Henry G.; Vernon, John M.; and Thomas, Lacy G. 1976. "The Effects of Regulatory Policy on the Incentives to Innovate: An International Comparative Analysis." In *Impact of Public Policy on Drug Innovation and Pricing*, edited by S. A. Mitchell and E. A. Link, pp. 47-82. Washington, D.C.: The American University.

Grossack, Irvin M. 1972. "The Concept and Measurement of Permanent Industrial Concentration." *Journal of Political Economy* 80 (July/August): 745-60.

Gumbhir, Ashok K. 1971. "The Determination and Evaluation of the Economic Significance of the Consumer Price Differentials Between Generic and Brand Name Prescriptions." Ph.D. dissertation, The Ohio State University.

Halperin, Jerome. 1979. "Illusions about Brands and Generics." Paper delivered at Rutgers University, Annual Pharmaceutical Symposium, June.

Hansen, Ronald, W. 1977. "The Pharmaceutical Development Process: Estimate of Current Development Costs and Times and the Effects of Regulatory Changes," Working Paper No. GPB 77-10, pp. 1-60. Rochester, New York: Center for Government Policy and Business of the Graduate School of Management.

_____. 1979. "The Pharmaceutical Development Process: Estimates of Development Costs and Times and the Effects of Proposed Regulatory Changes." In *Issues in Pharmaceutical Economics,* edited by Robert I. Chien, pp. 151-87. Lexington, Mass.: D. C. Heath.

Harrell, Gilbert D. 1978. "Pharmaceutical Marketing." In *The Pharmaceutical Industry,* edited by Cotton M. Lindsay, pp. 69-90. New York: John Wiley.

Harris, Seymour E. 1964. *The Economics of American Medicine.* New York: Macmillan.

Health Care Financing Review 3 (September): 1-54.

Helms, Robert D. ed. 1975. *Drug Development and Marketing.* Washington, D.C.: American Enterprise Institute for Public Policy Research.

Hornbrook, Mark. 1976. *Market Domination and Promotion Intensity in the Wholesale-Retail Sector of the U.S. Pharmaceutical Industry.* Rockville, Md.: Intramural Research Section. National Center for Health Services Research.

_____. 1978. "Market Structure and Advertising in the U.S. Pharmaceutical Industry: Some Implications for Public Policy." *Medical Care* 16 (February): 90-109.

Hymer, Stephen, and Pashigian, Peter. 1962. "Firm Size and Rate of Growth." *Journal of Political Economy* 70 (December): 567-69.

Jadlow, Joseph M. 1976a. "The Application of Economic Theory to the Pharmaceutical Industry: 1958-1968." Paper presented at a Seminar on the Economics of the Pharmaceutical Industry, Northwestern University, Evanston, Ill. November, 18-21.

_____. 1976b., *Final Report on An Empirical Study of the Relationship Between Market Structure and Innovation in Therapeutic Drug Markets.* Oklahoma State University.

_____. 1977. "A Summary and Critique of Economic Studies of the Ethical Drug Industry: 1962-1968." Paper presented at a Seminar on the Economics of the Pharmaceutical Industry, University of California, Los Angeles, September, 8-10.

_____. 1979. "A Summary and Critique of Economic Studies of the Ethical Drug Industry: 1962-1968." In *Issues in Pharmaceutical Economics*, edited by Robert I. Chien, pp. 13-17. Lexington, Mass.: D. C. Heath.

Jaffe, Marvin E. 1976. "Drug Regulatory Patterns Worldwide: Trends and Realities." In *Impact of Public Policy on Drug Innovation and Pricing*, edited by S. A. Mitchell and E. A. Link, pp. 277-87. Washington, D.C.: The American University.

Johnson, Julius E. 1976. "Cost, Time and Product Safety." In *The Proceedings of the Second Seminar on Economics of Pharmaceutical Innovation*, edited by Joseph D. Cooper, pp. 23-33. Washington, D.C.: The American University.

Johnston, J. 1972. *Econometric Methods*, 2d ed. New York: McGraw–Hill.

Joskow, Jules. 1960. "Structural Indicia: Rank-Shift Analysis As a Supplement to Concentration Ratios." *American Review* 42 (February): 113-16.

Jucker, E. 1972. *Patents Why?* Basel: Buchdruckerei Gasser.

Kaldor, Nicholas. 1950–51. "The Economics Aspects of Advertising." *Review of Economic Studies* 18: 17-21.

Karch, Fred E., and Lasagna, Louis. 1975. "Adverse Drug Reactions." *Journal of American Medical Association* 234 (December 22): 1236-41.

_____. 1976. "Evaluating Adverse Drug Reactions." *Adverse Drug Reaction Bulletin* 59 (August): 204-07.

Kearney, A. T., Management Consultants. 1970. *A Study of Administration Costs Associated with Federal Drug Formulary Legislation.* Chicago: A. T. Kearney Management Consultants.

Kemp, Bernard A. 1975. "The Follow-on Development Process and the Market for Diuretics." In *Drug Development and Marketing*, edited by Robert B. Helms, pp. 255-76. Washington, D. C.: American Enterprise Institute for Public Policy Research.

Kendall, Mark C. 1974. "FDA Regulations, Patent Lives and the Pharmaceutical Industry." Paper submitted to Pharmaceutical Manufacturers Association, Washington, D.C., April 2.

Kessel, Reuben A. 1977. *Ethical and Economic Aspects of Governmental Intervention in the Medical Care Market.* Washington, D.C.: American Enterprise Institute for Public Policy Research.

Knapp, D. A. 1971. "Paying for Outpatient Prescription Drugs and Related Services in Third Party Programs." *Medical Care Review* 28 (August 28): 826-59.

Lancaster, Kelvin J. 1966. "A New Approach to Consumer Theory." *Journal of Political Economy* 74 (April): 132-59.

Landau, Richard L. 1973. *Regulating New Drugs.* Chicago: University of Chicago Press.

Lasagna, Louis. 1956. "Across-the-Counter Hypnotics: Boon, Hazard, or Fraud? *Journal of Chronic Diseases* 4 (November): 552-54.

————. 1958. "The Drug Industry and American Medicine." *Journal of Chronic Diseases* 7 (May): 440–43.

————. 1959. "Gripesmanship: A Positive Approach." *Journal of Chronic Diseases* 10 (December): 459-68.

————. 1964. "Problems of Drug Development." *Science* 145 (July): 362-67.

————. 1969a. "Constraints on the Innovation of Drugs." In *The Economics of Drug Innovation,* edited by Joseph D. Cooper, pp. 229-40. Washington, D.C.: The American University.

————. 1969b. "The Pharmaceutical Revolution: Its Impact on Science and Society." *Science* 166 (December 5): 1227-33.

————. 1972a. "The Nature of Evidence." *Triangle* 11 (November): 145-52.

————. 1972b. "Research, Regulation, and Development of New Pharmaceuticals: Past, Present, and Future." *American Journal of the Medical Sciences,* Part I: 263 (January): 9-18; Part II: 263 (February): 67-78.

————. 1976. "Consensus Among Experts: The Unholy Grail." *Perspectives in Biology and Medicine* 19 (Summar): 537-48.

Lasagna, Louis, and Wardell, M. William, 1975. "The Rate of New Drug Discovery." In *Drug Development and Marketing,* edited by Robert B. Helms, pp. 155-63. Washington, D.C.: American Enterprise Institute for Public Policy Research.

Laventurier, Marc. 1972. "Utilization and Peer Review by Pharmacists." *Journal of the American Pharmaceutical Association* 12 (April): 166-70.

Lee, Armistead. 1976. "Comparative Approaches to Cost Constraints in Pharmaceutical Benefits Programs." In *Impact of Public Policy on Drug Innovation and Pricing*, edited by S. A. Mitchell and E. A. Kink, pp. 115-70. Washington, D.C.: The American University.

Lindsay, Cotton, ed. 1978. *The Pharmaceutical Industry*. New York: John Wiley.

Little, Arthur D. 1962. *The Social Costs and Benefit of Promotion: The Case of Ethical Pharmaceuticals.* Boston: Arthur D. Little.

_____. 1967. *Trends in Market Share for Ethical Pharmaceutical Products.* Boston: Arthur D. Little.

Lucas, Robert E. B. 1975. "Hedonic Price Functions." *Economic Inquiry* 13 (June): 157-77.

Mach, E. P., and Venulet, J. 1975. "The Economics of Adverse Reactions to Drugs." *WHO Chronicle* 29 (March): 79-84.

Mancke, Richard B. 1974. "Causes of Interfirm Profitability Differences: A New Interpretation of the Evidence." *Quarterly Journal of Economics* 88 (May): 181-93.

Mann, H. Michael, 1974. "Advertising, Concentration, and Profitability: The State of Knowledge and Directions for Public Policy." In *Industrial Concentration: The New Learning*, edited by H. J. Goldschmid, H. M. Mann, and J. F. Weston, pp. 137-56. Boston: Little, Brown.

Mann, H. M.; Henning, J. A.; And Meehan, J. W., Jr. 1967. "Advertising and Concentration: An Empirical Investigation." *Journal of Industrial Economics* 16 (November): 34-39.

Mansfield, Edwin. 1968. *Industrial Research and Technological Innovation.* New York: W. W. Norton.

Mansfield, Edwin, Rapoport J.; Schnee, J.; Wagner S.; and Hamburger, M. 1971. *Research and Innovation in the Modern Corporation*, see especially Chapter 8. New York: W. W. Norton.

Markham, Jesse W. 1964. "Economic Incentives and Progress in the Drug Industry." In *Drugs in Our Society*. edited by Paul Talalay, pp. 163-78. Baltimore: Johns Hopkins University Press.

Martin, Christopher M. 1969. "Reliability in Product Performance in An Innovative Climate." In *The Economics of Drug Innovation*, edited by Joseph D. Cooper, pp. 63-82. Washington, D.C.: The American University.

Mayer, Jean. 1976. "America's Health System and Medical Research: Pluses, Minuses and Ethical Dilemmas." In *Impact of Public Policy on Drug Innovation and Pricing*, edited by S. A. Mitchell and E. A. Link, pp. 99-112. Washington, D.C.: The American University.

McCaffe, K. M., and Newman, H. F. 1968. "Prepayment of Drug Costs under a Group Practice Prepayment Plan." *American Journal of Public Health* 58 (July): 1212-18.

McGuire, Thomas; Nelson, Richard; and Spavins, Thomas. 1975. "An Evaluation of Consumer Protection Legislation: The 1962 Drug Amendments: A Comment." *Journal of Political Economy* 83 (June): 655-61.

Means, Gardiner. 1935. *Industrial Prices and Their Relative Inflexibility*, A Report to the Secretary of Agriculture published as Senate Document 13. 74th Cong., 1st sess., January.

Measday, Walter. 1977. "The Pharmaceutical Industry." In *The Structure of American Industry*, edited by Walter Adams, pp. 250-84. New York: Macmillan.

Melmon, Kenneth L.; Sheiner, Lewis B.; and Rosenberg, Barr. 1975. "Medical Benefits and Risks Associated with Prescription Drugs: Facts and Fancy." In *Drug Development and Marketing*, edited by Robert B. Helms, pp. 5-14. Washington, D.C.: American Enterprise Institute for Public Policy Research.

Mitchell, Samuel A., and Link, Emery A. eds. 1976. *Impact of Public Policy on Drug Innovation and Pricing*. Washington, D.C.: The American University.

Morgan, John P. 1977. "Watching the Monitors: 'Paid' Prescriptions, Fiscal Intermediaries and Drug-Utilization Review." *New England Journal of Medicine* 296 (February 3): 251-56.

Mueller, Dennis C. 1966. *The Determinants of Industrial Research and Development*. Ann Arbor, Mich.: University Microfilms.

Mund, Vernon A. 1970. "The Return on Investment of the Innovative Pharmaceutical Firm." In *The First Seminar on Economics of Pharmaceutical Innovation*, edited by Joseph D. Cooper, pp. 152-38. Washington, D.C.: The American University.

Mundy, Gregory R.; Fleckenstein, L.; Mazzullo, J. M.; Sundaresan, P. R.; Weintraub, M.; and Lasagna, L. 1974. "Current Medical Practice and the Food and Drug Administration: Some Evidence for the Existing Gap." *Journal of American Medical Association* 229 (September 23): 1744-48.

Murray, Martin H. 1974. "The Pharmaceutical Industry: A Study in Corporate Power." *International Journal of Health Services* 4 (Fall): 625-38.

Naert, Ph., and Swinnen, R. 1977. "Regulation and Efficiency in Drug Whole-saling." *Journal of Industrial Economics* 26 (December): 137-49.

Norwood, George J. 1970. "An Analysis of New Product Market Failures in the Pharmaceutical Industry Including an Econometric Evaluation of the Influences of Promotional and Research and Development Expenditures on Pharmaceutical Sales." Ph.D. dissertation, The University of Mississippi.

Oates, John. 1975. "Commentary." In *Drug Development and Marketing*, edited by Robert B. Helms, p. 185. Washington, D.C.: American Enterprise Institute for Public Policy Research.

Office of Technology Assessment. 1974. *Drug Bioequivalence.* Reports of Drug Bioequivalence Study Panel. Washington, D.C.: U.S. Government Printing Office.

Oliker, L. Richard. 1965. "The Pharmaceutical Industry: Institutional Character-istics and Statutory Review." Ph.D. dissertation, Indiana University.

Olsen, Paul C. 1974. *Marketing Drug Products.* New York: Topics Publishing Co.

Peltzman, Sam. 1973. "An Evaluation of Consumer Protection Legislation: The 1962 Drug Amendments." *Journal of Political Economy* 81 (September/October): 1049-91.

_____. 1974. *Regulation of Pharmaceutical Innovation: The 1962 Amendments.* Washington, D.C.: American Enterprise Institute for Public Policy Research.

_____. 1975a. "The Benefits and Costs of New Drug Regulation." *Proceedings of the Conference on Regulation of New Pharmaceuticals.* Chicago: University of Chicago Press.

_____. 1975b. "The Diffusion of Pharmaceutical Information." In *Drug Development and Marketing*, edited by Robert B. Helms, pp. 15-25. Washington, D.C.: American Enterprise Institute for Public Policy Research.

_____. 1975c. "An Evaluation of Consumer Protection Legislation: The 1962 Drug Amendments, A Reply." *Journal of Political Economy* 83 (June): 663-67.

Pharmaceutical Manufacturers Association. 1967. *Ethical Pharmaceutical Industry Operations and Research and Development Trends 1960-1966.* Washington, D.C.: Pharmaceutical Manufacturers Association.

_____. 1968. *Bibliography on Biopharmaceutics.* Washington, D.C.: Pharmaceutical Manufacturers Association.

_____. 1976a. *Prescription Drug Industry Fact Book.* Washington, D.C.: Pharmaceutical Manufacturers Association.

_____. 1976b. *Prices and Profits in the Pharmaceutical Industry.* Washington, D.C.: Pharmaceutical Manufacturers Association.

_____. 1977a. *Competition in the International Pharmaceutical Industry.* Washington, D.C.: Pharmaceutical Manufacturers Association.

_____. 1977b. *Research and Development in the Pharmaceutical Industry.* Washington, D.C.: Pharmaceutical Manufacturers Association.

_____. 1978. *The Pharmaceutical Industry: Prices, Profits, Patents and Promotion.* Washington, D.C.: Pharmaceutical Manufacturers Association.

Pradhan, Suresh B. 1963. "Involvements of Packaging in Drug Marketing." Masters dissertation, The Ohio State University.

_____. 1965. "Research Trends in the American Pharmaceutical Industry and the Survival Rate of New Products 1954-1963." Ph.D. dissertation, University of Pittsburgh.

Primeaux, Walter, J., and Smith, Mickey C. 1976. "Pricing Patterns and the Kinky Demand Curve." *Journal of Law and Economics* 19 (April): 189-99.

Reekie, W. Duncan. 1975. *The Economics of the Pharmaceutical Industry.* New York: Holmes & Meier.

_____. 1977. *Pricing New Pharmaceutical Products.* London: Croom Helm.

_____. 1978. "Price and Quality Competition in the United States Drug Industry." *Journal of Industrial Economics* 26 (March) 223-37.

_____. 1979. "Pricing in the Pharmaceutical Industry in the United Kingdom and the United States." In *Issues in Pharmaceutical Economics,* edited by Robert I. Chien, pp. 101-104. Lexington, Mass.: D. C. Heath.

Report of the Committee of Enquiry into the Relationship of the Pharmaceutical Industry with the National Health Service, 1965-1967 1967. (Sainsbury Report). London: Her Majesty's Stationery Office.

Report on Phase I of a Study Conducted for the Pharmaceutical Manufacturers Association. 1971. *The Role of the Full Service Pharmaceutical Manufacturer.* Boston: Harbridge House, December 31.

Report on Phase II of a Study Conducted for the Pharmaceutical Manufacturers Association. 1971. *Innovation in the Pharmaceutical Industry and its Social Benefits.* Boston: Harbridge House, December 31.

Report on Phase III of a Study Conducted for the Pharmaceutical Manufacturers Association. 1971. *Present and Future Profits Levels in the Pharmaceutical Industry.* Boston: Harbridge House, December 31.

Robinson, Joan. 1933. *The Economics of Imperfect Competition.* London: Macmillan.

Rucker, T. Donald. 1970. "The Need for Drug Utilization Review." *American Journal of Hospital Pharmacy* 27 (August): 654–58.

_____. 1971. "Basic Methods for Optimizing the Rational Prescribing of Psychoactive Drugs." *Journal of Drug Issues* 1 (October): 326–32.

_____. 1972. "Economic Problems in Drug Distribution." *Inquiry* 9 (September): 43–28.

_____. 1974a. "Drug Use: Data, Sources, and Limitations." *Journal of American Medical Association* 230 (November): 888–90.

_____. 1974b. "Public Policy Considerations in the Pricing of Prescription Drugs in the United States." *International Journal of Health Services* 4 (Winter): 171–78.

_____. 1976. "Drug Information for Prescribers and Dispensers: Toward a Model System." *Medical Care* 14 (February): 156–64.

Sarett, Lewis H. 1974. "FDA Regulations and Their Influence on Future R&D." *Research Management* 27 (March): 18–20.

Schankerman, Mark. 1976. "Common Costs in Pharmaceutical Research and Development: Implications for Direct Price Regulation." In *Impact of Public Policy on Drug Innovation and Pricing,* edited by S. A. Mitchell and E. A. Link, pp. 3–26. Washington, D.C.: The American University.

Scheidell, John M. 1973. "The Price Reducing Potential of Advertising." *Southern Economic Journal* 39 (April): 535–43.

Scherer, F. M. 1970. *Industrial Market Structure and Economic Performance.* Chicago: Rand McNally.

_____. 1980. *Industrial Market Structure and Performance,* 2d ed. Chicago: Rand McNally.

Schifrin, Leonard G. 1964. "The Ethical Drug Industry: Practices and Perform-ance." Ph.D. dissertation, University of Michigan.

———. 1967. "The Ethical Drug Industry: The Case for Compulsory Patent Licens-ing." *Antitrust Bulletin* 12 (Fall): 893–915.

Schmalensee, Richard. 1972. *The Economics of Advertising*. Amsterdam: North Holland Publishing Company.

Schnee, Jerome. 1973. *The Changing Pattern of Pharmaceutical Innovation and Discovery*. Columbia University Graduate School of Business.

———. 1978. "Governmental Control of Therapeutic Drugs: Intent, Impact, and Issues." In *The Pharmaceutical Industry*, edited by Cotton M. Lindsay, pp. 9–21. New York: John Wiley.

Schnee, Jerome, and Caglarcan, Erol. 1976. "The Changing Pharmaceutical R&D Environment." *Business Economics* 11 (May): 31–38.

———. 1978. "Economic Structure and Performance of the Ethical Pharmaceutical Industry." In *The Pharmaceutical Industry*, edited by Cotton M. Lindsay, pp. 23–40. New York: John Wiley.

Schumpeter, Joseph. 1950. *Capitalism, Socialism, and Democracy*. New York: Harper.

———. 1975b. "Pharmaceutical R&D Expenditures and Rates of Return." In *Drug Development and Marketing*, edited by Robert B. Helms, pp. 63–79. Washington, D.C.: American Enterprise Institute for Public Policy Research.

Schwartzman, David. 1975. *The Expected Return from Pharmaceutical Research*. Washington, D.C.: American Enterprise Institute for Public Policy Research.

———. 1976a. *Innovation in the Pharmaceutical Industry*. Baltimore: Johns Hopkins University Press.

———. 1976b. "Research Activity and Size of Firm." In *The Proceedings of the Second Seminar on Economics of Pharmaceutical Innovation*, edited by Joseph D. Cooper, pp. 185–210. Washington, D.C.: The American University.

———. 1979. "Pricing of Multiple-Source Drugs." In *Issues in Pharmaceutical Eco-nomics*, edited by Robert I. Chien, pp. 97–100. Lexington, Mass.: D.C. Heath.

Seidman, David. 1976. *Protection and Overprotection: The Politics and Economics of Pharmaceutical Regulation*. Washington, D.C.: Social Science Research Council, Center for Coordination of Research on Social Indicators.

_____. 1977. "The Politics of Policy/Analysis—Protection or Overprotection in Drug Regulation." *Regulation* 1 (July/August): 22–37.

Siegfried, John J., and Tiemann, Thomas K. 1974. "The Welfare Cost of Monopoly: An Inter-Industry Analysis." *Economic Inquiry* 12 (June): 190–202.

_____. 1975. "Further Comment on the Welfare Cost of Monopoly: An Inter-Industry Analysis." *Economic Inquiry* 13 (December): 607–10.

Siegfried, John J., and Weiss, Leonard W. 1974. "Advertising, Profits, and Corporate Taxes Revisited." *Review of Economics and Statistics* 56 (May): 195–200.

Silverman, Milton, and Philip R. Lee. 1974. *Pills, Profits, and Politics.* Berkeley: University of California Press.

Simmons, Henry E. 1974. "The Drug Regulatory System of the United States Food and Drug Administration: A Defense of Current Requirements for Safety and Efficacy." *International Journal of Health Services* 4 (Winter): 95–107.

Siskind, David A. 1978. "Contributions of the Pharmaceutical Industry to Improved Health." In *The Pharmaceutical Industry*, edited by Cotton M. Lindsay, pp. 41–67. New York: John Wiley.

Smith, Gary H; Sorby, Donald L.; and Sharp, Lawrence. 1975. "Physician Attitudes Toward Drug Information Resources." *American Journal of Hospital Pharmacy* 32 (January): 19–25.

Smith, Rodney F. 1974. "Ethical Drug Industry Return on Investment." Ph.D. dissertation, University of Massachusetts.

Soloman, Ezra. 1970. "Alternative Rate of Return Concepts and Their Implications for Utility Regulation." *Bell of Journal of Economic and Management Science* 1 (Spring): 65–80.

Stauffer, Thomas R. 1971. "The Measurement of Corporate Rates of Return: A Generalized Formulation." *Bell Journal of Economic and Management Science* 2 (Autumn): 434–69.

_____. 1975. "Profitability Measures in the Pharmaceutical Industry." In *Drug Development and Marketing*, edited by Robert B. Helms, pp. 97–119. Washington, D.C.: American Enterprise Institute for Public Policy Research.

_____. 1976. "Discovery Risk, Profitability Performance and Survival Risk in a Pharmaceutical Firm." In *The Proceedings of the Second Seminar on Economics of*

Pharmaceutical Innovation, edited by Joseph D. Cooper, pp. 93–123. Washington, D.C.: The American University.

Steele, Henry. 1962. "Monopoly and Competition in the Ethical Drugs Market." *Journal of Law and Economics* 5 (October): 131–63.

———. 1964. "Patent Restrictions and Price Competition in the Ethical Drugs Industry." *Journal of Industrial Economics* 12 (July): 198–223.

Step, E. L. 1978. "The Pharmacist-Industry Team," Interview. *National Association of Retail Druggists*, 100 (July): 5–9.

Stigler, George J. 1947. *The Theory of Price*, 1st ed. New York: Macmillan.

———. 1955. *Business Concentration and Price Policy*, Princeton, N.J.: Princeton University Press.

Stigler, George J., and Kindahl, L. 1970. *Behavior of Industrial Prices*. New York: Columbia University for National Bureau of Economic Research.

Sweezy, Paul M. 1939. "Demand under Conditions of Oligopoly." *Journal of Political Economy* 47 (August): 568–73.

Talalay, Paul, ed. 1964. *Drugs in Our Society*. Baltimore: Johns Hopkins University Press.

Teeling-Smith, G. 1965. *Science, Industry and the State*. New York: Pergamon Press.

———. 1975. *The Canberra Hypothesis*. London: White Crescent Press.

———. 1976. "Comparative International Sources of Innovation." *The Proceedings of the Second Seminar on Economics of Pharmaceutrical Innovation*, edited by Joseph D. Cooper, pp. 59–72. Washington, D.C.: The American University.

Telser, Lester G. 1964. "Advertising and Competition." *Journal of Political Economy* 72 (December): 537–62.

———. 1968. "Some Aspects of the Economics of Advertising." *Journal of Business* 41 (January): 166–73.

———. 1975. "The Supply Response to Shifting Demand in the Ethical Pharmaceutical Industry." In *Drug Development and Marketing*, edited by Robert B. Helms, pp. 207–23. Washington, D.C.: American Enterprise Institute for Public Research.

Telser, Lester G.; Best, W.; Egan, J. W.; and Higinbotham, H. 1975. "The Theory of Supply with Applications to the Ethical Pharmaceutical Industry." *Journal of Law and Economics* 18 (October): 449–78.

Thompson, Arthur. 1975. "Corporate Bigness—For Better or For Worse?" *Sloan Management Review* 17 (Fall): 37–61.

Trapnell, Gordon R. 1976. "On Measuring the Effect of State Reimbursement Policy on Medicaid Spending for Prescription Drugs." In *Impact of Public Policy on Drug Innovation and Pricing*, edited by S. A. Mitchell and E. A. Link, pp. 195–222. Washington, D.C.: The American University.

U.S. Congress. Senate. Committee on the Judiciary. 1959-62. *Administered Prices— Industry Kefauver Hearings before a Subcommittee on Antitrust and Monopoly of the Committee on the Judiciary.*

_____. 1960 *Administered Prices in the Drug Industry. Hearings before the Subcommittee on Antitrust and Monopoly.* 86th Cong., 2d sess.

_____. 1965. *Testimony in Hearings on Economic Concentration, Senate Subcommittee on Antitrust and Monopoly*, Parts 1-8A.

U.S. Congress. Senate. Committee on Labor and Public Welfare. 1973-74. *Examination of the Pharmaceutical Industry, 1973–74.* Parts I-VIII, 93rd Cong., 1st and 2nd sess.

U.S. Congress. Senate. Committee on Labor and Public Welfare and The Committee on the Judiciary. 1974. *Regulation of New Drug R & D by the FDA. Joint Hearings*, 93rd Cong., 2d sess.

U.S. Congress. Senate. Select Committee on Small Business. Subcommittee on Monopoly. 1967-75. *Competitive Problems in the Drug Industry. Hearings before the Monopoly Subcommittee of the Select Committee on Small Business.*

_____. 1967a. *Critique of Presentations by Economists for PMA. Hearings before the Monopoly Subcommittee of the Select Committee on Small Business.*

_____. 1967b. *Hearings before the Monopoly Subcommittee of the Select Committee on Small Business*, December 19.

_____. 1967c. *Present Status of Competition in the Pharmaceutical Industry. Hearings before the Monopoly Subcommittee of the Select Committee on Small Business.*

_____. 1967d. *Statements of Cootner, Plotkin, Firestone, Markham, Conrad, Whitney. Hearings before the Monopoly Subcommittee of the Select Committee on Small Business.*

_____. 1968a. *Conrad-Plotkin Profit/Risk Hearings before the Monopoly Committee on Small Business.*

_____. 1968b. *Hearings before the Monopoly Subcommittee of the Select Committee on Small Business*, January 19.

_____. 1968c. *Rebuttal to Testimony given by Dr. Willard F. Mueller. Hearings before the Monopoly Subcommittee of the Select Committee on Small Business.*

_____. 1968d. "Risk and Return in American Industry; An Econometric Analysis." *Competitive Problems in the Drug Industry. Hearings before the Monopoly Subcommittee of the Select Committee on Small Business*, Part 5, 90th Cong., 1st sess.

U.S. Department of Health, Education and Welfare. 1968a. *Current American and Foreign Programs*. Background Papers, Task Force on Prescription Drugs. Washington, D.C.: U.S. Government Printing Office.

_____. 1968b. *The Drug Makers and the Drug Distributors*. Background Papers, Task Force on Prescription Drugs. Washington, D.C.: U.S. Government Printing Office.

_____. 1968c. *The Drug Prescribers*. Background Papers, Task Force on Prescription Drugs. Washington, D.C.: U.S. Government Printing Office.

_____. 1968d. *The Drug Users*. Background Papers, Task Force on Prescription Drugs. Washington, D.C.: U.S. Government Printing Office.

_____. 1968e. *Second Interim Report and Recommendations* of Task Force on Prescription Drugs. Washington, D.C.: U.S. Department of Health, Education and Welfare.

_____. 1968f. "Coverage of Drugs Under Medicare." *Third Interim Report* of Task Force on Prescription Drugs. Washington, D.C.: U.S. Department of Health, Education and Welfare.

_____. 1969a. *Approaches to Drug Insurance Design*. Background Papers, Task Force on Prescription Drugs. Washington, D.C.: U.S. Government Printing Office.

_____. 1969b. "Quality and Cost Standards For Drugs." *Fourth Interim Report* of Task Force on Prescription Drugs. Washington, D.C.: U.S. Department of Health, Education and Welfare.

_____. 1969c. "Organization of HEW Pharmaceutical Activities." *Fifth Interim Report* of Task Force on Prescription Drugs. Washington, D.C.: U.S. Department of Health, Education and Welfare.

_____. 1969d. *Final Report* of Task Force on Prescription Drugs. Washington, D.C.: U.S. Department of Health, Education and Welfare.

_____. 1969e. *Report of the Secretary's Review Committee of the Task Force on Prescription Drugs.* Washington, D.C.: U.S. Department of Health, Education and Welfare.

Updegraff, Gail E. 1979. "Commentary" to Hansen, "The Pharmaceutical Development Process: Estimates to Development Costs and Times and the Effects of Proposed Regulatory Changes." In *Issues in Pharmaceutical Economics*, edited by Robert I. Chien, pp. 189–91. Lexington, Mass.: D. C. Heath.

Vanlommel. E.; Brabander, B., and Liebaers D. 1977. "Industrial Concentration in Belgium: Empirical Comparison of Alternative Seller Concentration Measures." *Journal of Industrial Economics* 26 (September): 1–20.

Vernon, John M. 1971. "Concentration, Promotion, and Market Share Stability in the Pharmaceutical Industry." *Journal of Industrial Economics* 19 (July): 246–59.

Vernon, John M., and Gusen, Peter. 1974. "Technical Change and Firm Size: The Pharmaceutical Industry." *Review of Economics and Statistics* 56 (August): 294–301.

Virts, John R. 1979. "The Economic Regulation of Prescription Drugs." In *Issues in Pharmaceutical Economics* edited by Robert I. Chien, pp. 195–209. Lexington, Mass.: D. C. Heath.

Virts, John R., and Weston, J. Fred. 1980. "Returns to Research and Development in the U.S. Pharmaceutical Industry," *Managerial and Decision Economics* 1 (September): 103–11.

Walker, Hugh D. 1971. *Market Power and Price Levels in the Ethical Drug Industry.* Bloomington: Indiana University Press.

Wardell, William M. 1973. "Introduction of New Therapeutic Drugs in the United States and Great Britain: An International Comparison." *Clinical Pharmacology and Therapeutics* 14 (September/October): 773–90.

_____. 1974a. "Therapeutic Implications of Drug Lag." *Clinical Pharmacology and Therapeutics* 15 (January): 73–97.

_____. 1974b "Drug Development, Regulation, and the Practice of Medicine." Journal of American Medical Association 229 (September 9): 1457–60.

_____. 1975. "Development in the Introduction of New Drugs in the United States and Britain, 1971–74." In *Drug Development and Marketing*, edited by Robert B. Helms, pp. 165–81. Washington, D.C.: American Enterprise Institute for Public Policy Research.

_____. 1976a. "Analysis of the Federal Drug and Devices Bill." In *Impact of Public*

Policy on Drug Innovation and Pricing, edited by S. A. Mitchell and E. A. Link, pp. 305–11. Washington, D.C.: The American University.

———. 1976b. "Monitored Release and Postmarketing Surveillance: Foreign and Proposed U.S. Systems." In *Impact of Public Policy on Drug Innovation and Pricing:* edited by S. A. Mitchell and E. A. Link, pp. 289–327. Washington, D.C.: The American University.

———. 1976c. "Regulatory Assessment Models Reassessed." *The Proceedings of the Second Seminar on Economics of Pharmaceutical Innovation*, edited by Joseph D. Cooper, pp. 235–67. Washington, D.C.: The American University.

———. 1979a. "The History of Drug Discovery, Development, and Regulation." In *Issues in Pharmaceutical Economics*, edited by Robert I. Chien, pp. 3–11. Lexington : D. C. Heath.

———. 1979b. "The Impact of Regulation on New Drug Development." In *Issues in Pharmaceutical Economics*, edited by Robert I. Chien, pp. 145–49. Lexington, Mass.: D. C. Heath.

Wardell, William M., and Lasagna, Louis. 1975a. "The Rate of New Drug Discovery." In *Drug Development and Marketing*, edited by Robert Helms, pp. 155–63. Washington, D.C.: American Enterprise Institute for Public Policy Research.

———. 1975b. *Regulation and Drug Development*. Washington, D.C.: American Enterprise Institute for Public Policy Research.

Weiss, Leonard W. 1965. "Factors in Changing Concentration." Statement in Hearings on Economic Concentration, U.S. Senate, Committee on the Judiciary, Subcommittee on Antitrust and Monopoly. Part 2, p. 737.

———. 1969. "Advertising, Profits, and Corporate Taxes." *Review of Economics and Statistics* 51 (November): 421–30.

———. 1979. "Commentary" to Clarkson, "The Use of Pharmaceutical Profitability Measures for Public Policy Actions." In *Issues in Pharmaceutical Economics*, edited by Robert I. Chien, pp. 125–27. Lexington, Mass.: D. C. Heath.

Wesolowski, Jeremii W., and Wesolowski, Zdzislaw P. 1970. "The Economics of Research and Development in the Pharmaceutical Industry." *Marquette Business* 14 (Fall): 158–72.

Weston, J. Fred. 1972. "Pricing Behavior of Large Firms." *Western Economic Journal* 10 (March): 1–18.

———. 1979. "Pricing in the Pharmaceutical Industry." In *Issues in Pharmaceutical Economics*, edited by Robert I Chien, pp. 71–95. Lexington, Mass.: D. C. Heath.

Weston, J. Fred, and Lustgarten, Steven. 1974. "Concentration and Wage-Price Change." In *Industrial Concentration: The New Learning*, edited by Harvey J. Goldschmid, H. Michael Mann, and J. Fred Weston, pp. 307–32. Boston: Little, Brown.

Weston, J. Fred; Lustgarten, Steven; and Grottke, Nanci. 1974. "The Administered-Price Thesis Denied: Note." *American Economic Review* 64 (March): 232–34.

Whitney, Simon N. 1968. "Economics of the Ethical Drug Industry: A Reply to Critics." *Antitrust Bulletin* 13 (Fall): 803–48.

Wills, Richard A. 1972. "An Investigation of Consumer Goods Classification Systems with Particular Reference to Prescription Pharmaceuticals." Ph.D. dissertation, University of Colorado.

Worcester, Dean A., and Nesse, Ronald. 1978. *Welfare Gains from Advertising*. Washington, D.C.: American Enterprise Institute for Public Policy Research.

AUTHOR INDEX

SUBJECT INDEX

ABOUT THE AUTHORS

JOHN W. EGAN is Vice President in charge of Federal Government Operations for A. T. Kearney, Inc., a Chicago-based international management consulting firm. Before joining Kearney in 1968, Mr. Egan earned a B.A. degree in economics at Northwestern University and completed preliminary Ph.D studies at the University of Chicago. He has been responsible for the management and conduct of studies in transportation, regulatory, and industrial economics.

HARLOW N. HIGINBOTHAM, a manager in the Government Group of A. T. Kearney, Inc., received his Ph.D. in economics from the University of Chicago in 1976. His educational background includes a B.A. in applied mathematics at Harvard University and graduate course work at the London School of Economics in 1968–69. With A. T. Kearney since 1976, he has conducted a wide variety of public- and private–sector industry economics studies.

J. FRED WESTON began teaching at the University of Chicago in 1940 and in 1949 joined the staff of the University of California, Los Angeles, where he has been professor of Managerial Economics and Finance in the School of Management since 1955, and variously Chairman of Finance and Chairman of Business Economics. Weston received his Ph.D degree from the University of Chicago in 1948.

Dr. Weston is the author or editor of a number of books, including, PROCUREMENT AND PROFIT RENEGOTIATION, THE ROLE OF MERGERS IN THE GROWTH OF LARGE FIRMS, MANAGERIAL FINANCE, DEFENSE-SPACE MARKET RESEARCH, SCOPE AND METHODOLOGY OF FINANCE, PUBLIC POLICY TOWARD MERGERS, THE IMPACT OF LARGE FIRMS ON THE U.S. ECONOMY, INDUSTRIAL CONCENTRATION: THE NEW LEARNING, and FINANCIAL THEORY AND CORPORATE POLICY.